THE MOON'S A BALLOON

IS UP, UP AND AWAY THE BIGGEST HIT OF THE YEAR!

"The book is bloody marvelous!"
—PETER SELLERS

"First-rate, suprisingly frank and genuinely entertaining!"
—*Newsday*

"A really smashing autobiography!"
—*Detroit Free Press*

"Delightful, blithe, earthy, funny, and outrageous!"
—*San Francisco Examiner*

AND THE PRAISE SOARS

HIGHER AND HIGHER!

"If David Niven's savoir-faire has been a delight in pictures, it's even more so in print!"

—*Saturday Review Syndicate*

"Whatever he writes about—the army, Hollywood, his many amorous escapades—he is doing it honestly."

—*Chicago Tribune Book World*

"A present-day rarity—a truly funny book!"   —*Fort Worth Press*

"Outrageously funny, riotous, heartbreaking, incredible and revealing. . . . On every level it's a book worth reading!"

—novelist PETER VIERTEL

"David Niven is known among his friends as, quite simply, an incomparable companion. Always, when asked why, they were never able to communicate his particular magic. Now all we have to do is say: read his book. It's all here."

—WILLIAM F. BUCKLEY, JR.

THE MOON'S A BALLOON

A BALLOON

DAVID NIVEN

A DELL BOOK

Published by
DELL PUBLISHING CO., INC.
1 Dag Hammarskjold Plaza
New York, New York 10017
Reprinted by arrangement with
G.P. Putnam's Sons
New York, New York 10016
Printed in the United States of America
First Dell printing—January 1973
Second Dell printing—January 1973
Third Dell printing—December 1975
Fourth Dell printing—February 1976

For Kira Kanuphyladafodilos

who knows if the moon's
a balloon, coming out of a keen city
in the sky—filled with pretty people?
(and if you and I should

get into it, if they
should take me and take you into their balloon
why then
we'd go up higher with all the pretty people

than houses and steeples and clouds:
go sailing
away and away sailing into a keen
city which nobody's ever visited, where
always
            it's
                Spring) and everyone's
in love and flowers pick themselves.

e. e. cummings

INTRODUCTION

Evelyn Waugh penned these words: "Only when one has lost all curiosity about the future has one reached the age to write an autobiography."

It is daunting to consider the sudden wave of disillusionment that must have swept over such a brilliant man and caused him to write such balls.

Nearer the mark, it seems to me, is my friend, Professor John Kenneth Galbraith of Harvard University, who wrote: "Books can be broken broadly into two classes: those written to please the reader and those written for the greater pleasure of the writer. Subject to numerous and distinguished exceptions, the second class is rightly suspect and especially if the writer himself appears in the story. Doubtless, it is best to have one's vanity served by others; but when all else fails, it is something men do for themselves. Political memoirs, biographies of great business tycoons *and the annals of aging actors* sufficiently illustrate the point." The italics are mine.

I apologize for the name-dropping. It was hard to avoid it. People in my profession, who, like myself, have the good fortune to parlay a minimal talent into a long career, find all sorts of doors opened that would otherwise have remained closed. Once behind those doors, it makes little sense to write about the butler if Chairman Mao is sitting down to dinner.

My offering is a period piece. I hope you may enjoy looking back over my shoulder.

DAVID NIVEN
Cap-Ferrat A.M.

THE MOON'S
A BALLOON

1

Nessie, when I first saw her, was nineteen, honey-blond, pretty rather than beautiful, a figure like a two-armed Venus de Milo who had been on a sensible diet, had a pair of legs that went on forever, and a glorious sense of the ridiculous. She was a Piccadilly whore. I was a fourteen-year-old heterosexual schoolboy and I met her thanks to my stepfather. (If you would like to skip on and meet Nessie more fully, she reappears on page 42.)

I had a stepfather because my French mother had married a second time. This she did because my father, along with 90 percent of his comrades in the Berkshire Yeomanry, had landed with immense panache at Suvla Bay in 1915. Unfortunately, the Turks were given ample time to prepare to receive them. For days, sweltering in their troopships, the Berkshire Yeomanry had ridden at anchor off Suvla Bay while the high command in London argued as to the best way to get them ashore. Finally, they arrived at their decision. The troops embarked in the ship's whalers and on arrival held their rifles above heads and gallantly leaped into the dark waist-high water. A combination of barbed wire beneath the surface and machine guns to cover the barbed wire provided a devastating welcome.

Wood pigeons were calling on a warm summer evening, and my sister, Grizel (that's a hell of a name for a girl, incidentally), and I were swapping cigarette cards on an old tree trunk in the paddock when a red-eyed maid came and told us our mother wanted to see us and that we were not to stay too long.

The house was near Cirencester, and after a rather incoherent interview with my mother, who displayed a telegram and tried to explain what "missing" meant, we returned to the swapping of cigarette cards and resumed our perusal of

endless trains lumbering along a distant embankment loaded with guns and cheering young men . . . 1915.

I am afraid my father's death meant little or nothing to
me at the time; later it meant a great deal. I was just five
years old and had not seen him much except when I was
brought down to be shown off before arriving dinner guests
or departing fox-hunting companions. I could always tell
which were which because although they all pinched and
chucked and clucked in the same hearty manner, the
former smelled of soap and perfume and the latter of sweat
and spirits.

I lived with Grizel in a nursery presided over by a warm
enveloping creature, Whitty.

Rainy days were spent being taught Highland reels by a
wounded piper of the Argyll and Sutherland Highlanders,
and listening to an "His Master's Voice" gramophone
equipped with an immense horn. Our favorite record had
"The Ride of the Valkyrie" on one side and, on the other, a
jolly little number for those days called "The Wreck of the
Troopship." We were specially fascinated by the whinnying
of the horses as the sharks moved in (the troops were on
the way to the South African War), the horses on the "Valkyrie" sounded very much the same as the ones on the
"Troopship," and if I had known as much about show business then as I do now, I might have been suspicious of the
entire production.

Occasionally, I was taken to the hospital in Cirencester
to "do my bit." This entailed trying not to fidget or jump
while young VAD's practiced bandaging any part of me
they fancied.

The war days sped by and the house in Gloucestershire
was sold. So, too, was one we had in Argyllshire. Everyone,
my mother included, thought that my father was very rich.
As a part-time lieutenant in his part-time regiment, he had
cheerfully gone off to war like a knight of old, taking with
him as troopers his valet, his undergardener and two
grooms. He also took his hunter, but these were exchanged
for rifles in Egypt en route, and my father and his valet and
one groom were duly slaughtered—cavalrymen ordered to
land as infantry, at night, on a strongly defended beach
without any training whatsoever for it.

He was hugely in debt at the time.

We soon moved to London to a large, damp house in

Cadogan Place, and the sweaty, hearty, red-faced country squires were replaced by pale, gay young men who recited poetry and sang to my mother. She was very beautiful, very musical, very sad and lived on cloud nine.

A character called Uncle Tommy* soon made his appearance and became a permanent member of her entourage. Gradually the pale, gay young men gave way to pale, sad, older men.

Uncle Tommy was a second-line politician who did not fight in the war. A tall ramrod-straight creature with immensely high white collars, a bluish nose and a very noisy cuff-link combination which he rattled at me when I made an eating error at mealtime.

I don't believe he was very healthy really. Anyway he got knighted for something to do with the Conservative Party and the Nineteen Hundred Club, and Cadogan Place became a rendezvous for people like Lord Willoughby de Broke, Sir Edward Carson, KC, and Sir E. Marshall Hall, KC. I suppose it bubbled with the sort of brilliant conversation into which children these days would be encouraged to join, but as soon as it started, Grizel and I were removed to a nursery upstairs. It had a linoleum floor and a bag of apples hanging outside the window during the winter. Grizel, who was two years older, became very interested during this period in the shape and form of my private parts; but when after a particularly painful inspection, I claimed my right to see hers too, she covered up sharply and dodged the issue by saying, "Well, it's a sort of flat arrangement."

At about this time, the Germans began their air raids on London. High in the night sky, I saw a Zeppelin go down in flames near Shepherds Bush. The airplanes were to come next. On the day my mother took me down Sloane Street to buy a pair of warm gloves I saw my first Fokkers. Everyone rushed into the street to point them out to each other. Then as the possibility of what might be about to drop out of the Fokkers dawned on them they rushed back indoors again.

* Sir Thomas Comyn-Platt. Liked to be known as the mystery man of the Conservative Party. Contested Portsmouth Central in the election of 1926 . . . soundly beaten by Miss Jenny Lee, wife of Aneurin Bevan.

My mother never left the glove shop. She was busy giving a splendid discourse on the superior quality of French gloves when the manager said, "This place will come down like a pack of cards." By that time the Fokkers must have been fifty miles away, but I was nevertheless lugged across the street and we joined the undignified Gadarene swine movement down the steps of the Knightsbridge Tube Station. One woman had a parrot. Another had hysterics and, between screams, ate handfuls of marmalade out of a stone jar, a spectacle I found highly enjoyable.

After sufficient time had elapsed for the Fokkers to be cozily bedded down at their home base outside Hamburg, we all emerged well equipped to tell long dull stories about our experience in air raids during World War I. I suppose we gave these up about September, 1940.

Uncle Tommy's marriage to my mother coincided with my sixth birthday. The wedding took place at All Saints, Sloane Street. Purple with embarrassment, I was press-ganged into being a page and pressure-fed into a primrose-colored suit with mother-of-pearl buttons, a white lace collar, shorts and socks.

I did everything I could to wreck the show and fidgeted and picked my nose till an aquiline creature, later identified as the famous Lady Oxford and Asquith, came and knelt in the aisle to comfort me. I decided she was a witch and again and again informed the congregation of this discovery in a shrill treble.

I was removed, and Uncle Tommy, forever politically sensitive, treated me from that moment on with frosty distaste.

My eldest brother, Henri (known as Max), was a naval cadet at Dartmouth, longing to get into the war. My eldest sister, Joyce, was at home helping my mother, and Grizel had gone away to boarding school in Norfolk. I was the youngest.

Cadogan Place we soon could not afford to live in, so it was sold and a smaller house on Sloane Street, across on the unchic side of the garden, was purchased.

A pink Gawblimy cap was obtained for me and I was sent to Mr. Gibb's day school down the street. It became clear to me very early that I was not going to be long in the house on Sloane Street.

The little room which my mother had set aside for me

was appropriated by Uncle Tommy as his dressing room and I was packed off to boarding school at Elstree.

I can't say I was miserable at being snatched away from the bosom of my family because the bosom had not seemed, so far, to be a particularly warm and cozy place.

Apart from the Chinese, the only people in the world who pack their sons off to the tender care of unknown and often homosexual schoolmasters at the exact moment when they are most in need of parental love and influence are the British so-called upper and middle classes.

I don't suppose I particularly minded going away, but I had not been long at Elstree before I discovered that life could be hell.

There was a great deal of bullying, and for a six-year-old, the spectacle of a gang of twelve-year-olds bearing down, cracking wet towels like whips, can be terrifying.

For the most part, the masters were even more frightening. It would be charitable to think that they were all shell-shocked heroes returned from the hell of Mons and Vimy, but it seems more probable that they were sadistic perverts who had been found at the bottom of the educational barrel and dredged up at a time of acute manpower shortage.

One, a Mr. Christie, when he tired of pulling ears halfway out of our heads (I still have one that sticks out almost at right angles thanks to this son of a bitch) and delivering, for the smallest mistake in declension, backhanded slaps that knocked one off one's bench, delighted in saying, "Show me the hand that wrote this," and then bringing down the sharp edge of a heavy ruler across the offending wrist.

He took the last form on Friday evening, and I remember praying every week that he would die before then so that I could somehow reach the haven of Saturday and Sunday and the comparative safety of the weekend.

I don't think I have ever been so frightened of a human being in my life. Once he made me lean out of a fourth-floor window—a stupefying height for a little boy—then he shut the window across the small of my back, ordered two other equally terrified boys to hold my feet, and laid into me mightily with a cane. All this for some mistake in "common are *sacerdos dux vates parens et conjux. . . .*"

Years later, when I was at Sandhurst and playing in the Rugby football fifteen, big enough and by then ugly enough

to take care of myself, I had an overpowering urge to see
the bastard again, face-to-face.

I went down to Elstree, filled with vindictiveness. I don't
know what I intended to do really, and when I got there I
found the school empty. The prisonlike exercise yard was
full of rubbish and old newspapers. The fourth-floor window, out of which I had dangled, was broken and open to
the rain—it didn't even look very high.

My mother, at that time, would not believe my tales of
woe or rather Uncle Tommy persuaded her that they were
nonsense, telling her that all boys exaggerated and that anyway she could not be expected to know anything about
English schools.

After two years of this purgatory, I got a huge boil as a
result of the bad food. "Oh!" said the matron. "That's nothing. Don't make such a fuss!" and lopped off the top of it
with a pair of scissors.

The ensuing infection was pretty horrible and put me in
the sanatorium.

Finally, greatly urged on by my brother, who believed
me, my mother saw the light and at the end of term gave
me the glorious news that I would never have to go back to
Elstree again.

The next term, I was sent to Heatherdown at Ascot.

At this point, I don't believe my mother was actually taking in washing, but, as sure as hell, she was sending very
little out, and it must have been a fearful drain on her resources. Heatherdown was far more expensive than Elstree;
certainly only a token subscription to the family coffers was
being made by Uncle Tommy and she still had her thumb
in the dike of my father's debts; but I was blissfully unconscious of all this and found myself wallowing in a veritable
flood of good fortune.

Heatherdown was a very different cup of tea, very carriage trade, very protected; compared to Elstree, very soft
and compared to anywhere else, very snobbish. Everybody
went from there to Eton. Gone were the sadistic masters
and the school bullies tying small boys to hot radiators; no
more mad matrons; no more ex-naval cooks with finger-
nails like toenails doling out their nauseous confections;
and receding like a bad dream were the flinty playground
and the evil-smelling doorless lavatories, open to the elements and the helpful advice of schoolmates.

Instead, I found a world of cleanliness and kindly masters, motherly matrons, green playing fields, a lake, delicious food and a swimming pool. In short, schoolboy heaven.

The only grown-ups who hit me were the headmaster who, under great provocation, would uncork an occasional dose of the cane, and a dear old gentleman who taught divinity, called Mr. Hodgson, who occasionally wielded a clothes brush known as Dixon and Parker because if, as rarely happened, he hit hard enough, the name of the maker was left imprinted on the bum.

After the appalling apprenticeship of Elstree, I could not believe that life could be so perfect. Released from fear and oppression, the whole thing went to my head, and I bloomed like a rather questionable rose.

Almost nine, I became something of a clown. This was hastened on when, for some strange reason, my balls dropped three years earlier than they should have done.

I was in the choir at the time, no Eddie Lough to be sure, but the possessor of a voice of guileless purity. Sometimes I was entrusted with solo passages, and it was on such an occasion, and in front of a full house, that disaster struck.

Ascot Sunday, parents staying in smart country houses nearby for the Race Meeting had filled the chapel to capacity. Alone, I was piping my way through "There is a green hill far away, without a city wall. . . ." Suddenly, on the word "wall" a fearful braying sound issued from the angelic face of the soloist. I tried for the note again; this time it sounded like a Rolls-Royce klaxon of the period. The paper-thin discipline of the choir quickly disintegrated . . . repressed laughter became contagious and finally, general.

Almost immediately after chapel, I was caned by the headmaster, Sammy Day. He had once played cricket for England and still had one of the best late cuts in the business. It hurt a lot and considering the medical evidence that was from then on permanently with me, was rather unfair.

Boys are terrible snobs, and I was annually unnerved when the school list came out, to see some of my contemporaries sniggering because in between the young marquesses and dukes with their splendid addresses was:

Niven, D., Rose Cottage, Bembridge. I.W.

It had become necessary for the house in Sloane Street

to go and our permanent address was as advertised in the school list—a converted fisherman's cottage which had a reputation for unreliability. When the east wind blew, the front door got stuck, and when the west wind blew, the back door could not be opened; only the combined weight of the family seemed to keep it anchored to the ground. I adored it and was happier there than I had ever been, especially because, with a rare flash of genius, my mother decided that during the holidays she would be alone with her children.

Uncle Tommy was barred—I don't know where he went—to the Carlton Club, I suppose.

After the sudden descent of my testicles, I was removed from the choir as a bad risk and was told to blow the organ; that is to say, I was the "bellows man" and the musical success of each service (we suffered through two a day) depended entirely on me.

I had by now perceived that a certain popularity could be mine if I became a figure of fun, and although this was a position of great trust, the newly found clown in me could not resist the opportunities it offered. For a very small price—two chocolate whirls, one Cadbury's Milk Flake or a brace of Turkish delights—I could be bribed to let the air out of the bellows on important occasions. The whole school, on the selected day, would be in the know, and hugging itself with delicious anticipation, would sit through an endless sermon.

It took careful preparation, but I could generally arrange matters so that a rude noise could be subtly injected into the proceedings usually just after an Amen. I could redress the situation rapidly by quick pumping and only the connoisseurs could detect that it was not a mistake . . . the boys were all connoisseurs.

Once I tried it when the Bishop of Ripon was in the middle of a special address. This was my masterpiece and also my downfall, but the bribes were mountainous.

It was a highly technical job and involved surreptitiously and noiselessly keeping the bellow half-filled for several minutes after the end of the preceding hymn. I had intended to let the air out in a series of well-spaced small squeaks and trills, thus keeping the boys happy during what promised to be a long, trying period, but something went wrong and it all came out at once and on a most unfortunate cue

. . . a quotation from Proverbs 7: "I have perfumed my bed with myrrh, aloes and cinnamon. . . ."

It was as if the bellows could not contain themselves any longer—a tremendous fart rent the air. All was confusion.

The school was infiltrated with informers, and I was soon dealt with once more by the long-suffering Sammy Day.

I loved Heatherdown and tried hard to uphold the agricultural standards of the landed gentry with whom I was rubbing shoulders. Every summer on the First Sunday after the Derby (it is not thus described in the Book of Common Prayer, but so many boys of noble birth had race-horse owner fathers that at Heatherdown, it far out-ranked Rogation Sunday, the Sunday after Advent, and the twenty-first Sunday after Trinity) a prize was given to the boy with the most beautiful garden.

Each boy had a garden about the size of a lavatory mat in a small commercial hotel, and immense ingenuity and forethought were displayed by the owners. Actually, these gardens were status symbols of the worst kind, and boys whose family estates employed an army of gardeners proudly displayed the most exotic flowers and shrubs, de-livered for planting hot from the family greenhouses, while the more modest smallholders nurtured colorful annuals and arranged them in intricate patterns.

I could only manage a biannual crop of mustard and cress.

The year that Humorist won the Derby was the year of one of the phenomena of the world—a drought in England —and my crop, carefully timed for the flower show, failed, burned to a crisp.

By now the self-appointed jester to the upper classes, I decided to fill the gap, and creeping out of the dormitory after dark, I made my way downstairs and flitting from tree to tree in the moonlight, arrived at a well-known gap in the wall which separated Heatherdown from Heathfield, the girls' school next door.

From preliminary reconnaissance, I knew that this gap opened onto the kitchen garden. I selected a huge vegetable marrow plant, pulled it up by the roots, and once safely back on the male side of the wall, hid it behind a piece of corrugated iron.

It took some while and several near heart attacks, but I

finally made it back to bed. The next morning I retrieved
the marrow and, in the hubbub caused by the arrival of
other boys' parents in Daimlers and Rolls-Royces, managed
to plant my prize on top of my poor piece of desert.

It didn't go down very well. The Countess of Jersey, one
of the parents, presented the prizes.

She didn't give one to me, and later I was caned again by
a no-longer-affable Sammy Day: not for making a nonsense of the flower show which could have been justified,
but for *stealing* which put a totally different connotation on
the thing.

After this, I went rapidly downhill from popular school
clown to unpopular school nuisance. Striving to maintain
my waning popularity, I fell in the lake and nearly
drowned, purposely split my trousers on the school walk
through Ascot one Sunday, and was caught trying to get
into Ascot Racecourse—a hideous crime. Poor Brian
Franks, a Bembridge friend, near death's door with pneumonia at Wixenford, a school nearby, received from me on
the day of his "crisis," a large chocolate box inside which
was a smaller box, then a smaller box and so on until finally a matchbox with a piece of dog's mess in it.

Not a funny joke, especially for the matron who opened
it, but then I didn't know Brian was ill.

Brian overcame his illness and my gift and has remained
a lifelong friend, but the matron took a dim view, the
smoke signals went up between Wixenford and Heatherdown, and Sammy Day decided that his school could get
along without me.*

I was ten and a half when I was expelled.

* Later as a lieutenant colonel in the Special Air Services in
World War II, Brian, for great gallantry after being dropped
behind the German lines, was decorated with the DSO and MC.
It is rather depressing to think that his mother complained to
mine because I told him the facts of life when we were both ten
years old. He, not believing this phenomenal piece of news, had
asked her for up-to-date information.

2

There is a Chinese proverb to the effect that when everything in the garden is at its most beautiful, an ill wind blows the seeds of weeds and, suddenly, when least expected, all is ugliness.

The decision to expel me from Heatherdown, I am sure, was not taken lightly because in those days expulsion from school was tantamount to ruin for a boy of my age. Public schools with bulging waiting lists could pick and choose among far more desirable applicants, and any boy without a public school education started life at an incalculable disadvantage. Sure enough, my mother soon received a polite letter from Mr. Tuppy Headlam for whose house at Eton I had hopefully been entered, saying that, unfortunately, he had decided that he was going to have to "shorten his entry list, etc., etc."

But of this I knew nothing. It was the end of term anyway, and in the excitement I noticed no chill on the part of Sammy Day, nor any of the other masters, as I said goodbye and went off whooping and hollering with the rest of the boys to board the school train at Ascot for the trip to Waterloo.

On arrival at Waterloo, the shouting, laughing, hysterically happy boys were clutched to parental bosoms while parental eyes were averted from filthy nails, grease spots and ink stains.

I braced myself for my usual encounter with Uncle Tommy. He was enlisted on these occasions to meet the school train at one platform, collect my trunk, and see me safely ensconced in a third-class compartment on the train for Portsmouth Harbour where my mother would be waiting to take me on the boat across The Solent to Ryde and thence to my beloved Rose Cottage, Bembridge, I.W. Once this had been accomplished, his contribution to the proceedings ended.

Occasionally, he gave the guard half a crown to keep an eye on me and make sure that I did not get off at the stop before Portsmouth Town.

Uncle Tommy was easily identifiable. Above his beetling eyebrows and Duke of Wellington nose, he wore a top hat, the wont of his ilk whenever the king was in London. He bore down upon me, uttered no word of greeting, and with an imperious gesture of his umbrella commanded me to follow. Everything so far had been perfectly normal. He hardly ever wasted conversation on me, so the silent march through the station following a porter with my trunk gave me no sense of foreboding.

Soon I was alone in a sooty compartment that smelled of stale smoke and orange peel, watching the retreating figure of my stepfather stalking toward the exit. Hanging out of the window I saw him pause and speak to the guard and point in my direction. The guard nodded his understanding. Soon we were off.

I sat back and savored the delicious aroma of my compartment, then, after examining the framed faded pictures of Freshwater Bay and Shanklin, I snuggled into my corner seat, gazed out the window, and gave myself up to delicious anticipation of the four-week holiday ahead.

My mother had beautiful teeth and a beautiful smile. I imagined her standing by the barrier, the harbor behind her, waiting for me when the smile broke out as she saw me. Would I run to meet her as I longed to do? No, I thought not, the little kids at Waterloo had looked pretty soppy doing that; I would play the whole thing cool, saunter—that's what I'd do—saunter, and then suddenly, shove out my hand and give her the wooden bracket I had made for her in the carpentry class. I had clutched this bracket wrapped in brown paper in my hand ever since I left Heatherdown.

Two hours later, the green Hampshire countryside gave way to the drab outskirts of Portsmouth, and as the train slowed down for its first stop, I looked down into the busy heart of the city; another five minutes, ten at the most and I would see my mother and the holidays really would start. I wondered if the tires of my bicycle were flat and if Grizel and Joyce were there and, above all, if Brian Franks was back from Wixenford yet. Max, I knew, was away on a six months' training cruise as a cadet on HMS *Thunderer*, but I squirmed with excitement, little knowing that the Chinese wind had blown a whole carload of weeds into my garden and I was, at that very moment, waist deep in nettles.

The train stopped. The guard opened the door, jerked his thumb in my direction, and addressed someone behind him. "That's the little bastard."

A gigantic man in a trench coat, with a magenta-colored face and tufts of hair sprouting on his cheekbones, filled the doorway.

"Get your things," he commanded, "you are coming with me."

"No, sir," I quavered, "my mother is waiting for me at the next stop."

"Don't argue, get your bloody things."

Stupefied with fear, I cowered into my corner.

"Oh, Christ!" said the man to the guard. "Get his bloody things down, will you? I'll lug him out."

With that, while the guard lowered my suitcase and mackintosh, this huge creature picked me up bodily. I grabbed wildly at the luggage rack as I was carried out and dropped my mother's bracket. I don't think I fought much or even cried. I was paralyzed with terror.

I was dragged along the platform, outside into the station yard and shoved into an ancient car.

"What are you doing with that little boy?" asked a woman with a baby.

"Mind your own fucking business" was the answer. I noticed a heavy smell of spirits.

Through Portsmouth we lurched and out to the genteel suburbs of Southsea. I now sobbed uncontrollably. My brain refused to consider what could be happening to me. I cried for my mother.

"Stop that bloody noise, and when you do, I'll tell you where you are going."

My sobs dried up into a sniveling kind of hiccups.

"First of all, you have been expelled from Heatherdown because you are a dirty little shit. You are not going home for the holidays, you are staying here with me, and if you don't behave yourself, I'll tan the arse off you. Any questions?"

I shall always remember Southsea Common: flat greasy,

wet and windswept, with a dejected flock of dirty sheep
morosely munching its balding surface.

Halfway across he stopped the car and slapped me hard
several times across the face.

"Stop it, for Christ's sake . . . You're not a bloody girl."

I was still whimpering with fear when we arrived at a
dreary house in a shoddy row. Grimy net curtains and an
aspidistra filled half a bleak downstairs window which
looked onto a brick path and a muddy garden; the other
half was filled by the curious faces of a half dozen boys.

Commander Bollard ran a school for "difficult" boys.

I don't know how my stepfather found him. He was not
a lovable man. The object of a certain amount of misdirect-
ed sympathy because he fulminated constantly against the
terrible injustice he had suffered by being "axed" from the
Navy when a promising lieutenant commander. It was
nearer the truth to say that he had found it more expedient
to resign his commission at the time rather than face a
court of inquiry convened to trace the disappearance of
several hundred pounds' worth of bonded gin and whiskey
during his tenure as stores officer in Gibraltar.

Now he and his thin-lipped, blue-veined, tweedy, terribly
"refained" wife added to his meager pension and indulged
their mutual passion for pink gin by taking in a dozen or so
boarders.

The boarders were without exception pretty hard cases.
Nearly all had been expelled from one or more schools and
despairing parents had committed them to the tender care
of Commander and Mrs. Bollard hoping that stern discipline would work where kindness or indifference had so far
failed.

A few eventually pulled themselves together and clawed
their way back to acceptance by lesser public schools. Others ran away and joined the Merchant Navy. Several ended
up in Borstal.

The gallant commander laid about him with a will on the
smallest excuse, and there was hardly a bottom in the house
that did not bear witness to his Dickensian brutality.

We were treated like young criminals and soon began to
feel that we might as well behave like them.

Pocket money was not allowed as part of our "cure."

Extra food was essential because the gin-sodden labors
of Mrs. Bollard only half-filled our bellies.

I was welcomed by the other boys as a natural front. I had some fairly respectable clothes and a fresh pink-and-white complexion. When I opened my eyes wide, I could look fairly innocent. I was also, by at least eighteen months, the youngest.

The house was a three-storied rabbit warren and terribly overpopulated, but, oh, it was clean! We scrubbed and re-scrubbed every inch of it daily. It must have been the only building in existence where the wooden floors were holy-stoned twice a day. Oil lamps had to be spotless too—there was no electric light—and an ill-trimmed wick was evil-smelling evidence of highly punishable inefficiency.

The ghastly dining room was called the Gun Room, the kitchen the Galley, the cellar the Brig and so forth.

We did not sleep in hammocks but on wooden shelves, four to a room. The commander and his wife prowled about at night in stockinged feet hoping to catch us talking.

A couple of gray-faced ex-schoolmasters came every day to give us almost continuous lessons and there were no games. Saturday afternoons were free and we made full use of them.

One of the few useful things I learned there was the Morse code, which the commander taught himself. I sus-pect it was all he knew, but it made it unnecessary to speak when talking after lights out. It did however make flash-lights and batteries an essential part of our survival kit. These were procured in the same way as food—by stealing.

On Saturday afternoons, "the ship's company," as the commander liked to refer to his charges, split up into high-ly organized gangs of four or six and went shoplifting for chocolate, condensed milk, cakes, the batteries and torches, and other essentials.

Every day was torture for me. I received no word from my mother, and when once I borrowed enough money—sev-en pence, I believe—to put through a telephone call to wish her a happy Easter, somebody at Rose Cottage hung up as soon as they heard my voice. Feeling a complete out-cast and, worst of all, within sight of Bembridge seven miles away across the water, I gradually became the best and most dedicated front man in the establishment.

"Curly" and "Dusty" were the two unchallenged gang leaders. I worked mostly in Curly's group. A large foxy-faced boy with a mop of sandy hair, protruding teeth and freckles, he called the shots on Saturdays. He was a brilliant organizer.

On Saturday mornings he decided exactly what was to be lifted during the afternoon and it was never an excessive amount. Food for consumption during the coming week or salable goods to provide purchasing power. Curly knew a fence in Southampton who worked with smugglers in the Merchant Navy, and with the exception of our most ambitious effort, a hot motorcycle, which had to be dumped in a chalk quarry on the Downs, this man took everything we had to offer.

Curly had decided that as summer was coming on, thin cotton shirts and singlets would be most acceptable to the fence's regular customers—men heading for the Indian Ocean, Dakar or Panama.

We lifted in all that day, working half a dozen big stores, about two-dozen salable articles. As front man for candy, cigarettes and buns, my job was simple: to open big blue eyes wide in a small chocolate, tobacconist's or cake shop and engage some dear old lady in long conversation about the price of various things which I hoped to be able to buy for my crippled uncle in the hospital. While this was going on one or two of the rest of the gang lifted a few items from the far end of the counter. It was easy.

The big stores with their possibility of store detectives called for a more advanced technique: the marbles.

Once I saw that the lifters were exactly in position for a quick grab, I burst a large paper bag full of glass marbles.

The crash of falling glass turned all heads; many willing souls stooped to aid the poor little boy, who even on occasions could summon up a few tears of embarrassment.

We never worked the same store twice.

Three weeks passed, and as a relief from the crude and vicious discipline of the commander—I once spent a whole day in the Brig, alone in the darkness of the cellar listening to the rats scrabbling about among piles of old newspapers around me—Saturday afternoons became oases in the desert of my loneliness.

Thrashed by the commander for the smallest offense, ill-fed, apparently deserted by the family, expelled from a well-known school and facing my future through a bead curtain of question marks, I was, after ten years of life, already at a very low ebb.

But if, Dear Reader, you should think that at that point I felt I was a victim of circumstances, a magnet for bad luck, or just plain "hardly done by," while you might be right, I beg you to consider the possibility that I was also a thoroughly poisonous little boy.

After a month under the command of Commander Bollard, his wife one day came to find me. A cigarette permanently waggled from her mouth like a small French fonctionnaire Hooverizing at his Gauloise. Her upper lip was yellow.

"May husbind wants yew," she announced.

I followed her to the "Captain's Cabin"—a dreadful little study full of leather furniture and old Navy lists. Around the place plenty of bottles were in evidence—none held sailing ships.

The commander lounged behind his desk. "All right, you little bugger, you have been sprung. Get packed, don't steal anybody else's stuff because you go through customs here before you leave—you're catching the three o'clock ferry to the island."

My heart nearly stopped beating. I could hardly believe it. I rushed upstairs and started packing furiously, terrified that he would change his mind.

No mother met the ferry on which I was dumped unceremoniously by the gallant commander. With a strange last-minute change of character, he thrust a stick of Southsea rock in my hand along with my ticket.

At Ryde, an elderly porter who was on the lookout for me took charge.

On the short train trip to Bembridge, I reflected on what sort of welcome would be awaiting me.

It was my ally, Grizel, very distressed bless her, who met the train, and as we walked up the hill to the cottage, she filled me in, as best she could, as to my immediate fate.

I was to be sent into the Navy, if they would have me, and if I could pass the exam, about two years hence.

"How is Mum? Is she very angry with me?"

"I think she is terribly unhappy about Heatherdown. They wouldn't have you at Eton after being expelled, you know."

I had a poor welcome at Rose Cottage, but it was no worse than I had expected.

My mother was in her room. I went upstairs with leaden feet and watery knees.

Briefly she went over my miserable performance at Heatherdown. The damage was done, she said, but it was far more serious than I realized—I wouldn't be able to get into anything now. The Navy might take me, but everything depended on getting very high marks in the exam. If I got those, they might overlook my being expelled from school.

My mother explained that I had been brought over from Portsmouth, not for a holiday but to repack my trunk and to leave the very next morning for Penn Street, in Buckinghamshire, where Uncle Tommy had arranged for me to go to a "crammer" who would try to get me past the entrance examination for Dartmouth.

Another of Uncle Tommy's selections? I quailed at the thought but I couldn't see that things could get very much worse than they had been lately, so after a silent family supper, I borrowed Grizel's bicycle—the tires of mine were flat—and pedaled up to the Mill House where Brian Franks lived, knowing I would find a sympathetic ear.

Still shaky from his illness, Brian gave me an eyewitness account of the opening of my gift. It seemed that the matron had unwrapped the box with quite a flourish and the contents had flown into a medicine cabinet whence it had been extracted with forceps. It was all rather grubby one way or another, but Brian said he had begun to feel better from that moment.

I have noticed again and again that when things are really black and one feels that they can't possibly get any worse, they often do. This time, however, things improved.

The crammer at Penn Street was the vicar, the Reverend Arthur Browning, a magnificent-looking grandson of Robert Browning—clear blue eyes and white wavy hair.

Chorus: It's the roast beef of old England,
           That makes us what we are today!
Verse: What makes the Vicar's hair so nice and wavy?
           It's simply becos he was brought up on the gravy,
           Of the Roast Beef of old Engerlund
           That makes us wot we are today.

So we dutifully and sycophantically warbled at the village fete a week after I arrived.

Sycophantically because beneath his benign and exotic

exterior he was an evil-tempered, vain old tyrant.

The parents uniformly adored him; the boys, without exception, loathed him.

The Victorian vicarage nestled next to the Victorian church in a damp valley, enfolded by dripping beech woods, part of the well-known pheasant shoot of Lord Curzon's Penn House Estate, three miles away.

Mrs. Browning was a plump partridge of a woman who wore pince-nez which were attached to a little chain. These in turn were controlled by a spring concealed inside a round enamel receptacle pinned to her generous left bosom.

There was a nice sporting master called Mr. Keeble who took us for long walks to Amersham and bicycle rides to Beaconsfield and a nice scholarly old gentleman called Mr. Woodcote, whose ill-fitting false teeth had a distressing habit of flying out onto the carpet or into soup. At the village fete they became embedded in a macaroon.

Ma Browning was immensely greedy, and the high fees paid by our parents enabled her to provide a very good board indeed. She had a brace of daughters aged eighteen and twenty, whose woolen bloomers hung in festoons in the bathroom, and an elder son who enlivened Sunday luncheons by arriving very flushed and rather late with garrulous business friends from London.

All in all, with the exception of Pa Browning's rages, which were the twittering of little birds compared to the exhibitions of Mr. Christie of Elstree and of more recent memory, Commander Bollard of Southsea, Penn Street vicarage was a very pleasant interlude.

I worked hard but many of Pa Browning's tantrums were certainly brought on when it became apparent to him that mathematics of all sorts would forever be beyond me.

It began to look probable that the Royal Navy would not entrust the navigation of several million pounds' worth of battleship and several hundred lives to an officer who could not work out his position; but there was still some hope as the most important part of the naval entrance exam was said to be the interview by the Board of Admirals, and many encouraging stories were in circulation to prove that he who impressed the admirals personally was well on his way to conquering the written papers.

There were about a dozen boys at the vicarage, some of

my age trying to pass the common entrance exam to public
schools and an older group who had finished with school
and were trying to pass examinations for universities. Some
of these had been expelled or superannuated from public
schools.

Having been expelled from Heatherdown, I had a certain
amount in common with these, but not nearly so much in
common as one large ex-Etonian thought.

At first I was flattered by his attentions and was naïve
enough to think he liked me for myself. He took me for bicycle rides and stood me ice-cream cornets by the gross.
Then one day he took me for a walk in the beech woods.

It was a very dreary experience, and the laws on homosexuality being what they still are, I am certainly not going
into it in any great detail here. Suffice to say that I came
out of the wood with a ten and sixpenny secondhand accor-
dion which I had admired in a junk shop in Loudwater.

I think I had visions of owning a whole orchestra. In any
event, I could not wait to tell everyone how easy it was to
obtain musical instruments.

I was interrogated by Pa Browning and a large, black
taxi came and took the large ex-Etonian away.

The day of the naval entrance exam finally dawned. I
was scrubbed from head to toe and shining like a new sixpence, was dumped with several hundred other applicants
in a forbidding morgue of a building, next to Burlington
Arcade.

My French, English, history and geography all were
pretty reliable, and I had been primed with a few questions
in arithmetic, algebra and geometry that Pa Browning was
sure would come up. I had those answers down pat, but
above all I was rehearsed in how to behave in front of the
admirals.

"Be quick and intelligent without being smug or
cheeky," said Pa Browning.

"If you don't know the answer to a question, make one
up quickly—don't just dither.

"Remember above all the boy who was asked to give the
names of the three most famous admirals in British naval
history—'Admiral Nelson, sir; Admiral Drake, sir; and I
didn't quite catch your name, sir.' "

The first exam was the medical one.

Half a dozen at a time, we were stripped naked and to

test our hearts, made to climb ropes without using our legs;
then the usual tapping of knees and peering into ears,
mouths and eyes took place.

Finally, "get on your marks as though you are going to
run a hundred yards." Once in position, a large hand
grabbed our testicles from the rear. "Cough!" came the
order. One poor little brute thought the man said "Off!"
and leaped eagerly forward. He was still being rubbed with
ice when I was fully dressed and waiting to be summoned
by the admirals.

A bemedaled master-at-arms approached me in the anteroom.

"All right, you, you're next. Now go and sit at that desk.
You'll find a pencil and paper there. You have five minutes
to write a funny story—got it?"

I repressed my urge to indulge in lavatory humor and I
don't remember what I wrote, but it was certainly plagiarism in its finest form, as I had read it the day before in an
old *Punch*.

Clasping my funny story, I followed the master-at-arms
into a long paneled room. Seated around a table was a drift
of admirals. One or two wore beards; all were bound to the
elbows with gold braid and festooned with medals.

They seemed rather bored. One took my funny story and
read it, then passed it to his neighbor. Out of the corner of
my eye I watched it progress as questions were fired at me.

"Have you had any relations in the Navy?"

I skipped my brother and dug up a distant cousin who
fought at Jutland.

"How does a petrol engine work?"

I knew.

"What was the number of the taxi you came in this
morning?"

"I walked, sir."

"There is a blank map on the wall over there. Go and
point out Singapore."

I jabbed a desperate finger in the region of Bangkok.

"Why do you want to go into the Navy?"

"I want to be an admiral, sir."

I think I overdid it a bit there.

After a few more fairly inane questions to which I gave
answers of equal nondistinction, the most heavily bound up
and festooned of the admirals spoke up.

"One last question: Why were you expelled from Heath-erdown?"

That really rocked me, but I should have realized they would have done their homework.

"I put some dog's mess in a box, sir, and sent it to a sick friend, sir."

A long silence followed my announcement.

"You thought that was funny?"

"Yes, sir."

"But your headmaster did not—correct?"

"Yes, sir."

"I see. Well, fortunately, we don't have dogs aboard ship."

Hearty laughter greeted this sally.

I believe I passed the interview and I was bullish after most of the written papers. The last one to confront me was mathematics.

Not one of the carefully learned problems so confidently predicted by Pa Browning came up and my total score in the subject was 28 out of a possible 300.

Naturally, I failed and the Royal Navy decided that it could rub along without me. So aged twelve and a half, it was back to the old drawing board.

Tommy it was who unexpectedly saved the day. Not yet his far-reaching and inadvertent introduction to the whore, Nessie, but he thrust into my path a character who definite-ly arrested the downward graph of my fortunes.

3

The English public schools have been operating for a long time; some for a very long time indeed. Eton was founded in 1440, and Winchester even earlier in 1378. Rugby, where that horrible little boy picked up a soccer ball and charged off with it, opened in 1567, and Oundle, thirteen years before that. Cheltenham and Marlborough, having opened their doors for the first time in the early eighteen forties, were probably the youngest additions to the well-known list, until in 1923 Stowe came along.

Stowe School was started not as were the others, by kings, archbishops or lord mayors but by a consortium of educators and hardheaded businessmen who saw the possibilities for a new public school and hoped to make a good thing out of it.

Stowe House, the vast Georgian home of the extinct dukes of Buckingham, had become the debt-ridden property of a kinsman, the master of Kinloss.

He, like my father, was slaughtered during the war to end all wars, and his mother like mine was forced to liquidate.

The consortium obtained the magnificent house and several hundred acres of grounds. Clough Williams-Ellis, the architect of Portmeirion in North Wales, was enlisted to transform it. A prospectus was issued and Stowe was on its way, heralded as "the new great public school."

In these early postwar years, a whole strata of suddenly well-to-do industrialists found the established public schools, to which they longed to send their sons, already bulging at the seams, so the consortium had no problem whatever in finding clients. Finding an aggressive headmaster with new ideas was far more difficult. They made a most fortuitous choice: a young housemaster from Lancing College, J. F. Roxburgh.

In May of 1923, the school opened with fewer than a
hundred boys. Somewhere in the depths of the Carlton
Club, Tommy heard rumblings; they could have been ful-
minations because a leading article in the *Times* and the
headmaster of Eton, Edward Lyttelton, both opined that
year that instead of starting a new public school it would be
far more sensible to enlarge the facilities of the old ones;
but whatever they were, the rumblings sank in. Pa Browning was instructed to investigate this last resort, and in July,
I was sent over to Stowe, thirty miles in the dilapidated village taxi, to be interviewed by J. F. Roxburgh.

Stowe has to be the most beautiful school in England.
Golden stone colonnades, porticoes by Vanbrugh, sweeping
lawns, huge lakes, long green valleys, glorious avenues, a
Corinthian arch, a Palladian bridge and scores of assorted
grottoes and *"temples d'amour"* from each of which,
through spectacular beech woods, rides open up to show
other more fascinating "Follies." Robert Adam, Grinling
Gibbons, William Kent, Valdré and Borra combined to
produce glowing, beautifully proportioned interiors.

Roxburgh, in his first public speech as headmaster, said,
"Every boy who goes out from Stowe will know beauty
when he sees it for the rest of his life."

How true, but the apprehensive small boy who waited in
the headmaster's flower-filled garden on that warm summer
evening saw nothing of the architectural and landscaped
beauties around him. All he knew was that he had never in
all his life wanted anything so much as to be accepted for
that school—it just felt right and he longed passionately to
be part of it.

Roxburgh finally appeared. Very elegant, he seemed,
with a spotted bow tie, very tall, curly hair parted in the
middle.

He came out through the French windows of his study
and crooked his finger at me. Then he smiled, put an arm
around my shoulders and led me to a stone bench.

"Now, my dear man," he said, "you seem to have had a
lot of ups and downs. Tell me all about it."

I don't pretend to have total recall, but I do remember
those words—I will never forget them.

He listened sympathetically as I told him my version of
my life so far. When I had finished, he remained silent for
what seemed like an eternity. Then he stood up and said,

"I'll walk with you to the car." On the way through the school, he showed me the assembly hall and the library and pointed out the fabulous view from the top of the south front steps across sloping, green pastures to a lake, then up to the towering Corinthian arch. Several times he spoke to boys who passed us, each time addressing them by their Christian names.

When he reached the ancient taxi, he looked down at me and smiled again, then he said. "There will be two hundred new boys coming next term and you will be in Chandos House. Your housemaster will be Major Haworth."

I mumbled something, then climbed into the taxi. If I didn't weep then, I should have.

In September I arrived at Stowe along with the other new boys. As we outnumbered the old boys by two to one, everybody, masters included, for the first couple of weeks, sported a piece of white cardboard pinned to his coat showing his name in bold print, rather like a dentists' convention in Chicago.

All the boys wore gray flannel suits, as one of Roxburgh's better new ideas was to break with the traditional prison garb of the older establishments; no top hats, stiff collars or straw boaters for us . . . gray flannel suits on weekdays and blue suits on Sunday.

Rules were sensible and good manners were encouraged; for instance, hands had to be removed from pockets when passing a master. There were no bounds and boys were allowed to have bicycles. However, one still had to pedal three miles to get out of the school grounds so that was a little more strenuous than it sounded.

I could not believe my good fortune. The boys seemed nice and friendly, albeit as bemused for the first few days as I was, and Major Haworth, lately a company commander at Sandhurst, was one of the kindest and gentlest of men.

People are sharply divided about their school days and contrary to what one tells one's children about their being the best days of one's life, most people remember them as being pretty ghastly.

Stowe, in those early days, had to be different from any other school. At the start, we were all the same age—around thirteen. Within four years, as the number of boys swelled

from 300 to 500, there was an annual intake of younger
ones, but somehow it seemed as though we all grew up together and I for one enjoyed the whole thing immensely.
Later, my inherent weakness of not being able to stand
prosperity got me into trouble, but for the first couple of
years, I was a fairly reliable citizen.

Roxburgh dominated the scene and I worshiped the
man.

The first to notice some special interest being shown by a
boy, Roxburgh nurtured it, fostered it and made the boy
feel a little bit special because of it. How he did this, I shall
never know, but he made every single boy at that school
feel that he and what he did were of real importance to the
headmaster. Boys were always addressed by their first names
and encouraged to build radio sets; to fence and play golf
and tennis besides the usual school games; to paint, play
the piano or the bagpipes; and to keep pets, though this last
got a little out of control as the boys grew older and instead
of rabbits and ferrets being the status symbols, monkeys,
bears, hyenas and skunks filled the cages. Finally, the
school zoo was shut down for reasons of noise and smell.

I played the trombone and the drum in the school band
and started a house magazine, to which "J.F." subscribed,
called *The Chandosian.* I also, by the age of fourteen, fell
in love once more with milk chocolate and became almost
entirely conical in shape. My nickname was Podger or
Binge and I went bright pink after Rugger. Another boy,
named Smallman, was even fatter than I was; his nickname
was unoriginal—Tiny. Tiny Smallman was very large indeed and we both became self-conscious about our physical
defects. Tiny found an ad in a boys' paper and we spent
our pocket money on strange tubes containing a foul-smell-
ing green paste which, when rubbed onto the stomach or
bottom, was guaranteed to reduce it in size. After football,
we waited till the others had left the changing room rather
than take a shower in public and thereby risk the ribald remarks and the towel flicking that was apt to accompany
our appearance.

Because of my shape, I was enlisted in the school plays
usually playing a mushroom or something fairly unobtru-
sive . . . I got the call of the greasepaint, however, and before I left school, I was running the school concerts and
giving myself all the best parts.

I studied fairly hard, though permanently stymied by mathematics, and my immediate goal was the school certificate, a public exam for which one sat between fifteen and sixteen and which, provided one obtained enough credits, was comparable with O and A levels today. One of the credits one had to obtain in order to get the school certificate was mathematics, so from a very early date, "J.F." saw to it that I took special tuition to try and defeat the monster.

My long-term goal, thanks to some pretty nifty salesmanship by Major Haworth, became the Royal Military College, Sandhurst, followed by a commission in the Argyll and Sutherland Highlanders.

School, between thirteen and fifteen, therefore, presented no great problems and the holidays, too, went along very nicely during this period of formation . . . Tommy being persona non grata at Rose Cottage, the summers were bliss. For Christmas Grizel and I were packed off to spend the holiday at Nanpanton, in Leicestershire, with the Paget family, where the children, Peter and Joan, were of identical vintage.

Edmund, the father, was, with a splendid figure named Algy Burnaby, joint master of the Quorn Hunt; and Barbara, the mother, was a garrulous, gossipy, enchanting, shop-talking fox huntress who rode sidesaddle under a top hat bigger than Tommy's, swore like a trooper and, along with the rest of her family, never could grasp the fact that Grizel and I were not actually afraid of horses—we were just too impecunious to hunt. We loved the Pagets.

Easter holidays in English schools being short—three weeks—Tommy would arrange to be away while my mother found a variety of places in which to house us. Sometimes, it was Bembridge, but Rose Cottage was barely habitable at that time of year. Once we were sent to a sister of Tommy's who lived in a noisome little flat in Portsmouth—far too near the Bollards and the scenes of my crimes for comfort—but the worst was when Tommy decided to be a real-estate tycoon.

He bought a poky little house in a back street behind Windsor Castle. It was a dark-paneled purgatory, whose sole charm lay in the fact that it had once belonged to Nell Gwyn and much royal thrashing around was said to have gone on in the four-poster upstairs. It poured with rain for the entire holiday and Grizel and I played mah-jongg in semidarkness for three weeks.

I hope I never again have to set eyes on the bamboos, the flowers, the winds, the seasons and all those miserable dragons. I couldn't wait to get back to Stowe.

The memorable Easter holiday of this period came just after my fourteenth birthday.

Tommy's real-estate operations found us, for a while, the inhabitants of 110 Sloane Street, a small house of many floors which shook as the buses went past the door: gasoline-driven red metropolitan buses, Nos. 19 and 22, and far more fascinating to me because they were driven by steam, the white Nationals, No. 30.

My brother, who had left the Navy because of chronic seasickness and sensibly switched to the Army, was abroad with his regiment in India. Joyce and Grizel both had tiny bedrooms, but there was no room for me, so I slept in a minute cubicle in a boardinghouse in St. James's Place, some distance away.

Every night after dinner, I walked to Sloane Square, boarded a 19 or a 22 headed for Piccadilly, got off at the Ritz Hotel and proceeded down St. James's Street to my iron bed, wooden floor, stained jug and basin and pot under the bed.

The next morning, I had to be back for breakfast at eight o'clock and I was given fourpence a day for the round trip. Even my rudimentary mathematics could work out that by walking four miles a day, I could save almost half a crown a week.

I enjoyed my nocturnal travels very much and soon gave up going straight from Sloane Street to St. James's Place and took to going all the way down Piccadilly to Piccadilly Circus to watch the electric signs.

Every night, I became most adventurous and after a week or so, I knew the area bounded by Park Lane, Oxford Street, Regent Street and Pall Mall like the back of my hand. This was a pretty safe area for a fourteen-year-old—indeed, it never crossed my mind that it could be otherwise—and apart from being spoken to a few times by strange men who asked me if I would like to go home with them to meet their dogs or see their paintings, I tramped around unhindered.

It seemed to me perfectly normal for a boy to be walking around the West End of London at night, so I saw nothing out of the ordinary in the number of girls who were doing the same thing; cloche hats, flesh-colored stockings and the forerunner of the miniskirt being the vogue, I saw a vast amount of female legs and ankles twinkling their way up and down the same streets that I frequented.

Bond street was a great favorite of mine because many of the shop windows were lit up all night, and I made it a point, after watching BOVRIL, IRON JELLOIDS and OWBRIDGE change colors in Piccadilly Circus, to pause on my way to St. James's Place and check on how things looked in the windows of Garrards, Aspreys and Ciros Pearls.

Some of the girls, I noticed, were walking every night on the same streets, and I was soon on nodding terms with them, although I didn't understand at all the remarks made as I passed, nor the giggles that followed me.

One night, on Bond Street, I noticed a really superior pair of legs in front of me and I became so fascinated by them that I followed them for quite a distance. The girl seemed to have many friends and stopped and spoke to them from time to time.

The next night, I skipped going to watch the electric signs and went looking for those legs instead. I searched up and down Bond Street and cased the side streets too—Clifford Street, Savile Row and even Burlington Street, the scene of my naval debacle.

Just as I was about to give up, the girl came out of a house right in front of me and walked rapidly off toward Piccadilly. I followed, and when she stopped on a corner to talk to a couple of lady friends, I crossed the street and pretended to look into a shop window. I managed to get a fairly good view of her face. She was laughing and talking . . . very lively, very gay, and her face looked beautiful in an open, fresh English rose kind of way—blond, blue eyes, high color—you know the sort of thing.

She stayed there talking to her friends, and as I didn't want to be conspicuous, I moved off toward my boarding-house.

When I woke up in the morning I knew I must be in love. At least, I suspected that I was because I could think of nothing else but this girl. The day dragged on interminably, a shopping morning with my mother and in the afternoon, playing among the stunted, grimy bushes of the gardens opposite our house with some stunted, grimy Spanish children.

That night, after dinner, I didn't walk. I was in a hurry. I took the bus and was lucky. After I had cruised up and down for what seemed an age, my patience was rewarded and my heart gave a lurch as I saw her lovely, long legs approaching from the Piccadilly direction. She was with a distinguished-looking, gray-haired man in a dinner jacket, about the same age as Tommy. He wore an opera hat and was smoking a cigar—obviously her father. Together they went into a house on Cork Street, and deliriously happy that I had found out where my dream lived, I took myself off to bed.

It took three days or rather nights of patient toil and careful sleuthing before I finally met Nessie.

I was following her down Cork Street at what I imagined to be a discreet distance, my eyes glued to her wondrous underpinnings, when she stopped and turned so suddenly and so unexpectedly that I nearly bumped into her.

"Wot the 'ell are yer followin' me for?" she demanded.

I went purple.

"I wasn't following you," I lied. "I was just on my way to bed."

"Well, for Gawd's sake, go on 'ome, mate. For the last four nights you've been stuck to me like my bleedin' shadow. Wot d'yer want anyway?"

I stammered and looked wildly to right and left. Suddenly she softened and smiled.

"All right, it's still early and you're a bit young but come on home and I'll give yer a good time."

Soon she turned into her doorway, and in a daze I followed, unable to believe my good fortune.

"A good time," she had said—it had to be at least a ginger beer and listening to the gramophone . . . Aileen Stanley singing "When It's Moonlight in Kaluha" or Jack Hulbert and Cicely Courtneidge in excerpts from *Clowns in Clover*. In a high state of expectancy, I mounted to the second floor behind my glorious new friend.

The flat, above a tailor's shop, was small and smelled of cabbage. In the living room there was a large divan with a lot of satin cushions and some dolls on it and nearby a small lamp with a red shade. A small kitchen stove was behind a screen. The other room was a bedroom, also rather poorly lit; a tiny bathroom was just discernible in the gloom beyond the huge bed that seemed to sag quite a lot in the middle.

"Three quid," she said, as she took off her coat.

I didn't quite get the message, so she came very close to me and peered into my eyes.

"Three quid," she repeated. "That too much?"

I gulped and floundered. "For what?"

"For the best yer've ever 'ad, mate, but then you 'aven't 'ad a lot, 'av yer? 'Ow old are yer anyway?"

I was still unsure as to exactly what ground I was on and I kept wondering if her father lived downstairs, but I managed to mumble the truth.

"*Fourteen!!*" she practically shrieked. "Wot the 'ell d'yer think I am—a bleedin' nannie?"

Then she started giggling. "Oh, my Gawd, wot a larf. 'Ow old d'yer think I am anyway?"

"Twenty," I suggested tentatively.

"Three years yet before that 'appens," she said. "Well, come on, let's get on wiv it. *Fourteen* . . . Gawd, yer are a one aren't yer?"

I watched half in fascination, half in apprehension as she walked about the living room, taking off her little hat and blouse and unhooking her skirt.

" 'Ere, take a look at these in case you need any 'elp." With that she sat me down on the divan and left me to look at a large album of photographs.

"I'll be ready in a jiffy, dear." She disappeared into the bedroom.

I had not so far been exposed to any pornography so the contents of that album very nearly finished off my sex life before it got under way. Hideous overweight ladies, clad only in shoes and stockings, being mounted from every angle by skinny little men with enormous "dongs": combinations of every sort in threes and twos, all with expressions of the greatest sincerity—and all apparently in advanced middle age.

The awful truth began to filter through my brain.

When Nessie appeared in the bedroom door dressed in the same uniform as the buxom ladies in the album—naked except for black stockings, held up above the knees by pink garters with blue roses on them and pink high-heeled shoes—she had a small towel in her hand.

"Come along, ducks, let's see 'ow good yer are . . . yer can wash in 'ere . . . I've put in pomegranate," she added. In a daze I followed her into the dark little bedroom . . . another red-shaded lamp was beside the bed. "Over there, dear," she said, indicating a kidney shaped enamel bowl on a collapsible knee-high stand. She threw me the towel, lay down on the bed, and put a record on a portable gramophone. The tune was one I knew well; it has, rather naturally, haunted me ever since. "Yes . . . we have no bananas." As I was to discover later, Nessie had a wonderful native wit but I still believe her selection at that particular moment was a random one.

"Get a move on, ducks. You don't get all night for three quid, yer know. Get your shirt off for a start."

I took off my coat and my shirt and started to wash my hands in the bowl.

"Christ!" she yelled, sitting bolt upright. "Not yer bleedin' 'ands—yer dickie bird! Just a minute," she went on more gently, "come 'ere, come and sit on me bed. I want to talk to you . . . Now look me in the eye, straight. . . . Is this the first? . . . 'Ave yer ever done it before . . . ever done any fuckin'?"

Miserably, I shook my head.

"And you 'aven't got three quid either, I'll bet?"

Again I shook my head and mumbled some inane explanation.

"Aw, you poor little bastard," she said, "you must be scared out of yer fuckin' wits." She looked at me reflectively. "Ever seen a naked woman before?"

"No," I confessed.

"Well, this is wot it looks like—'ow d'yer like it?"

I smiled weakly and tried not to lower my eyes. Nessie snuggled down and started to giggle again, a deliciously infectious sound.

"Well, you've got this far—why don't you take the rest of your clobber orf and pop into bed?"

"What about the . . .," I began.

"Oh, you owe me three quid," she interrupted. "Christ, I never thought I'd be seducing children. . . . FOURTEEN . . . come on, jump in then."

"Yes . . . we have no bananas" was replaced by something a little more encouraging; the bedside lamp with the red shade was left and Nessie with her wondrous skin became a most understanding teacher. "There we are, dear, that's it now—take a little weight on your elbows like a gentleman. Slowly, dear, more slowly. Whoa! yer not a fuckin' woodpecker, yer know . . . slowly . . . *that's* it, enjoy yerself . . . there, that's nice, isn't it, dear? . . . Are yer 'appy? . . . 'Appy now?"

By the time the Easter holidays ended Nessie had become the most important thing in my life; my education at her hands and, in a way, at her expense had continued. She worked at night and slept late, but on many afternoons, we met, usually at the entrance to a small movie house—she loved W. S. Hart—or we went to the music halls, the Coliseum, the Alhambra or the Palladium, to see Herbert Mundin, Lily Morris, Rebla the juggler, or a marvelous pair of young acrobats—Nervo and Knox. The seats cost one shilling and threepence and after the shows we had a cup of tea and a bun in a little tea shop or we skipped the tea and the bun and went directly back to her flat. Afterward, I would walk down to Sloane Street for a dreary family dinner during which Tommy would rattle the damn cuff links in his starched shirt to draw attention to the fact that I was dozing at the table.

Quite early in my relationship with Nessie, I made the elementary mistake of asking her why she did it . . . "a sweet girl like you." She rounded on me like a tigress: "Now don't yer start tryin' to reform me. About three times a week some silly bugger asks the same friggin' question.

"Look . . . I'm three years older than you and I'm doing it because I want to do it. . . . Why I want to do it is none of your fuckin' bizness so if yer don't like it, piss off back to school."

Back at school for the summer term, I found that my life had fundamentally changed. Nessie or the thoughts of Nessie became the focal point of my existence. What I saw in her was fairly obvious, but there were other things, too, quite apart from the normal and very special physical attachment to "the first"; she gave me something that so far had been in rather short supply—call it love, understanding, warmth, female companionship or just ingredient X—whatever it was, it was all over me like a tent.

I can't believe that I contributed very much to Nessie's well-being or peace of mind during this period—a fat fourteen and a half with no money and less experience—but apart from the "hurly burly of the chaise longue," as Mrs. Patrick Campbell once described a splendid activity, there also grew up between us a brother-sister relationship that was to last for many years.

Thanks to Nessie's insistence, I lost weight, a lot of extra padding turned to muscle, and I became quite a proficient athlete of the second rank . . . house colors for practically everything and a frequent performer before I left Stowe in the 1st. XI cricket, the 1st. XV Rugby football and on the fencing and boxing teams.

Nessie came down to Stowe to see me in summer and brought a picnic basket and a tartan rug. Together we took full advantage of the beauties of the school grounds. She had never been out of London before, and these trips to the country, she told me later, gave her a peace she never knew existed. She took a great interest in my progress at the school and became so intrigued by my hero worship of Roxburgh that she insisted on meeting him. Basely, I tried to avoid this confrontation, but Nessie was not easily put off.

"Look, dear, 'e'll never know I'm an 'ore. 'E'll think I'm yer bleedin' aunt or somefin'." . . . "Do I look like an 'ore?"

I told her she looked beautiful and like a duchess—not that looking like a duchess was much of a compliment but she was as easily flattered as she was hard to dissuade.

"That's 'im, innit?" she cried one Saturday afternoon, looking across toward the cricket pavilion. Roxburgh was approaching our tartan rug. resplendent in a pale-gray suit topped by the inevitable spotted bow tie.

Nessie stood up, bathed in sunlight. She was wearing a short white silk summer dress that clung lovingly to her beautiful body; her honey-colored hair was cut in the fashion of the time—the shingle; she had a small upturned nose; she looked wonderfully young and fresh.

Roxburgh came over smiling his famous smile. "May I join you?"

I introduced him.

" 'E's just like you told me" said Nessie to me. " 'E's beautiful," and then to Roxburgh, "Don't look a bit like a schoolmaster, dew yer. dear?"

J. F. settling himself on the rug, missed a tiny beat but thereafter never gave any indication that he was not talking to a beautiful duchess.

THE MOON'S A BALLOON

He stayed about ten minutes, extolling the glories of Stowe House and its history, and Nessie bathed in the full glow of his charm. Never once did he ask any loaded questions, and when he got up to leave, he said, "David is very lucky to have such a charming visitor." The charming visitor nearly got me expelled almost a year later, but it was certainly not her fault.

In the summer of 1926, by now a robust sixteen-year-old and appreciably ahead of my time in worldly experience, I must have seemed changed to Roxburgh. He sent for me and told me that I was one of four boys he had selected to become monitors in a new house—Grafton—which was to open the following term.

The housemaster was coming from Fettes, Mr. Freeman, and the boy chosen as prefect or head of the house was Bernard Gadney.* It was a huge compliment, an enormous boost for any boy, but for me to feel that J. F. had this faith in me, it was a bonanza. However, before I could bask in the glories of my new responsibilities, I had to overcome a slight hazard—the school certificate. I was to sit for the exam in two weeks' time. It was a sort of long shot really; if I failed this first time, I would still have three more chances but I had to obtain the certificate soon in order to qualify to sit for the entrance exam to the Royal Military College, Sandhurst, eighteen months hence.

Apart from the dreaded mathematics, I was quite confident that I could pull it off this first time. My prospects in the new house were very exciting, my fat had disappeared, I had many friends at school and at Bembridge. I had Nessie in the background, and I was at last beginning to get to know and to love my mother. In fact, everything was roses for me. Then that damn wind started puffing those weeds in my direction once more.

I sat for the exam in the big school gymnasium and made mincemeat of the first two papers, French and history, and after the science, geography and English papers, I remained supremely confident. The last two papers were mathematics and Latin translation. In mathematics, as already explained, a credit (about 80 percent) was obligatory, otherwise the whole exam was failed. When the questions

* B. C. Gadney was later to captain the English XV in many Rugby Internationals.

were put on my desk—and all over the country at that
particular moment identical papers were being put in front
of thousands of nervous boys—I took a deep breath and
started to read.

One glance was enough. It was hopeless. I knew that I
just couldn't cope and there is no more suffocating feeling
than that when sitting for a public examination.

I made a few vague stabs at the geometry questions and
a token effort at the algebra, but there was no point in my
even trying to tackle the arithmetic.

I was the first boy to hand in his answers and leave the
gymnasium. I went out to the cricket nets and faced the
fact that the school certificate was certainly not going to be
mine this time.

Nessie was coming to see me the next day—a Saturday—and her train was due at Buckingham Station at
midday. The Latin exam was scheduled from ten o'clock
till eleven thirty, so I decided to get through this now-useless
and unprofitable period as quickly as possible, pedal down
to the station, and surprise her there instead of meeting her
as planned near the Corinthian arch at twelve thirty.

It so happened that my Latin teacher was the supervisor
of the candidates on that Saturday morning; this meant
that it was he who would hand out the questions at the
start, collect the answers at the end, and in between,
wander about the rows of desks making sure that there was
no talking, or, perish the thought, any use of notes.

He knew that I could easily pass the Latin exam, but
only I knew that it was now useless to try.

However, if I handed in a half-finished paper in half the
allotted time, he would most certainly make me go and sit
down again and do the job properly. The trick then was to
complete the whole paper in half the time and be on my
way to Buckingham Station. Archie Mongomery-Campbell
was a good and outstanding friend who occupied the desk
on my right during the whole week of exams. He was also
an excellent Latin scholar, so I enlisted his help.

The Latin paper was in two parts, prose and verse. It
was agreed that I would quickly dispose of the prose while
Archie coped first with the verse. Then, after making his
fair copy, he would crumple up his first draft and drop it
on the floor between the two desks. It was clearly understood between us that if anything went wrong, Archie

would merely say that he had thrown away his first translation after he had made his fair copy and if somebody picked it up it was none of his business. The dirty work was to be done by me alone, he was to be blameless.

It all went beautifully according to plan.

I copied out Archie's verse translation beneath my own effort at the prose, handed in my paper, and bicycled happily off in plenty of time to surprise Nessie.

We spent a blissful day together, eating shrimp paste sandwiches and sausage rolls, drinking shandy-gaff* and rolling around on the tartan rug. Nessie had begun to tell me a little more about herself and I listened adoringly that afternoon to her descriptions of her childhood in a Hoxton slum: six children in a tiny room, the three youngest in the bed, the others sleeping on the floor and all cowering away from the Friday night battles between the parents.

At fifteen she and her sister of a year older had run away. For a while, they found work as waitresses in dingy tea shops and restaurants in Battersea and Pimlico. A few months later they were engaged as hostesses in a sleazy "club" in Wardour Street. Then the sister started taking drugs and one night told Nessie she was going north with a boyfriend to avoid the police. Nessie didn't miss her much and soon was employed by Mrs. Kate Merrick at the 43 Club. She had to be on hand in evening dress as a dancing partner, making a fuss of Ma Merrick's rather high-class clientele and persuading them to buy champagne at exorbitant prices.

She was not allowed to solicit on the premises—a rule that was strictly enforced because Ma Merrick's establishment was often infiltrated by police officers in evening clothes, posing as the tipsy aftermath of regimental dinners or bachelor parties—but, in fact, contacts were easily enough made and Nessie soon built up the basis of an enthusiastic clientele.

"I'm not an 'ore wiv an 'eart of bleedin' gold, yer know, dear. I'm out for everything I can get out of this game for another couple of years—then I'm going to marry some nice Yank or Canadian and fuck off abroad and have kids.

"The only reason I work the streets is that I'm on me own. I don't 'ave to sit up all bleedin' night talkin' to a lot

* A mixture of beer and ginger beer.

of drunks. When I git tired, I can go 'ome an' lock me door. . . . I make much more money, too, an' the best bit, it's not like bein' one of those who sit on the end of a phone all night. I can see wot I'm gettin'. If I don't like the look of a bloke, I don't ask 'im up, see?"

Watching Nessie while she talked, it seemed incredible that she could be leading this sort of existence—her very youth and, yes, her very freshness were in complete contradiction to everything she was describing.

"A lot of blokes want to 'ave me all to themselves . . . you know, set me up in a bleedin' flat in Maida Vale wiv a maid an' a fuckin' puppy, but when the time comes, I'll set meself up. I've got to move out of Cork Street tho', it's gettin' so fuckin' noisy, dear, with that big ginger who's moved in above. An Army officer by all accounts. 'E goes 'round the coffee stalls at Hyde Park Corner an' picks up them corporals in their red tunics an' all, then 'e brings them 'ome an' dresses 'imself up as a fuckin' bride, make-up, white satin, 'igh 'eels, a bleedin' veil, orange blossom—the lot. Then 'e chooses one of these blokes—'e always 'as about a 'arf a dozen 'em up there at the same time—and 'e fuckin' *marries* 'im. Goes through a sort of service, then arm in arm wiv 'is 'usband, 'e walks under a fuckin' arch way of swords 'eld up by the other blokes. I've talked to a coupla the soldiers—they're not gingers, mark you, far from it, but they pick up a coupla quid apiece for the job an' a fiver for the 'usband.

" 'E doesn't lay an 'and on any of them, just shoots 'is wad walking under them fuckin' swords. But the noise, dear—Christ! I can't stand it! Everything is very military, 'im being an ex-officer an' all, an' when it's all over 'e gets back into 'is nice blue suit, sits down be'ind a table with a fuckin' Army blanket on it an' they all form up like a bleedin' pay parade. 'Guardsman so-and-so.' 'Sir!' One pace forward march . . . crash! 'Forty shillings . . . SIR!' 'About turn' . . . crash! 'NEXT MAN' . . . CRASH! 'SIR!!' . . . CRASH! CHRIST! . . . those fuckin' Army boots, dear, I'm goin' to 'ave to move. . . ." She shook with delicious laughter.

"Of course, I don't get mixed up wiv no funny business meself . . . it's just me an' a bloke, that's all. . . . No exhibitions, none of that stuff. Of course, I'm not sayin' I don't occasionally pick up a little fancy money—there's this Aussie millionaire, dear, about fifty, who gets about eight of us up to 'is 'otel, then we all strip down to the stockin's and 'igh 'eels an' 'e takes off everything! Then 'e gives us each an 'en pheasant's tail feather to stuff up the arse—'ell of a job keepin' it in there, it is, because we 'ave to walk 'round in a circle—then, would you believe it, dear, 'e stands there in the middle wiv a cock pheasant's feather up 'is own arse an' sprinkles corn on the fuckin' carpet—of course we 'ave a terrible time not larfin' but if we do larf, we don't get paid an' it's a tenner each too. . . . Well, there 'e stands, kind of crowin' or whatever the 'ell pheasants do, an' we all 'ave to kinda peck at the fuckin' corn . . . it's amazin' really, he shoots off right there all by 'isself in the middle of the circle. We never 'ave to touch 'im . . . pathetic really when you think."

When Nessie went back to London after these outings, I always felt terribly lonely. I loved walking about the fields and woods with her. I've never seen anyone get such real pleasure out of trees and flowers and birds, and it gave me a feeling of importance to be able to point out different animals and to tell her about life in the country.

Sadly, I waved her away at Buckingham Station and pedaled up the long avenue in time for evening chapel.

The whole school attended chapel twice a day, and after the evening service, announcements of special importance were made by the headmaster.

In chapel about three weeks after Nessie's visit, J. F. motioned the boys to remain in their places; an expectant murmur arose.

"All over the country," J. F. began, "overworked examiners have been correcting several thousand papers sent in for this year's examinations.

"Stowe is a new school and these same examiners have been looking at the papers sent in by us with special interest.

"Boys who sit for a public examination are representing their schools in public and they, therefore, have a very great responsibility. Schools are judged by the boys who represent them—

"It is, therefore, with grief and great disappointment that I have to tell you that two boys representing Stowe in the school certificate have been caught cheating. I shall question the two concerned this evening and I shall deal with them as I see fit."

Only when I saw Archie Montgomey-Campbell's ashen face did the horrible truth sink in. As the school rose to leave the chapel, my legs turned to water.

4

Ratings of the Royal Navy have always prided themselves on the fact that without any official signals being made, news and gossip passes between ships at anchor with a rapidity that makes African tribesmen blush over their tomtoms. The ratings themselves would have blushed that day: Ten minutes after chapel, the whole school knew who were the two culprits. Perhaps like people being attacked by dogs or run away with on horses, Archie and I smelled of fear.

Poor Archie was the first to be summoned to the headmaster's study; he went off like Sydney Carton at the end of *A Tale of Two Cities*. A quarter of an hour later, I was located near the lavatories, where I had been spending the interim.

No smile on J. F.'s face this time, just a single terse question: "Have you anything to say for yourself?"

For the lack of any flash of genius that might have saved me, I told him the truth: that I had failed the exam anyway and wanted to get out early. I also added that Archie was completely guiltless and stood to gain nothing by helping me.

J. F. stared at me in silence for a long time, then he crossed the quiet, beautifully furnished room and stood looking out of the open French windows into the flower garden where he had first interviewed me. Cheating in a public examination is a heinous crime and it seemed inevitable that I would be expelled. I braced myself for the news as he turned toward me.

"Montgomery-Campbell made a stupid mistake in helping you with your Latin translation and I have given him six strokes of the cane. Until you stood there and told me the truth, I had every intention of expelling you from the school. However in spite of your very gross misbehavior, I still have faith in you and I shall keep you at Stowe. Now, I propose to give you twelve strokes of the cane."

My joy at not being thrown out was quickly erased by the thought of my short-term prospects . . . Twelve! That was terrifying! J. F. was a powerfully built man and his beatings, though rare, were legendary.

"Go next door into the Gothic Library. Lift your coat, bend over and hold onto the bookcase by the door. It will hurt you very much indeed. When it is over, and I expect you to make no noise, go through the door as quickly as you wish. When you feel like it, go back to your house."

The first three or four strokes hurt so much that the shock somehow cushioned the next three or four, but the last strokes of my punishment were unforgettable. I don't believe I did make any noise, not because I was told to avoid doing so, or because I was brave or anything like that; it hurt so much, I just couldn't get my breath.

When the bombardment finally stopped, I flung open the door and shot out into the passage. Holding my behind and trumpeting like a rogue elephant, down the stone passage, past the boiler rooms, I went out into the summer evening and headed for the woods.

After the pain subsided, the mortification set in. How was I going to face the other boys—cheat? Obviously, my promised promotion to monitor would be canceled and my remaining time at Stowe would be spent as an outcast.

Eventually, about bedtime, I crept up to my dormitory. It was a large room that accommodated twenty-five boys. The usual pillow fights and shouting and larking about were in full swing. They died away to an embarrassed silence as I came in. I took off my clothes, watched by the entire room. My under-pants stuck to me and reminded me of my physical pain. I put on my pajamas and slunk off to the bathroom next door. An ominous murmur followed my exit.

In the bathroom mirror, I inspected the damage. It was heavy, to say the least. Suddenly, Major Haworth's cheery voice made me turn. "Pretty good shooting, I'd call that . . . looks like a two-inch group!" He was his usual smiling, kindly self. "When you've finished in here, get into bed. I'm going to read out a message the headmaster has sent 'round the school. . . . Nothing to worry about."

When everyone was in bed and quiet, the major stood by

the dormitory door and read from a piece of paper. "I have interviewed the two boys connected with the school certificate irregularities. Their explanations have been accepted by me and the boys have been punished. The incident is now closed and will not be referred to again by anyone."

"Good night, everybody," said the major, and then with a wink at me: "When that sort of thing happened to me, I used to sleep on my stomach and have my breakfast off the mantel-shelf."

In the darkness the whispers started: "How many did you get?" . . . "Did you blub?" . . . "What sort of cane is it?" . . . "Promise to show us in the morning." All friendly whispers. In the darkness, I buried my face in my pillow.

I determined there and then that, somehow, I would repay J. F. I never could, of course, but I became, I think, a good and responsible monitor the next term, and in due course, after squeaking past a mathematical barrier, I passed into the Royal Military College, Sandhurst, and became one of the first three Stowe boys to gain commissions in the Regular Army.

Summer holiday at Bembridge followed immediately after ten days of Officers' Training Corps camp on Salisbury Plain. It was at one such camp that I first smelled success in front of an audience. Several hundred boys from many different schools were attending the camp concert in a huge circus tent. Someone had told Major Haworth that as Stowe was a new school, it would be a good thing if we were part of the program and he had asked me to do something about it.

There was, at that time in England, a monologist named Milton Hayes. I had one of his records at school and had memorized some of his stuff for the benefit of my friends. I must now belatedly apologize to Milton Hayes for stealing from his material, which is what in part I did, adding topical touches of my own to fit the situation at the camp.

His monologue was a takeoff of a half-witted politician electioneering. I made mine a half-witted general inspecting the camp. On the night of the concert, I sat outside the tent, waiting for my turn to go on. The boys were a rowdy audience and the noise from inside was deafening. There were a lot of boos. I experienced, for the first time, that delicious terror that has never left me—stage fright—and with rubbery knees, dry lips and sweating palms, I fought against the urge to dash madly away, grow a beard and emigrate to the Seychelles. At last I was called, and I heard the master of ceremonies announce, "Niven of Stowe."

Miserably, I mounted the steps onto the stage, wearing the baggy general's uniform which Major Haworth had concocted for me. In my eye was a monocle and on my upper lip a huge gray mustache

Scattered applause and some laughter greeted my appearance.

The M. C. put up his hand: "Major General Sir Useless Eunuch!" More laughter.

I gulped and prayed that the stage would open and swallow me up. Hundreds of boys in khaki filled the benches. The first three rows were occupied by officers in red mess kit. I screwed my monocle into my eye and gazed at the officers. . . .

"Sergeant Major, why is it that these members of the band have no instruments!" I asked. A roar of delighted laughter filled the tent, and suddenly, it was easy.

Then lapsing into pilfered Milton Hayes: "What we must do with this camp, Sergeant Major, is find out where we stand, then get behind ourselves and push ourselves forward. We must get right down to the very roots, right down to rock bottom, then bring the whole thing up into one common pool . . . and looking around here at Salisbury Plain—and how very plain it looks—we should keep the ships at sea . . . the harbors will be much cleaner for one thing . . ." and so on for about ten minutes.

Milton Hayes and I were a riotous success that night and the harpoon of craving success as a performer was planted very insidiously deep inside me.

Sailing entered my life about this time. My mother bought Grizel and me a twenty-five-year-old 14-foot sailing dinghy for £12. It was called *Merlin* and is still being sailed by children at Bembridge. I became a good hand and the pinnacle of my sailing career came later while I was still at Sandhurst and was chosen as a member of Great Britain's International Crew in the Cumberland Cup, a race for 8-meter yachts, during Ryde Week. With Sir Ralph Gore, the famous helmsman in command, we in *Severn* easily defeated the French challenger *L'Etoile* in a best-of-three final.

First, however, Brian Franks and I formed the Bembridge Sailing Dinghy Club for children between twelve and eighteen. I was the first secretary, Brian, the first captain. At the end of the first year, the club showed a profit of £2.12.6, which Brian and I transferred into liqueur brandy. We were both found next morning facedown in the nettles, behind the Garland Club.

The Garland Club was on the beach and was pretty chic. Nobody under eighteen was allowed near the place. I was permanently scarred there at the age of seventeen.

Freddie James was the son of a fisherman. Freddie introduced Brian and me to a game called Ting Ting Spider. It was beautiful in its simplicity.

The equipment needed was as follows: one large thumbtack, one 4-ounce fishing weight, and about 50 yards of light fishing line.

The three of us would set off after dark, select a house with a big garden, and go into action. Two of us would wait in the shadow of the trees or bushes while the number-one man "sank the harpoon"—that is to say, stuck the thumbtack in the window frame of an occupied downstairs room. He then attached a 6-inch piece of line to the thumbtack and the fishing weight to the end of this piece of line. With the weight then neatly poised over an exposed pane of glass, the number-one man attached the long line just above the weight, paid it out, and delivered the end of it to the couple waiting in the shadows.

The "spider" or weight could thus be manipulated from a safe distance so that the resulting "ting ting" scared the hell out of the people inside the room.

We had a certain code of ethics about these proceedings: Old ladies living alone and women with small children were exempt from our attentions. We much preferred targets which represented a certain element of risk. The most formidable of these was a purple-faced retired major general who lived with several large dogs in a huge house just behind the Garland Club.

The night we decided to tackle the general started ominously. Freddie James announced his intention of bringing along a friend of his from St. Helens, the village next door. . . . "Beautiful bit of stuff," he said, with a ghastly leer. . . . "Seen more stiff pricks than she 'as 'ot dinners."

So Doris joined us for the evening and the first intimation I had that Freddie's description was a just one was

when we were all tiptoeing in Indian file up the grass verge
of the general's driveway, Doris, with a dreadful "crunch"
stepped off onto the gravel.

"Get on the grass," I hissed.

"Wot 'ere—now?" she asked, expectantly.

The general was just finishing his dinner, and his first
reaction to the initial two or three "ting tings" was perfectly normal. He parted the curtains and peered out into the
darkness to see who was there. Not noticing the little sta-
tionary weight, he returned to his port. "Ting ting," we
went again. He reacted in the same manner. The third time
he reacted differently. The front door suddenly flew open
and he appeared, flanked in silhouette by two huge dogs
and bearing a shotgun.

"Who's there?" he shouted.

"Christ!" whispered Freddie. "The old bugger's goin' to
kill us."

Brian, always the leader, said, "When he goes in again,
we'll give him another couple of 'tings,' then down the
bank quick, over the railings and into the Garland."

Doris began to whimper, "I thought we wos goin' to 'ave
some fun."

"Shut up, you silly twat," was Freddie's gallant re-
joinder.

I just sweated.

The fourth and fatal salvo of "ting tings" went off just
after the general went back into his house. Out he shot, like
a jack-in-the-box, firing from the hip, luckily not in our direction, but when the dogs joined in with a frenzy of bark-
ings, our little mixed commando panicked. We broke cover
and ran for the bank. It was very high and very steep but
fear was the spur. We all fell down it, and I still have a vision of the sizable, white buttocks of Freddie's guest as she
performed a perfect parabola over my head.

Brian, our gallant commander, said, "Over the railings."

The railings were about eight feet high, rusting and
spiked at the top, but there was a helpful tree that made it
just possible to climb over them.

The dogs were barking, the general was roaring, and the
gun was going off in every direction, so it is not surprising
that mistakes were made. I was last to go over, not from
any sense of gallantry, believe me; I just happened to be the
last of the four to arrive at the tree. On the top of the rail-

ings I slipped and pitched forward. One of the rusty spikes went, like a red-hot poker, into my leg and there I hung, head down like a side of beef, till Brian and Freddie lifted me off. No blood poisoning by a miracle, but weeks of painful convalescence and a huge scar for the rest of my life.

When you are a senior boy in an English public school, you perhaps reach the pinnacle of your self-importance. Given hitherto undreamed-of responsibilities and privileges, often receiving the acclaim, even the adulation, of your juniors and sometimes served by "fags,"* it is very easy to get carried away.

The Royal Military College, Sandhurst, soon took care of that. . . . It is never pleasant to be treated like mud but Sandhurst, at least, did it with style and no malice aforethought; it just came naturally.

We were called gentlemen cadets. The officers and noncommissioned officer instructors were the pick of the whole British Army and the drill instructors were exclusively the pick of the Brigade of Guards. Knowing you were due to become an officer in eighteen months' time, the NCO's could call you anything they liked, provided they prefaced it with a "Mr. So-and-So, sir."

There were about one thousand cadets at Sandhurst divided into seniors, intermediates and juniors. The course was eighteen months, so one spent six months in each category.

The commandant was Major General Sir Eric Girdwood, DSO, etc., etc,; the adjutant was the famous Major "Boy" Browning, Grenadier Guards, DSO, etc., later to command all British Airborne troops in World War II.

In No. 1 Company, my company commander was Major Godwin Austen, South Wales Borderes, MC; my chief instructor was The Honorable Major "Babe" Alexander,† Irish Guards, DSO; and the company sergeant major was "Robbo" Robinson, Grenadier Guards.

All these were completely splendid soldiers, with impec-

---

* American friends are often appalled by this description of younger boys who clean the rooms and run messages for their seniors. They don't have to be; it is not an abbreviation of faggot.

† Brother of the famous wartime "Alex."

cable and gallant records, and however tough they may sometimes have been, they always had a deep understanding and sympathy for the cadets under their command.

The cadet underofficer* in charge of the junior platoon to which I was assigned was a shifty-looking customer with a broken nose named Wright—a singularly, unattractive piece of work. It was small wonder to any of us who knew him at Sandhurst that later, after changing his name to Baillie-Stewart and joining the Seaforth Highlanders, he was caught selling military secrets to the Germans, court-martialed and imprisoned in the Tower of London.

The "mud treatment" started on the first day of our ten weeks of concentrated drill "on the square." We were paraded in civilian clothes in which we had arrived the day before. A strange assortment wearing suits, tweed jackets, plus fours, hats, caps, boots, shoes and even umbrellas, we smiled nervously at each other as we awaited the ministrations of Robbo.

Rapidly and with the minimum of trimmings, Robbo explained that although it looked unlikely at the moment, we were supposed to be officer material and it had fallen to his unfortunate lot to try, within eighteen months, to transform this " 'orrible shower" into being worthy of the king's commission.

"I shall address you as 'sir' because that's orders, but when you speak to me, you'll stand at attention, look me right in the eye, and call me 'staff'. . . got it?"

A few murmurs of "Yes," "Right-ho" and "Jolly good" were silenced by one of the mightiest roars in the British Army.

"GOT IT!!!!??? Now let me hear the answer, gentlemen . . . ONE, TWO, THREE."

"GOT IT, STAFF," we roared back.

Quickly and efficiently we were stripped of umbrellas and walking sticks and shown how to come to attention, how to march and how to halt. Then, at a hair-raising speed we were marched one and a half miles to be issued boots and canvas uniforms. Around and around the college

---

* In each company, the five top cadets from the senior term became underofficers. They were the elite and wore Sam Browne belts.

we whizzed, sweating and apprehensive beneath the patronizing glances of beautifully turned-out older cadets to the barbers to be shorn like sheep; to the gym to be fitted with physical training outfits; to the stables for breeches, brown boots and leggings; to the laundry "because I don't want to see a speck of dirt for the next year an' 'arf, mind"; and finally to the chapel "because 'ere, gentlemen, you can thank Almighty Gawd at the end of each week if you are still breathin'. Got it?"

"GOT IT, STAFF!"

It was very hard and very exhausting; for the ten weeks on the square, we never stopped running, saluting, marching, drilling, climbing ropes, riding unmanageable chargers, and polishing and burnishing everything in sight—boots, belts, chin straps, buttons, bayonets and above all our rifles —"the soldier's best friend, mind."

Normally, there were about fifteen minutes between being dismissed from one parade and being inspected for the next in a totally different and spotless outfit. The slightest lapse—a finger mark on a brass button, a cap at the wrong angle or hair not mown like a convict's—was rewarded with "defaulters"—a particularly grueling extra drill in full battle order at the end of the day when everyone else was resting.

A rifle barrel imperfectly cleaned invariably meant pack drill. At the hands of the dreaded Wright—full battle order but with a difference—the pack was filled with sand and in place of normal drill movements, it was a case of being forced, after supper, to run up and down several flights of stairs with the offending rifle at arm's length above the head, shouting at the top of our lungs "Parade, parade."

The cadets incarcerated in their rooms, cleaning their equipment, made bets on how long each individual could stand the punishment. Many defaulters found it a matter of honor to prolong their own agony in order to impress listening friends. I was a firm supporter of the doctrine of another group who sought kudos by pretending to pass out long before they would normally have collapsed.

In the riding school, the rough-riding sergeant majors were particularly heartless. We had a beauty, an Irishman, from the Enniskillen Dragoons called McMyn. At six thirty on a Monday morning, winter and summer, he would be waiting for us with the same grisly joke: "Now then, gentle-

men, I'm supposed to make mounted officers of all of you
so let's see how many dismounted showers we can have here
on this lovely morning. . . . Knot your reins. Cross your stir-
rups. Fold your bleedin' arms and split ass over the jumps
. . . . Go!" Carnage, of course, but in those strange days,
even in infantry regiments, all officers had to know how to
ride and ride well.

The great thing about those first ten weeks was that although one was being treated like mud it was at least
grown-up mud. We were treated like men for the first time
in our lives, and as men we were expected to react.

Those weeks "on the square" were sheer, undiluted hell.
At weekends we were allowed no dining-out passes, but by
Saturday night we were so exhausted anyway that all we
wanted to do was to fall into bed, underneath which was a
dreadful receptacle described in military stores as "one pot,
chamber, china with handle, gentlemen cadets for the use
of."

At the end of the purgatory, we "passed off the square"
and settled down to learning other things in addition to
physical training, drill, riding, bayonet fighting and more
drill; instruction was given us in organization and administration, in the manual of military law and of course in tac-
tics and man management.

Of the two hundred and fifty juniors who passed off the
square and still remained in one piece, four in each
company were promoted to lance corporal. I was one of
the lucky four in No. 1 Company, and as there was now a
little more time for leisure, I managed also to get a Rugger
Blue and played regularly for two seasons with the 1st. XV.

I furthermore performed in a couple of college concerts,
writing my own sketches, and played the lead opposite
Mrs. Barcus, the wife of one of our company officers, in *It
Pays to Advertise*.

Nessie came down one Saturday to see the show, which
opened after a particularly grueling afternoon's Rugger
battle against the RAF College, Cranwell.

"Yew looked ever so nice up there on that stage, dear,
but the sport's better for yew, isn't it? More balls, if you
know what I mean."

My liaison with Nessie continued more or less full time
all through my year and a half at Sandhurst. She still insisted that "pretty soon I'm goin' to find that nice feller an'

fuck off to the Fiji Islands." In the summer term, she came down for the June Ball, the big social event of the year. For the occasion she borrowed a magenta-colored taffeta ball gown from a friend who danced in competitions on the outer London circuit. Her very great beauty and, again I say, her freshness, overcame this extraordinary garment and I basked in her success as we waltzed and fox-trotted around the gymnasium to the fluctuating rhythms of the Royal Military College Band.

Nessie was very specific about my seeing other girls: "We're just together for the larfs an' the fuckin', dear, so don't go gettin' serious wiv me or yew'll spoil it."

Cadets in their intermediate and senior terms were allowed cars. Obviously, I did not own one, but the wheels of friends were always available and Saturday night in London on a late pass became the focal point of the week.

In the intermediate term, I was promoted to full corporal and received the ultimate accolade for that rank. Along with one other corporal, Dick Hobson of No. 3 Company, I was appointed commandant's orderly for six months. This post was highly coveted, and besides announcing to all and sundry that the holder of it was practically bound to become an underofficer in his senior term, it also carried various "perks." One was excused from Saturday morning drill parade, which meant early to London, and on Sunday came the big moment: breakfast with the general, Sir Eric Girdwood.

The breakfast must have been pure hell for this splendid officer, but week after week he toyed with toast and coffee while Dick and I plowed through acres of scrambled eggs and miles of sausages. Afterward, while the general was being dressed in highly polished riding boots, Sam Browne belt and sword, Dick and I waited in the garden decked out with silver sticks, on which were engraved the names of a hundred years of commandants, orderlies, with white pipe-clayed belts across our chests to which, between our shoulder blades, very beautiful and heavily embossed silver Victorian message boxes were attached. Upon the appearance of the general, we formed up on either side of him and escorted him onto the parade, slowly marching together ahead of him up the front rank and down the rear as he inspected the battalion of one thousand spotless cadets; then into chapel, trying not to skate with our hobnailed

boots on the black marble of the nave and, afterward, leading the commandant's Sunday morning inspection of the
college buildings, gymnasium, hospital, stables and so on.

The general was a most imposing and awe-inspiring figure with his chest full of medals and his bristling white
mustache. He was also God. A creature so far above the
lowly cadet as to make his every word and gesture seem to
us divine. Of the thousand at that moment under his command, perhaps one would ultimately attain his exalted
rank.

The silver message box nearly proved to be my undoing.
So many cadets asked me what was in it that I decided to
give them a little food for thought and I filled it with
various commodities. Thereafter upon being asked the
usual question, I would reply, "Commandant's personal
supplies—take a look." Inside they were delighted to find a
packet of Woodbines, a box of Swan Vestas matches, a roll
of toilet paper and a dozen condoms. I had completed
about three months as commandant's orderly and I believe
my purchases went a long way toward relieving the tedium
of those Sunday mornings, and cadets kept standing to attention far too long in all weathers were deeply apprecia-
tive of the fact that visiting dignitaries, kings, presidents,
prime ministers and archbishops were invariably preceded
in their inspection of the ranks by the pompous passing of
this curious cargo.

One cloudless Sunday morning after breakfast, Dick
Hobson and I were waiting for the general amidst the rho-
dodendrons of his garden when he suddenly changed his
routine. Normally, he would issue from the house, booted,
spurred, shining like a new pin and clanking with medals.
Then we would fall into step on either side of him, listening
to his extremely engaging and relaxed small talk as he
headed toward the old college buildings where the battalion
would be drawn up ready for inspection by him and on occasion by his VIP guests.

Some five hundred yards from his house and just out of
sight of the parade, it was taken for granted that all infor-
mality would melt away and Dick and I would put our
silver-headed orderly sticks under our left armpits and start
our slow march for the tour of the ranks.

This beautiful June morning, however, he came out of
the garden door and stopped in front of us.

"I think I'd better inspect you two fellers today," he said.

We immediately sprang to attention secure and relaxed in the knowledge that we, too, were faultlessly turned out. I was on Dick's right, so the general looked first at my cap, chin, my buttons, my belt, my creases and my boots. Then, with a pace to the side and in the usual Army fashion, he started on Dick from his boots up to his cap. Around the back he went, inspecting Dick from the rear when, Christ! I heard a little click as he opened Dick's message box.

The joke of what mine contained had long since been over; hardly anybody bothered to ask me anymore what was in it—everyone knew—in fact I had forgotten all about it myself. The few seconds that it took the commandant to inspect Dick's rear view seemed to me to take until autumn. Finally, I heard him move and heard his breathing directly behind me. I prayed he would move around to the front again without looking into my box. I promised God all sorts of rash things if he would arrange this for me, but he failed me. I felt rather than heard the general open my box and I sensed him rustling about among its horrible contents—Woodbines, matches, lavatory paper and condoms. My military career was obviously over before it had even started and I toyed with the idea of falling on my bayonet among the rhododendron petals. Dick, too, had realized the full possibilities of the situation and started to vibrate like a harp string on my left, a condition brought about by a mixture of concern for his partner, suppressed laughter and keen anticipation of impending doom.

After an eternity, Major General Sir Eric Girdwood stood before me. He stared for a long time at my sea-green face without saying a word. Staring blankly ahead, I waited for the ax to fall.

"Niven," he said, "I had heard about that . . . thank you very much . . . you are very considerate. . . ."

It was never referred to again, but immediately after church parade that day I cleared out my message box.

Life at Sandhurst was tough, but it was exhilarating and the cadets were a dedicated *corps d'élite*. Some went on to command divisions and even armies. Several among the dignified Sikhs and Pathans became leaders in their countries, but a heartbreakingly high percentage were destined in a little more than ten years' time to meet death on the beaches, deserts and hillsides of World War II, for this was the vintage of professional soldiers that suffered most heavily when the holocaust came.

Led by Major Godwin Austen and goaded almost beyond endurance by the much loved Robbo Robinson, No. 1 Company became the Champion Company and for the eighteen months I was at Sandhurst, I was one of the privileged, proudly wearing the red lanyard of the Champions.

In my platoon was a charmingly "fey" little Jordanian, the Emir Talal, uncle of the present king. He was really not cut out to be a soldier and single-handedly could have reduced the Champions to nonentities in the drill competition because of his inability to tell right from left. . . . It became a normal occurrence during rehearsal parades for the whole company to turn in a clockwork body smartly to the left only to come face-to-face with Talal, who was marching proudly in the opposite direction.

"Drill competition, tomorrow, gentlemen," announced Robbo, who was equal to every occasion. "My 'gawd, Mr. Emir Talal, sir, you look bleedin' 'orrible, you do. 'Ow d'you feel, sir?"

"Very well, thank you, staff."

"No you don't, sir, you're feelin' bleedin' ill. Report sick tomorrow morning, mind, and don't come back till after parade. . . . Got it?"

"Got it, staff."

If the work was hard, so was the play. Cadets in their senior term were allowed motorcars, and a few well-heeled young men could be seen whizzing up the Great West Road, London bound for weekends in an assortment of jalopies. Jimmy Gresham in my platoon owned a Hillman Huskie and was most generous about giving his friends lifts. A very bright fellow destined for the Welsh Guards, he was, like Robbo, highly resilient when it came to contretemps. For some misdemeanor he was not allowed to use his car for several weeks, but he solved this temporary inconvenience by keeping a chauffeur's uniform and a false mustache at White's Garage in Camberley and our weekly forays to the capital continued without missing a beat.

Reggie Hodgkinson, an old Bembridge friend, also headed for the Welsh Guards, was a member of No. 3 Company housed across the barrack square in the new buildings. One night, having persuaded some kind friend to sign in for him, he was almost caught by the watchful Robbo crossing our parade ground at 3 A.M. wearing a dinner jacket. Reggie arrived beating at my door, breathless: "Give me a pair of pajamas, for Christ's sake, that bloody Robbo nearly nabbed me." He quickly donned the pajamas over his dinner jacket and dashed out again.

From the window, I watched, fascinated, as Reggie, with closed eyes, gave it the full "I come from haunts of coot and hern" treatment: arms stretched out before him, he ambled in the bright moonlight, straight across the barrack square toward No. 3 Company.

Pretty soon it was obvious that Robbo had materialized and was walking beside him.

"Wot d'you think you're doin', Mr. 'Odgkinson, sir?"

"Sleepwalking, staff."

"Then sleepwalk into the bleedin' guardroom . . . lef' right, lef' right. . . . Smartly now, swing the arms, sir," and my pajamas disappeared at high speed in the direction of "the cooler."

It had long been decided that no stone would be left unturned for me to be commissioned into the Argyll and Sutherland Highlanders once I had successfully passed out of Sandhurst. When I say it had been decided, I really mean that my mother had gone to a great deal of trouble to raise old influential friends of my father's from the days when we had lived in Argyllshire. For my part I was delighted at the prospect of joining such a glamorous regiment and reveled in the meetings that were arranged by one of my mother's advisers, the colonel of the regiment, the McClean of Lochbuie.

The McClean, three times during my days at Sandhurst, took me, all spruced up, to visit Princess Marie Louise, sister of King George V, who was the honorary colonel of the regiment and who took a great interest in all things pertaining to that famous outfit.

The first time I was taken to visit her, I was instructed to meet the McClean at his London Club so that he could check me over and, among other things, teach me how to bow properly to royalty—never but never, any arching of the back or movement from the waist—that, he informed me, was strictly for headwaiters.

"Stand upright, my boy, look 'em right in the eye, then, with a completely stiff back, a sharp, very definite inclination of the head, bringing the chin almost to the chest."

I tried this rather painful maneuver several times and each time a peculiar squeaking sound issued from my undergarments. A minute inspection disclosed the fact that the new braces which I had purchased for the occasion, complete with a very complicated gadget—a sort of pulley effect . . . little wheels over which passed elastic straps— had been delivered with a faulty wheel and this was complaining bitterly at the unusual strain that was being placed upon it. The McClean solved the problem by oiling the offending part with a dab of hair lotion.

The elderly princess became a great ally, and it was at her suggestion that I was invited to spend the day with the officers of the regiment just before they embarked for service in the West Indies where I hoped to be joining them later. They were a fun and friendly group, and colonel and subalterns alike all made me feel confident of a warm welcome in about one year's time. All I had to do, they assured me, was to pass the final Sandhurst exams and I would be with them for sure.

Before I returned to Sandhurst for my last term and final exams, I spent what was to be my last holiday at Bembridge. The whole family, minus Tommy, was there. My mother, whom I had finally grown to love and to appreciate, presided over the gathering. Max was back from India, having become disenchanted with soldiering. He had resigned his commission and gone to work as the starter on the Bombay Racecourse. This, too, had palled and his adventurous spirit had taken him to Australia, where for the past five years he had been working as a jackeroo (cowboy) on a cattle station near Yarra Weir. Now he was having a last long look at England before sailing away to take a job as manager of a banana plantation on Norfolk Island in the South Pacific.

Looking back on that period, I now realize that at eighteen I must, by today's standards, have been a very square member of a very square group. There seems to have been the minimum of rebellion against the establishment. There was mass unemployment and appalling conditions in the mines and shipyards. There were hunger marches and general strikes, but my generation of students remained shamefully aloof. We did little or nothing in protest. Perhaps we were still very much in shock from realizing that the cream of the generation immediately before ours had been wiped out. Perhaps there was no one left worth rebelling against, and in my case, discipline was being pumped and bashed into me to such an extent that any sort of organized student revolt against authority, such as has now become the norm, was unthinkable. We drank a great deal, it's true, but we were immensely physically fit. Pot, hashish and LSD were as yet unheard of, so instead of sitting around looking inward, we rushed about noisily and were extroverted.

My final term at Sandhurst was a breeze. I had never had it so good. By now promoted to underofficer, I was also, for the second season running, a Rugger blue and even found time to produce a couple of concerts and to play the juvenile lead in *The Speckled Band*. I had also discovered girls in a big way, and although Nessie might with certain justification have been called the Head Mistress, I had a heart like a hotel with every room booked.

Nessie, as always describing herself as "an 'ore wiv an 'eart of fuckin' gold," was staying with a gentleman friend on a yacht for Cowes week, but she managed a few clandestine meetings with me in Seaview. She was still the same, as funny and as beautiful as ever and, as always, most solicitous as to my sexual well-being. "Gettin' plenty, dear?"

When I sat for the final exams, I discovered with pleasure mixed with surprise that they came quite easily to me, and as I had also accumulated a very nice bonus of marks for being an underofficer, my entry into the Argylls seemed purely a formality. Everything in the garden was beautiful —a fatal situation for me.

Just before the end of term, all cadets who were graduating were given a War Office form to fill in: "Name in order of preference three regiments into which you desire to be commissioned."

I wrote as follows:

1. The Argyll and Sutherland Highlanders
2. The Black Watch

and then for some reason which I never fully understood, possibly because it was the only one of the six Highland regiments that wore trews instead of the kilt, I wrote:

   3. Anything but the Highland Light Infantry

   Somebody at the War Office was funnier than I was and I was promptly commissioned into the Highland Light Infantry.

5

I cushioned my mother from the blow of my not being commissioned into the Argylls by a lot of military double-talk about vacancies and people with short-service commissions coming from the universities, and I told her with truth that, anyway, the HLI was a much older Highland regiment than the Argylls and persuaded her with a big, black lie that, also, I much preferred being sent to Malta instead of to Bermuda.

I had, however, a sizable problem explaining to her, when I displayed my uniform, why I was wearing "those funny striped trousers instead of a kilt." After reading up on the regimental history of the Argylls for eighteen months I was woefully short of material about the HLI, but I did remember hearing that this, the second oldest Highland regiment, had so distinguished itself at some point in its history that the men of the regiment were paid the supreme compliment of being allowed to dress like the officers in the other Highland regiments—in trews—the kilt being, they were told, the symbol of serfdom. An unlikely story, I always felt, particularly since the HLI insisted on wearing white spats with their trews to make quite sure that nobody confused them with the Lowland regiments, and a campaign to be allowed to wear the kilt was always simmering on the regimental hob. . . . It finally came to the boil a few years after I joined and a large number of Glaswegian* knees were from then on bared to the public gaze.

Nessie accompanied me to various pompous tailors and bootmakers in London while I was being outfitted, and eye-

---

* The Highland Light Infantry was "The City of Glasgow Regiment" and 70 percent of the men were recruited from that redoubtable town.

brows flew up and down like lifts at some of her observations.

"Don't like that fuckin' black bonnet at all, dear. Makes yew look like a bleedin' judge 'andin' out the death sentence.

"Better not sit down in them tight trousers, dear, or yew'll be singin' alto in the fuckin' choir."

When one considers that the most expensive tailors in London at that time charged only fourteen guineas for a suit, it must have come as a body blow to my mother to receive bills for £250 for tropical clothes all "suggested" in a list provided by the adjutant. Salt was doubtless rubbed into my poor mother's financial wound when I handed over my "Clothing Grant" from a grateful government—£50.

Nessie took me to a photographer in Piccadilly called Cannons of Hollywood and had me preserved for posterity. She also insisted on coming to see me off at Tilbury Docks on a bleak January morning when I embarked in the *Kaisar-i-Hind* for Malta, two months before my nineteenth birthday. At the last moment, my mother who had been suffering one of her increasingly frequent bouts of what the family called "Mum's pain" decided to get out of bed and come too.

"Don't worry about me, dear," said Nessie when I told her, "I won't embarrass yew, I'll hide behind a fuckin' packin' case or somefink. I just want to wave good-bye, that's all."

In the event it was my spats that brought them together. I put on my outfit, Glengarry, cutaway short khaki jacket with one "pip" on the shoulders, McKenzie tartan trews, and my mother took me, with a mound of tin mothproof uniform cases, in a taxi to the docks. Far from hiding behind a packing case, Nessie was very much in evidence, standing by the barrier wearing a little beret over her fair hair and a very short white tightly belted raincoat that took nothing away from her fabulous figure and long slim legs. She was doing a very poor job of pretending not to look in my direction; she looked ravishing and I realized with a lurch of the heart just how much I was going to miss her. As my mother and I walked toward the barrier, a noise like castanets came from the region of my feet. A few heads turned in our direction and suddenly Nessie doubled up with laughter. "Christ, yer fuckin' spats are on the wrong feet." My mother caught Nessie's laughter and I caught hers, and in the ensuing hysteria I introduced one to the other. My mother's famous disdain for punctuality had already brought our arrival at the docks perilously close to sailing time, so with Nessie in tow we barely had time to inspect the cabin which the aforesaid grateful government had arranged that I share with three others before the booming gong and a cry of "all visitors ashore please" sent them both scurrying back down the gangplank. I have always been embarrassed by long-drawn-out farewells; once I have got to the point of departure, like an operation, I want to get the damn thing over with, so I was really rather relieved to see them go. We had all agreed that there would be none of that business of smiling bravely and waving while swearing dockhands wrestled with gangplanks festooned with paper streamers, so the last I saw of them was walking away through the damp, dreary customs shed. Nessie was holding my mother's arm.

My small cabin contained three occupants, two homosexual civil servants returning from spending their leave together and a fat red-haired subaltern in the Indian Cavalry who smelled like a hot donkey. I spent very little time in it.

"Posh" was an adjective much used aboard and it was in this dingy P and O liner with its black hull and dung-colored superstructure that I learned what it meant; the best bookings, to avoid the heat of the Red Sea and Indian Ocean, were made thus Port Out, Starboard Home. It was in the good ship *Kaisar-i-Hind* that I also got my first unpleasant whiff of the suburban snobbery which polluted the air of garrison life everywhere in our then far-flung empire.

There were many officers of all three services on their way to join their units in Gibraltar, Malta, Egypt, Aden or India. Many had their families with them.

Naval officers were by far the most relaxed and friendly. Those in the Royal Air Force were rather hearty and condescending, and the Army officers were pretty much what I expected: firm believers in the doctrine that second lieutenants speak when they are spoken to and at no other time. Their wives were nearly all much worse than their husbands, so I clung like a drowning man to a very attractive Jewish couple whom nobody spoke to and who were simply taking a sea voyage as far as Alexandria.

One wonders what sort of welcome they would receive

there today, but at that time Mr. and Mrs. Marks were a boon and a blessing. On the voyage they invited me to sit at their table and took me with them when we went ashore at Marseilles. We spent the day at Arles, where I was initiated into the glories of the art galleries and the Roman amphitheater.

There was one other officer on board from my own regiment. I had spotted him from his uniform on the dock and I knew that he had also spotted me for the same reason, but he chose not to speak to me until the day we arrived at Malta. It was a pretty ridiculous situation because between us we represented 15 percent of the total complement of officers in the First Battalion, the Highland Light Infantry, and would presumably be living cheek by jowl for the foreseeable future; but for ten days on a smallish ship he preferred to avoid me. This behavior later turned out to be typical of a large percentage of my brother officers, but I was in no position to argue about it and as if somebody had left a door open somewhere, I had a nasty cold feeling that the comedian at the War Office might have passed on the happy news of my three choices of regiment.

The *Kaisar-i-Hind* dropped anchor in the deep-blue grand harbor of Valletta just as the sun was setting, and it was an unforgettable sight, tier upon tier of honey-colored houses rising on one side and Fort Ricasoli, built in 1400 by the Knights of Malta, brooding benevolently on the other. In between lay the leviathans of the greatest navy in the world. "Retreat" was being sounded by the massed bands of the Royal Marines on the flight deck of the giant carrier *Eagle* whilst astern of her lay three more—*Furious, Argus* and *Ark Royal*. Ahead there was a line of huge battleships—*Royal Oak, Resolution, Renown, Barham* and *Warspite*, among others—and beyond them again, the tall rather old-fashioned-looking county-class cruisers—*Norfolk, London, Suffolk, Shropshire, Newcastle*. The huge harbor was filled with these giants and their escorts, the light-cruiser squadrons, the destroyer and submarine flotillas, with their mother ships and oilers and the battered old target ship *Centurion*. Pinnaces, admirals' barges and shore boats slashed with white the blue water as they fussily dashed about on their errands leaving hordes of gaily colored local dghaisas with their lowly civilian passengers humbly bobbing about in their wake.

As the final plaintive notes of the "Retreat" floated out from *Eagle*, the sinking sun kissed the topmost houses and churches of Valletta with gold, and all over the Grand Harbour as the signal lights winked from a hundred mastheads, the white ensigns and Union Jacks of the Royal Navy were lowered, rolled up, and put reverently away for the night. If my vintage at Sandhurst was to be decimated in the war that the Germans were to unleash only ten years later, it is even more horrifying to speculate on the fate of those magnificent ships and their ships' companies that I glimpsed for the first time on that balmy evening.

Captain Henry Hawkins had been a trooper in the Life Guards, but through a combination of bravery and efficiency, he had been commissioned from the ranks and was now adjutant of my regiment. Tall, almost Phoenician-looking with his swarthy features and black mustache, resplendent in Glengarry, blue patrols and strapped evening tartan trews, he came aboard the liner to meet me. Flashing white teeth and a hearty handshake did much to decongeal me from the chilling apprehension that had descended upon me when I had put on my new uniform for the first time since I had left Tilbury Docks.

"Of course you have been with Jimmy for the whole voyage so at least you know somebody in the battalion."

"Jimmy, sir?"

"Don't call me 'sir' except on parade. Colonels and majors you address as 'sir,' always; everybody else by their Christian names once you get to know them. Jimmy McDonald—he's on board, isn't he? Ah! Here he is now."

Henry Hawkins then gave a rather restrained welcome to my shipmate and snorted when he learned that we had so far not met.

"How bloody silly," he said and introduced us.

Jimmy McDonald was a fairly senior subaltern with rather shifty eyes and the complexion of a hotel night porter. He had a blond mustache, yellowed in the middle by nicotine. I was relieved to learn from Hawkins that I was to be in C Company while he was to join the headquarters wing.

Hawkins brought McDonald up to date on various regimental news while we were gathering our hand baggage together and being ferried ashore by Carlo, the regimental boatman. The Marks pressed an antique Hebrew silver amulet into my hand for good luck and waved from the upper deck till I could no longer see them.

On the dock were several tough-looking Jocks from the regiment working under the supervision of a sergeant. They were busy loading our heavy baggage and a mound of regimental stores onto mule-drawn drays. Only a few years before the German *Blitzkrieg* would shatter the British Army, mechanization had still not come to our infantry regiments.

"Just room for two comfortably in the gharry," said Henry Hawkins, "so you and I'll go ahead to the mess. Jimmy knows the way so he can follow." Actually there was room for four in the rickety horse carriage that now transported us up from the landing stage down the main street of Valletta and out across the vast underground granaries to Floriana Barracks.

"Watch the driver," said Henry Hawkins. "They are so superstitious here that, now the sun has gone down, he'll keep changing his position so that the devil can't come and sit beside him."

We clip-clopped along at a good pace, but I had a chance to notice the ornate sandstone buildings on either side and the Sunday evening promenade in the streets, the men walking up and down on one side, the women on the other. All the men in dark suits and clean white shirts; the women in black and a large percentage wearing the *faldetta*, a large black crescent-shaped hood.

"Yells, bells and smells—that's how the Jocks describe Malta." Hawkins chuckled. "Just listen to their bloody bells now, Sunday evening is the worst. They all have a go but you'll get used to them. You may get used to the yelling too. Most of that is the poor sods trying to sell goat's milk, hot from the udder, but I don't think you'll ever get over the smells—I haven't.

"Now let me tell you a few things and ask me any questions you like. When we get to the mess, you'll meet Jackie Coulson—he's orderly officer today. He's about a year senior to you, and he's going to look after you and give you a shove in the right direction. Being Sunday evening, there probably won't be anybody else about. Incidentally, people in this regiment make it a point to take a long time to get to know newly joined officers. They reckon that they don't have to rush things because joining a regiment is for a lifetime. So don't worry if some of them, specially the more senior ones, are not very forthcoming for a little while. I had a hell of a time." He smiled to himself and tickled the back of his neck with his swagger cane.

Mine was a rather daunting prospect, being abroad for the first time in my life; joining a regiment in which I did not know one single soul; taking command of a platoon of forty hardened professionals, many of whom had been soldiering abroad for a dozen years or more, all under the watchful eyes of brother officers who, I gathered, were not going to be very helpful and my nineteenth birthday still some way off.

To say that I was relaxed during our half hour to Floriana would be a slight exaggeration. I was damp with apprehension which was not eased when H. H. told me that we would probably go on an active service "stand to" the following week.

"The whole Mediterranean Fleet is pulling out for two months for their spring exercises and we are expecting serious trouble—riots and sabotage at the dockyard—that sort of thing. The Italians have been stirring up the Maltese for a long time and getting them all excited about kicking out the British and becoming part of Italy. When the Navy leaves, we'll be on our own—just one miserable battalion to control this whole bloody island."

The officers' mess of Floriana Barracks was glued to the side of a huge church which housed the biggest and busiest and noisiest bells in Malta. They were banging away as we arrived.

Jackie Coulson met us at the door and Hawkins effected our introductions with sign language, then, roaring above the din, explained that his wife and his dinner were waiting for him; he was driven off in the evil-smelling gharry.

Coulson signed to me to drop my two pieces of hand luggage inside the courtyard and to follow him. We passed through a door in a far corner and I found myself in a monstrosity—typical of the living quarters of British Army officers at home and abroad: brown leather sofas and chairs; a few functional writing tables; a large round table in the middle of the room on which were elderly copies of English daily and weekly papers; a large fireplace and mantelshelf above which were two signed sepia reproductions of pictures of King George V and Queen Mary and beneath which was a large bum warmer. Two morose and, to my eyes, middle-aged officers in mufti were seated on this piece of furniture with drinks in their hands. The bells were a little fainter in here, but the room had a gloom all its own and was entirely covered with a thin layer of dust.

"This is Niven," said Coulson, jerking a thumb in my direction. Like the guns of a battleship, two pairs of cold eyes swiveled toward me. There was a long silence. The elder and more mauve-colored of the two finally spoke. "Oh," he said.

They both continued to stare at me.

Coulson pressed a bell on the right-hand side of the fireplace and a corporal appeared in a white mess jacket with two gold stripes on his arm. "Sir?"

"Double whiskey," said Coulson.

"Same," said the more mauve man, finishing his glass.

"Same," reiterated the less mauve man, draining his.

"If you want something," said Coulson to me, "order it yourself. We don't stand drinks in the mess."

"Same please," I said faintly.

Nothing very much happened till the drinks arrived; then the two mauve men returned to their interrupted conversation about Maltese priests.

"Not a bad job, really," said the more mauve man. "If some woman can't have a baby, she sends for the priest and he has to go to help things along in the name of the church."

"Always remembering to hang his umbrella on the doorknob to warn the husband to stay away till he's finished," said the less mauve man. Knowing winks and chuckles followed this exchange.

Coulson led me to a far corner of the anteroom, and in subdued whispers, or at least in subdued shouts against the clamor of the Sunday evening bells, he proceeded to bring me up to date. No one could have described Coulson as a warm and friendly man, but he was better at first sight than the two highly colored gentlemen on the bum warmer. He was thin, sandy and weedy. He exuded an aura of defeat.

"Malta is a sod of a place," he said. "You'll hate it. Nobody knows how long we'll be here. The second battalion is in India and we are supposed to be on home service for the next ten years, but they suddenly winkled us out of Aldershot and shipped us out here a couple of years ago. It's a

bloody mess being a home battalion on service abroad; they
don't even give us tropical kit. Just wait till you have to
wear full mess kit with a stiff shirt and waistcoat in August
when the sirocco is blowing. . . . Christ, you'll melt!"

"Who are those officers?" I asked, nodding at the other
occupants of the room.

"McDougall and Galt," said Coulson. "Subalterns both
in D Company. You are going to be in C."

"Subalterns"—I was amazed. "Both subalterns," said
Coulson, divining my thoughts, "about halfway up the list.
Nobody ever gets promoted in the regiment. It takes at
least ten or twelve years to become a captain."

"Twelve years!" I gasped—my dream of becoming a
general fading rapidly.

"At least," said Coulson, "and then it will be another
seven or eight till you have a chance of commanding a
company, and if you ever get that and become a major, it
will be four to one against you ever commanding a battalion. So the chances are that at the age of forty-five you will
be out on your ass with a pension of a hundred and eighty
pounds a year, after twenty-five years' service!"

I must have looked fairly shaken because he added almost kindly, "Well, we're all in the same boat, aren't we?
They never told us about this at Sandhurst, did they? Anyway if some silly bugger starts another war, we'll get plenty
of promotion, though it seems pretty quiet at the moment.
In the meanwhile, you get two months' leave a year; after
you've completed a year's service, you get nine shillings
and sixpence a day pay and messing allowance but whiskey
we get in Bond so that's only six shillings a bottle."

Coulson morosely painted thumbnail portraits of some
of the senior officers and ended by giving the following advice: "The only people you have to look out for are the
colonel, the adjutant, your company commander and, of
course, Trubshawe."

"Trubshawe?"

"Trubshawe, look out for him—he's nothing but trouble.
If it hadn't been for Henry Hawkins covering up for him, he
would have been flung out months ago. . . . He's a disaster!"

"Which company is Trubshawe in?"

"B Company, thank God, and they're over there on the

DAVID NIVEN

other side of Grand Harbour in Fort Ricasoli. He's confined to barracks anyway at the moment, so he's practically
locked up and a good job too!"

Just as I was about to ask a few pertinent questions
about this intriguing character, my erstwhile shipmate,
Jimmy McDonald, walked in, having temporarily mislaid
two pieces of baggage on the dock.

"These fucking Malts!" he said, addressing the mauve
men on the bum warmer. "They think they own the bloody
island—said I had to go through customs. Told 'em where
to get off, of course, but the Head Greaseball got quite offensive till I threatened to put him under close arrest." He
jabbed the bell with his finger and ordered a double whiskey.

"Have a good leave, Jimmy?" asked one of the mauve
men.

"Not bad, spent most of it at home. Nearly got married
but managed to talk my way out of it. Any supper left?"
The three of them disappeared into the dining room, carrying their glasses.

"Cold food on Sunday nights," said Coulson. "Go on in
if you want anything. . . . I've eaten."

I was very hungry, but the thought of sitting alone with
the three who had just gone in there filled me with alarm.

"So have I," I said. "I think I'll go and unpack."

Coulson showed me my room. "Your batman is Mc-
Ewan. He looks like a fairly decent sort of Jock. I'll tell the
mess corporal to send him over." He turned to go, then
paused at the door.

"Oh, you'll need a mosquito net. Did you bring one?"

"No, nobody told me."

"Well, I have a spare one you can have. It's never been
used so you can have it for what I paid for it."

"Very good of you, thanks!"

I've forgotten what I paid Coulson for his net, but it was
about double, I subsequently discovered, the going rate in
Valletta.

I looked around the room. It was large, stone-floored
and almost bare.

There was an iron bed by the window underneath which
reposed the usual receptacle, no different from the one
under my bed at Sandhurst except that this one bore the
Royal Crown and the king's initials; a washstand stand with

jug, bowl and soap dish similarly embossed stood against
one wall and a row of hooks were embedded in another.
There was no wardrobe.

The room was on the ground floor. Through the window
I could see the heads of people and various animals as they
passed in the street. The smell of horse, donkey, mule and
goat dung was very strong indeed. The bells were deafening
and white dust lay like a shroud over the whole unappetiz-
ing scene. I was very depressed.

"Private McEwan, sorr," said a voice behind me.

I turned to find a stocky, fresh-complexioned soldier of
about my own age.

"Corporal Deans sent me over tae help ye unpack."

My boxes and bags were in a corner, and in silence we
bent to the considerable job.

"I've no done this sort o' work before, sorr—ye'll have
tae tell me what ye want me tae do."

"What are you supposed to do, McEwan?"

The square bandy-legged figure stood up very straight.
"Sorr, in time o' war I'm yer runner. I carry yer messages
tae the platoon and see that ye have food and a place tae
sleep . . . in time o' peace, sorr, I look after ye as best I
can." He paused and then added, "That's what the
company sarnt major told me this morning."

When the recitation ended, we continued the unpacking
and I learned a little more about Private McEwan.

Like many others he had joined the Army because he
was sick of being unemployed. A day laborer from the
Glasgow slums, he had grown weary of standing in line in
drizzling rain, week after week, waiting to collect the dole.
A man of fierce pride and stainless-steel integrity, as I was
to learn during the four years he remained with me, for
him it must have been a degrading experience. So one day,
he and half a dozen cronies sauntered into Maryhill Barracks and announced that they were interested in joining
the Highland Light Infantry.

As was the custom, they were deloused, given a bath, a
hot meal and a bed for the night. A recruiting sergeant did
his gruff best to make them welcome and told them that in
the morning they could decide whether to sign on for a
total of seven years—five with the Colours and two with
the Reserve—or twelve years in a ratio of seven to five.

In the event, the next day four of the cronies disappeared before breakfast but McEwan signed on for five with the Colours and two with the Reserve. His remaining chum opted for seven and five because he was wanted by the Glasgow police for housebreaking, assault and battery. Like many others in that tough town he had decided that the best way to avoid civil justice was to change his name, join the Army, and disappear abroad while the statute of limitations ran out.

"Have ye no' had yer supper, sorr?" McEwan asked when we had got everything stowed away as best we could.

Before I had time to answer, he went on, "Corporal Deans said that maybe as this is yer furst night in the mess, yer'd like tae eat in yer room and he said tae tell ye that he has some cold grub and a bottle o' beer for ye. . . . I'll go an' get it the noo."

When McEwan came back with this most welcome repast, he also brought me the news that I was to report to my company commander at the company office at 0800 hours the following morning.

"I'll wake ye at seven o'clock, sorr, wi' a cup o' gunfire* an' then I can show ye the way to t'office."

I slept fitfully, and during the long periods I was awake, I became increasingly excited at the prospect of taking over my platoon.

In the morning I avoided the mess, as I was extremely apprehensive of meeting brother officers on an empty stomach, and fortified by "gunfire," I was escorted across the granaries by McEwan, past the guardroom, across the barrack square and deposited outside the door marked C COMPANY OFFICE.

Company Sergeant Major "Sixty" Smith was the sole occupant, arranging papers on a trestle table covered with a gray Army blanket. He sprang to attention as I came in and I caught a glimpse of the medal ribands of the DCM and MM on his chest. A rather portly figure with a friendly and revealing smile—revealing the absence of four front teeth.

"You'll be Mister Niven, sorr? The Company Commander will be here in a wee while. Welcome to C Company, sorr."

"Sixty" Smith was a regimental character recommended

---

* Tea the Jocks made—very strong and very sweet.

for the Victoria Cross in 1917. He was renowned for his toughness, and the fact that his company commander was hardly ever called upon to deal with small "offenses" was not so much a measure of the high standard of discipline in C Company as a tribute to the strong right arm of "Sixty" meting out his own brand of punishment behind the latrines with a big leather belt.

"Sixty" excused himself and I filled in the time waiting for my company commander by studying with interest the various training programs and duty rosters that covered the walls. Almost half an hour dragged by, then "Sixty" put his head around the door.

"Company commander crossing the Barrack Square, sorr."

I looked out of the window with interest well mixed with apprehension. For the foreseeable future the officer approaching would be both my boss and my judge; answerable only to the commanding officer, it would be in his hands alone to make my life pleasant or very unpleasant, interesting or deadly dull. I saw a long sleek Lagonda swing up to a stop outside the company office. The morning sun was beginning to beat down and the glare from the parade ground hurt my eyes. Dust from the sudden stop billowed up around the car. From the driver's seat a tall and powerfully built figure emerged. Major Harry Ross-Skinner was a man of about forty-five; on his chest his bravery DSO and MC; in his hand a battered briefcase; on his head nothing.

He unhurriedly addressed a well-turned-out soldier who was sliding over behind the controls: "Wash the car, then pick up my wife at eleven o'clock and take her shopping. At noon be back here for me and don't forget to tell Sergeant Fensham at the stables that I'll be playing six chukkas this afternoon." He picked up his Glengarry, Sam Browne belt and swagger cane from the back seat and ambled toward the door. As he entered, silhouetted against the fierce glare from outside, he was even larger than I had first thought. His complexion was florid; his eyes bright blue; his hair and rather scraggly mustache sand and salt. He gazed at me with vague alarm as I snapped off my best Sandhurst salute.

"Oh, hullo," he said amicably, "what can we do for you?"

"Niven, sir, reporting to 'C' Company."

"Well, that's nice," he said, "who told you so?"

"The orderly officer, sir, Coulson."

"I wonder why nobody told me." He raised his voice very slightly. " 'Sixty!' "

The company sergeant major could only have been out of sight by a couple of feet. He shot around the door and stood to attention. "SORR?"

"Do we know anything about this officer being posted to us?"

"Yes, sir, it was in battalion orders last week and the adjutant sent you a personal memo two days ago."

"Oh, I see . . . well, splendid. . . . Do you play polo?"

"I'm afraid not, sir."

"Why not?"

"I don't think I could afford it, sir."

It seemed to take an appreciable time for this to sink in, and when it finally did, it was too late and perhaps too difficult for him to make any observation.

"Which platoon have we given him?"

"Yer said No. 3, sorr," said "Sixty" Smith gently.

"Ah, yes. . . . Well, he can have that or No. 2 and No. 4, whichever he likes. . . ."

He brushed up his mustache between the forefinger and thumb of his left hand and looked down on me: "Any preference?"

"Er . . . no, sir . . . er, anything will do."

"All right then No. 3. . . . Let's see. 'Sixty,' who's the platoon sergeant of No. 3?"

"Sarnt Innes, sorr."

"Oh, yes, of course." Ross-Skinner was putting on his belt and cap during this conversation.

"Anybody for company office?" he asked.

"No charges today, sorr, but the storeman has reported the loss of seven blankets and a pickax. He thinks he can make them up before the next quartermaster's inspection."

"How's he going to do that, d'you suppose?"

"Sixty" chuckled. "Best not ask, sorr."

Ross-Skinner took off his belt and bonnet again and sat down behind the table with a sigh. Then he opened his briefcase and spread out on the gray blanket some saddlery catalogs.

"Better send for Innes, I suppose. . . . He can show Mr. Niven his platoon." Company commander and company sergeant major smiled secret smiles over this, but I had no time to reflect upon them because at that moment a solidly built old soldier appeared in the doorway with a great stamping of feet.

"Adjutant's compliments, sorr," he bellowed toward the ceiling. "Commanding officer wants to see Mr. Newton." He made this statement with such tremendous authority that it was a moment before I realized that he was referring to me.

"You'd better cut along then," said Ross-Skinner. "Pity about the polo," he added.

Across the barrack square, the old soldier set a rapid pace, and between keeping up with him and proudly answering meticulously the first salutes ever thrown in my direction, I was bathed in perspiration by the time I arrived at battalion HQ. I was shown into the adjutant's office.

Henry Hawkins smiled up from behind his desk. "Shaking down all right? It's very strange at first, I know. Just let me finish signing all this bumph and I'll take you in to meet the CO." For a few minutes the scratching of his pen was the only sound in the warm office, then he spoke again.

"Incidentally, when you were posted to us, some joker at the War Office sent us a memo about you, something about your preference for regiment."

My sweating increased a hundredfold. Hawkins never looked up, he continued signing documents.

"It came directly to me and it is now locked up in the adjutant's confidential file. Nobody else can see it."

He looked up, put down his pen and smiled again.

"Now . . . let's go and see the colonel."

This was an awesome moment. The commanding officer was seated behind his desk: that is to say, like Ross-Skinner, Henry Hawkins and everyone else in Floriana Barracks who was seated behind anything, he was seated behind a trestle table on which was spread a gray Army blanket.

"Mr. Niven, Colonel," announced Henry Hawkins, loosing off a salute. I did the same.

It took weeks for my commanding officer to address a word to me directly. I never discovered whether he thought it was impressive or whether he was shy or whether he just didn't know what the hell to say, but for whatever reason, he preferred to address the junior officers of his battalion through an intermediary. Nobody had warned me of this,

and it came as something of a shock when he turned to the
adjutant and said, "Did he have a good trip?"

"Yes, sir, very good," said Hawkins firmly.

"I hate those bloody P and O's. They always smell of
sick," said the colonel. "What sports does he play?"

Henry consulted with a file he had in his hand. "School
Rugby XV and cricket XI, school teams for boxing and
swimming. Rugby Blue at Sandhurst, good horseman and
passed for hunting."

"Is he going to play polo?"

Hawkins made a question mark face in my direction.

"I may not be able to, sir," I said now addressing Hawkins. "It might be a bit . . . er . . . too much for me."

"Well, tell him about the fifteen bobbers, Henry," said
the colonel, "and explain that people in the Navy always
have ponies they want exercised. . . . I think we can expect
him down at the Marsa."

To show that the interview was now concluded, the colonel rose from behind his desk. Unfortunately, he was so
short that his head remained almost exactly the same distance from the floor. Sitting down in the darkened office,
he had seemed quite impressive, large brown eyes set in a
deeply tanned face. Dark hair, gray at the temples and at
least three rows of medal ribands; but when he walked to
the window and displayed tartan trews that somehow managed to look both skimpy and baggy at the same time, he
looked like a little bird, a similarity that to my astonished
eyes became even more pronounced when, with his back to
the room, he raised both arms high above his head with the
palms flat and fingers extended . . . he reminded me instantly of a cormorant drying its wings.

"Wait behind, will you, Henry?" said the commanding
officer over his shoulder. I saluted his strange back view
and went out into the hot sunlight.

Back at the company office, Sergeant Innes was waiting
for me and a splendidly reassuring sight he was too. Strong
as an ox, he was also comparatively tall, about five feet ten.
Most of the men in the regiment were much stockier. He
had bright-red hair, very close cropped, and a deep scar
under his cheekbone which raised one corner of his mouth
in a permanent grin. It was probably a razor slash. The
Jocks had a great partiality for the razor as an offensive
weapon and invariably had a couple of safety blades sewn

just inside the peak of their Glengarrys. In a brawl, an adversary was well advised to stay out of range because with one quick movement, the bonnet was off and swinging in a wide arc held by the ribbons at the back.

"Ginger" Innes saluted. "I'll take ye tae the barrick room, sorr, so ye can see yer platoon."

So this was it—the moment of truth! At last I was about to come face-to-face with the forty professionals who would be under my command. This was the crunch. In a strange mood of exaltation, I marched confidently alongside Sergeant Innes. Outside a barrack room door, excitingly marked NO. 3 PLATOON, Sergeant Innes stopped, then flung it open. A stentorian bellow rent the sultry air.

"STAND TAE YER BEDS!!"

A sound of scuffling feet came from within. After that, silence.

"No. 3 Platoon ready for yer inspection, sorr."

Proudly, I passed him to confront for the first time my long-awaited charges.

Seven rather crestfallen soldiers in various stages of undress stood waiting for me beside their beds.

6

Only seven stood by their beds, but there seemed to be many other beds displaying kilts laid out for inspection.

"Why only seven, Sergeant Innes?" I asked.

"Four on regimental guard, sorr, six on palace guard, three on cookhouse fatigues, three on regimental fatigues, two on officers' mess fatigues, four awa' sick wi' sandfly fever, and two doing sixty-eight days detention in military prison for attempted desertion, sorr."

Even my faulty mathematics could work out that my platoon was woefully under strength, but I swallowed my disappointment and inspected my rather meager flock.

They were a hard-faced lot, and although they stared unblinkingly at some fixed point about two feet above my head, I was pretty sure that within thirty seconds of my having walked through the door they had all thoroughly inspected me.

Foot regiments in the Regular Army consisted of a regimental depot and two battalions; of these one battalion was permanently on service abroad in different parts of the empire, while the other, based in the British Isles, acted as a sort of holding and training battalion for the one overseas which, perforce, has to be kept up to full strength.

Back at "C" Company office "Sixty" Smith gently explained that for a young officer still in his teens, trained to the hilt and pumped full of ambition and enthusiasm to find himself in a home service battalion of very diminished strength, trying to fulfill overseas garrison duties while completing its own training program and at the same time being constantly drained of its newly trained men, the result was inevitable: deadening frustration. It didn't descend on me like a cloud that very first day, of course, but slowly, like the damp of a disused house, it bored its way into me during the next few months. In the meantime so much was new, so much was exciting and everything was different.

Nothing much happened during that first morning. My company commander disappeared in his Lagonda at about eleven thirty; two other subalterns of the company appeared briefly, peered at me, and went about their business. The other subaltern and the second-command were away on leave, so I hung about the company office till lunchtime, not knowing what to do.

Luncheon in the mess was torture. About twenty officers were present, including the birdlike colonel, but nobody spoke to me except Mr. Gifford, the civilian steward employed by the officers' mess. Mr. Gifford, a charming Jeeves-like character, was responsible for the catering and for keeping the officers' mess bills. At dinner time, in white tie and tails, he acted as a glorified butler, and at all times he was the supreme boss of Corporal Deans and two permanent mess orderlies. On guest nights or other highly charged occasions, a roster of officers' batmen was also pressed into service and these too he ruled with a rod of iron.

Mr. Gifford seated me at a long mahogany table, gleaming with vast pieces of Victorian silver donated by retiring officers—horses and pheasants mostly, but also a profusion of cigar and cigarette boxes, lighters, ashtrays and menu holders.

The menu displayed in the holders was extensive, but my nerves were not quite up to it so I settled for something cold off a groaning sideboard, washed it down quickly with some beer, and fled to my room.

Soon Private McEwan appeared. "Adjutant's compliments, sorr, ye'll be playing cricket fer the battalion at fifteen hundred hours this afternoon."

I must have looked a little dazed because he added, "We've a verra poor team just the noo, but the lads all say ye'll be a big help, an' we're playing against the gunners an' they're good."

"Christ," I said, "I haven't played cricket since I left school—I can't possibly play for the battalion."

McEwan smiled encouragingly. "Ye'll be one o' the best if ye've played at all, sorr." He was explaining that in a regiment recruited from Highland villages and slums of Glasgow cricket was an almost unknown sport.

At three o'clock that afternoon, I presented myself at the

Marsa Cricket Ground. The heat was like a blast furnace.
A jovial deaf major, the shape of a football, called with
heavy humor Roundy by his contemporaries, greeted me
and introduced me to the team, mostly elderly sergeants
and young officers. They seemed a friendly and cheerful lot
and I began to relax.

Suddenly, an earsplitting belch rent the air. I spun
around and perceived a truly amazing sight. Trubshawe
was approaching. Six feet six, with legs that seemed to start
at the navel, encased in drain-pipe-tight white flannels, he
sported a blue blazer with so many brass buttons on it that
he shone like a gypsy caravan on Epsom Downs on Derby
Day; on his head a Panama hat with an MCC riband; on
his face the biggest mustache I had ever seen: a really huge
growth which one could see from the back on a clear day.
Part of it was also miraculously trained to branch off and
join the hair above his ears. It was in fact not so much a
mustache as an almost total hirsute immersion.

"My dear fellow," boomed this splendid apparition,
"welcome! I'm delighted to meet you." A row of very white
teeth blazed out of the foliage as Trubshawe shook my
hand. The sergeants, I noticed, were nudging each other
and smiling with great affection in his direction, but the officers tended to drift away and busy themselves with their
cricket gear.

"This, old man," said Trubshawe, tapping a briefcase he
was carrying, "is an invention of mine. It's called the Dipsomaniac's Delight." He flicked the lock, and inside, set in
green baize slots were, I perceived, a bottle of whiskey, a
soda water siphon and two glasses.

"Come, let us drink to your most timely arrival with a
stoop of mead, or a posset of burnt sack." In the heat of
that blazing afternoon I downed what was to be the forerunner of many thousands of toasts in the company of this
amazing and wondrous creature.

Never in the history of human conflict has there been a
more unlikely officer in a Highland regiment. Just for a
start, he was English—a felony which he compounded by
not being Sandhurst-trained but by arriving via Cambridge
University and the supplementary reserve of a smart cavalry regiment. He was also highly eccentric with a wild and
woolly sense of the ridiculous, an unabashed romantic who
had a grand piano in his room on which for hours he

played sixteenth-century folk music and Peter Warlock's haunting melodies. His reading matter was influenced by an old Cambridge chum, T. H. White. He was, in short, an Elizabethan with a hunting horn.

I don't remember too much about that afternoon's cricket, but I believe I acquitted myself adequately. With the shortage of bowlers I was made to trundle down my slow offbreaks for hours on end. The Royal Artillery gleefully dispatched these to various boundaries, but I managed to take a few wickets—one a glorious catch on the boundary by Trubshawe who was not supposed to be there at all; he was easing his way back to be close to the Dipsomaniac's Delight.

I made a few runs and for a brief spell was joined at the wicket by Trubshawe. He was a fascinating sight, full of confidence, taking guard before each ball, patting nonexistent divots on the matting wicket and inspecting the positions of the fielders with an imperious and disdainful gaze. But something was very wrong with his timing, for although each individual stroke was immaculate in style and execution, it was played so late that the ball was well on its way back to the bowler by the time he had completed his shot.

The match was drawn but not because our team was of the same standard as the gunners. Cook Sergeant Winters, who was extremely portly as befitted his station, had considerable difficulty in bending down while fielding—a shortcoming he gallantly overcame by stopping ground shots with his shins. A hard drive to mid off had just connected with a horrible "crack" just below his knee when a dispatch rider roared onto the field and gave "Roundy" Cavendish a message. "Roundy" gathered both teams together and somberly told us to return to our barracks at once. The situation caused by the Italian-inspired troublemakers, which Henry Hawkins had foreseen on the day of my arrival, had deteriorated rapidly, and we were to stand by for riot duty and for the guarding of important points against a possible coup.

Back at Floriana Barracks, everything was hustle and bustle, but I managed to locate Jackie Coulson and ask him what I should do. "Battle order, I should think, and report to your company office," he said curtly over his shoulder, hurrying away. Private McEwan, already himself capari-

soned like someone during the retreat from Mons, buttoned
me into webbing equipment, water bottle, revolver, map
case and steel helmet and with, admittedly, a certain
number of cabbage whites in my stomach, I made my way
across the granaries. At the company office, the other subalterns were already waiting. "Sixty" Smith was issuing
them with revolver, ammunition and maps. We all came to
attention when Major Ross-Skinner strode in. Gone was
the vague and bumbling sportsman and in his place was the
fully efficient, calm, professional commander. As we stood
in front of him, he quickly and lucidly issued his orders.

I scribbled frantically as he laid down the duties of No. 3
Platoon, the positions to be occupied, the organization of
rations and ammunition, the arrangements for communications, evacuation of wounded and numerous other pieces
of vitally important information. He even included a brief
résumé of the political situation that had just come to a
head; according to Ross-Skinner, the Maltese had been
British subjects for a hundred and twenty years but somehow during that time, while English had become the official language of the administration, Italian had remained
the legal language used in all disputes. The local Strickland
government had lately fallen out with the island's church
leaders. The Vatican had consequently become involved
with the British Foreign Office and now it had
mushroomed into a full showdown between Italy and
Great Britain.

It all seemed extremely complicated to me, but when I
recited it to my amazed platoon a few minutes later, it
sounded like one of the more unlikely plots by Gilbert &
Sullivan.

The platoon as presented to me that afternoon by Sergeant Innes had grown to more respectable proportions,
and I was relieved to note that fighting strength was now
about thirty. They were a tough-looking bunch—mostly
Glaswegians—and when I first entered the barrack room,
they were clustered around a very apprehensive middle-
aged Maltese in a sweat-soaked singlet. Like a man possessed, he was turning the heavy stone wheel of a giant
knife sharpener. One of the corporals stepped forward
proudly: "He hoppened tae be passin', sorr, so I persuaded
him tae come in wi' his wee contraption and touch up the
laddies' bayonets."

We soon embarked in two local buses that had been commandeered for the occasion and were driven to the customs sheds on the St. Elmo side of the Grand Harbour—our responsibility till relieved. I made a quick reconnaissance with "Ginger" Innes and issued my orders for the disposition of my troops. Later, Ross-Skinner arrived in his Lagonda and had a look around. To my great relief, he altered nothing, just made a few suggestions about drinking water and a better place to be used as a latrine.

For hours nothing happened. Then some confused shouting around midnight heralded a halfhearted attack by a few hooligans armed with stones and iron bars. A Jock standing next to me was hit on the steel helmet with a loud clang. "FOOK THAT!" he roared and charged out with his bayonet flashing in the moonlight. That was the last appearance of any opposition and, incidentally, the one and only piece of active service I was to take part in during four years with the Highland Light Infantry.

The next morning, the platoon was withdrawn and the general order to "stand down" was given. The crisis was over. The British Empire was intact.

Trubshawe, always a mine of information on questions political, told me later that it had all been very simply arranged. The British government had promptly suspended the Maltese Constitution; forbidden Italian as the official legal language; and put His Majesty's governor in sole charge of everything. "Thereby, old man, putting the whole place back at least a hundred and twenty years."

Once this little flurry of excitement was over, the battalion settled back into its dreary, soporific routine of garrison duties. Training programs were issued, but there were few men available to train.

With the advent of the hot weather, the leave season moved into high gear and many officers headed for England.

Aided by Trubshawe, whose period of incarceration in Fort Ricasoli was now ended and who had, much to my delight, appointed himself my guide and sponsor, my shaking-down period proceeded apace. First I had to make official calls on all the married officers. The routine was simple. First Private McEwan would find out from the batman at the quarters in question just when the people would be out and I would then slip a couple of calling cards into the silver tray just inside the door. The wives had a nasty habit of testing the surface of these cards with their thumbs to make sure they were engraved; no gentleman, of course, would ever have printed cards. I had also to make the rounds and sign my name in various visitors' books, the governors at Government House and various admirals' establishments were similarly visited.

After a few weeks, one or two officers apart from Trubshawe occasionally spoke to me and it was a great joy when Trubshawe's company was replaced in Fort Ricasoli by another company which included the uncommunicative Jimmy McDonald. Trubshawe's Company B (machine gun) arrived at Floriana Barracks and things perked up a lot. The major was "Tank" Ross, a famous Army and Scotland Rugby footballer; the second-in-command, a young captain, R. E. "Wallard" Urquhart. A serious soldier of great charm and warmth, he was unfailingly kind and helpful to me, and his splendid qualities, from all accounts, were never seen to greater advantage than in 1944 when as a major general he led the daring airdrop on Arnhem.

The first regimental guest night occurred about six weeks after I arrived. It was, quite simply, a nightmare. As the newly joined subaltern, in a sort of travesty of welcome, I was ordered to sit at the colonel's right hand.

About forty officers were present, including a few guests: Greville Stevens, ADC to the governor, an amusing pink-faced, sandy-haired captain in the 60th Rifles, known locally as "the amorous prawn"; a brace of admirals; an air marshal; some assorted soldiers; and two naval guests of Trubshawe's, a Lieutenant Anthony Pleydell-Bouverie; and a midshipman David Kelburn, now admiral, the Earl of Glasgow. Two, incidentally, of the most eccentric and brightest men ever to put on naval uniform.

Round after round of drinks in the anteroom, and finally just as I was headed for a most necessary trip to the lavatory, Mr. Gifford announced dinner. Like a lamb to the slaughter, I was led with bursting bladder to my chair next to my commanding officer. As he had still not spoken to me directly during my service, I was in no position to ask him if I might be excused, an unthinkable request, as officers and gentlemen never left the table under any circumstances until the end of the meal when the king's health had been drunk. Sweat broke out all over me as I contemplated the hours of agony ahead.

I've long since forgotten who sat on my right. Whoever he was, he, too, never directed a word in my direction.

So I sat in miserable silence with crossed legs, perspiration trickling down inside my shirtfront, my stand-up wing collar wilting with pain.

Cold soup (more strain on the bladder) was followed by other courses, each course washed down by a different wine. I continued to drink everything that was placed in front of me in the vague hope that something might act as an anesthetic and reduce my terrible pain.

By the time we arrived at the cheese I was desperate, past caring. As far as I was concerned, my career could end in a pool of urine right there under the polished mahogany and the regimental silver but succor was at hand. Mr. Gifford bent over and whispered in my ear, "With Mr. Trubshawe's compliments, sir, I have just placed an empty magnum underneath your chair." Relief, when I heard his words, did not flow over me—it spurted out of me, in an apparently endless stream, but thanks to a firm grip on the bottle with my knees, I was able to aim with one hand and leave the other available to crumble nonchalantly a water biscuit. This proved just as well because suddenly, the colonel zeroed in on me and spoke to me for the first time. I was so unnerved by this sudden reversal of form that I nearly released my grip on the warm and by-now-heavy receptacle below the table.

His words were few and his point was made with admirable clarity. "I have," he said, "fucked women of every nationality and most animals, but the one thing I cannot abide is a girl with a Glasgow accent. Pass the port." He never spoke to me again.

After the port completed its circuit, a toast was given to the king. Many glasses I noticed were ostentatiously passed over the top of a glass of water on their way to the lips in a rather juvenile gesture to show that Highlanders were still drinking to the exiled Stewarts—the king—over the water.

After the toast, the mess pipers filed in, eight in number. From the top drone of each instrument fluttered a heavily embroidered silken banner—the coats of arms of the senior regimental officers present. The eardrums of the diners, particularly those of the Sassenach guests, were subject in the confined space of the dining room to a veritable barrage of sound. Around and around the table marched the pipers, and around and around the table went the port, brandy, kümmel and Drambuie.

Finally, after the pipe major had played his solo pibroch, the hauntingly lovely "Desperate Battle of the Birds," the colonel tottered from the room followed by the survivors, who then indulged in a monstrous barging match, punctuated by wild cries which passed for Highland reels. These in turn further deteriorated into a competition to see who, by using the furniture, could make the fastest circuit of the anteroom without touching the floor. Trubshawe, Pleydell-Bouverie, Kelburn and I left in some alarm when a visiting air commodore ate a champagne glass whole, stem and all, and the majors decided to have a competition to see which one could pick up a box of matches off the floor with his teeth while balancing a bottle of champagne on his head.

Anthony and David borrowed some civilian clothes and the four of us, now more suitably attired—Trubshawe in a strange green almost knee-length hacking jacket—made a memorable tour of the late bars of the Shada Stretta known to the Jocks as the Gut.

At five in the morning, after Hooverizing down prairie oysters, raw egg yolks mixed with equal portions of port and Worcestershire sauce in Aunties—a plush red establishment run by an enchanting elderly ex-whore from Leeds—I was sick at the top of the Marsamuscetto Cliffs.

In the months that followed, my military ambitions began to seep away as slowly, but surely, it dawned on me that there was very little point in being a keen young officer—people who just went through the motions would still in the next ten years march inexorably up the Army list to the rank of captain. The fawn-colored Army list was kept in the mess, and the pages devoted to the Highland Light Infantry were gray from the probing fingers that endlessly traced the inevitable promotions that would come in the long, long years ahead.

However, there was so much new, so much to enjoy that it was almost two years before the deadening horror of the whole thing finally descended upon me and enveloped me like a black Bedouin tent. In the meantime Trubshawe's guidance continued apace. He explained to me that I could hire polo ponies for fifteen shillings a month and that apart from buying some mallets, I had nothing to worry about financially, the grooms being soldiers and the ponies all being on the regimental strength as officers' chargers. In addition, as I got better at the game, he assured me that many naval officers would be delighted to lend me their ponies just to keep them exercised during the long periods they would be away at sea.

All this was indeed true and I found myself soon with as many mounts as I could play and quite a respectable handicap.

The Marsa Polo Club was the smart place to be—smart in the most colonial sense of the word—it was mounted suburbia. It was parasols and fraightfully refained voices. It was "Boy bring me a stingar" and naval wives who announced with a smirk, "We're going in to have our bottom scrubbed next week," but it was still heady stuff compared with what I had been exposed to before and I thrived on it. Girls there were in plenty. Apart from the resident ones, daughters of senior officers and officials, there were also for several months a year hundreds of young and lonely naval officers' wives. There was, in addition, the "Fishing Fleet." A motley collection of passed-over debs and pink-cheeked country cousins who annually timed their arrival to coincide with the return, after many months at sea, of several thousand sex-starved mariners. Finally, there were the whores, although in spite of my lucky tutelage by Nessie, I had largely graduated from that particular kind of relaxation, but Valletta was full of whores busily catering to the needs of all ranks of the biggest fleet in the world. Many were mid-Europeans or Russians, refugees of impeccable lineage with sisters plying the same desperate trade in Singapore and fathers driving taxies in Paris.

Once, when sallying forth on a training march at the head of my handful of heavily laden troops, I was gladdened to see two gorgeous blond figures in bathing costumes waving and smiling from a balcony on the outskirts of Floriana. I made a mental note of the whereabouts of the house and a couple of days later paid them a visit.

I had not been mistaken, they were very beautiful indeed, very aristocratic looking with a distinct family resemblance.

The more mature one was about thirty-five while the

younger could have been no more than seventeen. The older one did all the talking—that is to say, she did all the hand flapping, nodding and smiling because they were Hungarians and the language barrier was a mile high. I was made to understand that she was either the mother or the aunt of the girl. I still hope, looking back on that appalling evening, that at least she was not the mother. It had certainly been in the back of my mind when I went to call that they might be whores, but when the sign language became more comprehensible, I was left in no doubt.

I also gathered that I had, rather naturally, been earmarked for the younger and that I was expected to be "understanding" because she had only just arrived in Malta. The sad and minimal financial arrangements once completed, with the style of a duchess showing an honored weekend guest to the Canaletto suite, I was ushered, with a strangely quiet girl clinging to my hand, to a tiny room with a single bed under the window.

Once inside, this beautiful creature sat frozen on the iron bed and watched with large luminous eyes as I started to undress. I must confess that for many years after my initiation, Nessie remained as a yardstick for my sexual activities. This night provided an extraordinary comparison.

When, with shirt off, I sat beside the girl, put my arm around her and kissed her in a possessive way on the ear, she tensed up. When I put a hand on her knee and without wasting too much time, let it travel north, she went rigid and jerked her head away. When I finally managed to get us both naked on top of that tiny bed, she lay like a mummy with clenched fists and teeth to match, staring at the mosquito-covered ceiling. I cannot say that she "resisted" but she certainly "avoided"; but in my massive ignorance, I pressed home the attack. After a short one-sided and, apart from one muffled cry, noiseless encounter, I rolled, semisatisfied, against the crumbling wall while the poor child buried her head in the pillow and sobbed her heart out. Utterly appalled at the havoc I had wrought for the evidence was by now only too apparent, I dressed, tiptoed downstairs and walked slowly through the hot, smelly night back to my own iron bedstead.

There was a professionally languid captain in the headquarters wing who wore a monocle and was reputed to be the tallest officer in the British Army. His wife was very pretty in a sort of chocolate-boxy way and could have been described in polite society as a flirt, anywhere else she would have been called a cock teaser.

I had, it is true, nibbled her ear and snapped her garter a couple of times while watching the polo from her car, but nothing more, so I was all unsuspecting when a runner informed me that the captain wished to see me immediately in his company office. I entered and saluted. He was busy looking over some ammunition returns with the quartermaster sergeant. I fidgeted around for a while but he still did not look up. Finally, head still down, he spoke, "Niven, are you very much in love with my wife?"

My toes tried to grip the floor through my brogues to stop me from keeling over.

"No, sir . . . not at all, sir," I murmured and then, for no apparent reason, I added, "Thank you very much, sir."

"Well, if you're not," said the captain, putting some papers in a folder, "be a good chap, don't go on telling her you are . . . upsets her, you know. Now, Quartermaster Sergeant, about the Range Allotment of 303. . . ."

I saluted the top of his head and withdrew.

After that I decided to be a good deal more selective in my nibbling and snapping.

As a matter of fact the fleet sailed several weeks later for exercises off the Greek Islands, leaving behind them not only their ponies but literally hundreds of ladies in different stages of availability. I discussed the situation with the wife of the signals officer of a destroyer who had made it very obvious that she had no intention of sitting around twiddling her thumbs waiting for his return.

It was a nasty little intrigue really but quite exciting especially when the husband gave a party in his cabin before he sailed and said to me, "Look after Eunice for me till I get back."

"I certainly will," I said, avoiding her eye.

When sailing time came, Eunice and I climbed to the top of the cliffs and watched the splendid spectacle of the entire Mediterranean Fleet steaming out of the harbor, Royal Marine Bands playing and bunting fluttering.

We used my field glasses and paid particular attention to her husband's destroyer. He was on the bridge. We had told him where we would be watching and with his binoculars, he found us. Lots of waving went on and we even staged a big amorous embrace to make him laugh. I wish I could report that I felt a twinge of shame at that moment, but I didn't. I had other feelings of a more animal nature to contend with.

The fleet sailed away into the sunset and disappeared over the horizon bearing the poor cuckold-to-be toward Corfu; never has a safer stage been set for infidelity but Eunice decided to savor the moment. After all, we had at least six weeks ahead of us in which to indulge ourselves so she insisted that I take her to the Sliema Club to a party with some others, escort her home to her house and then . . .

So we danced close and drank champagne and toasted each other over the rim of our glasses, all very high-powered romantic stuff; finally I found myself in her bed.

Some far-from-routine thrashing around was going on because Eunice was an expert at prolonging everything when, suddenly, she went rigid.

"Christ!" she hissed. "He's back!"

He was too and downstairs in the sitting room.

"Get in that cupboard," ordered Eunice.

It was pretty ridiculous because my clothes were all over the floor, but I did as I was told and stood quaking in a black hole that smelled of mothballs.

I didn't have time to reflect on the old French farce situation that I was in. All I could think of was the certain death that would soon come up those stairs.

Eunice was made of different stuff. She went down naked to meet him.

"Darling, how did you get back?"

"Stripped a bloody turbine thirty miles out . . . towed back."

Somehow she persuaded him to get in the car and go to get a bottle a champagne so they could celebrate.

I dressed in about eleven seconds and with my shoes on the wrong feet shot downstairs and out of the house. I was impotent for days.

So long as the ex-ranker Henry Hawkins was adjutant, my interest in things military at least remained dormant. Somehow, he could even revive it after telling me the frustrating news that after months of training, the twenty best men in my platoon had been posted to the Second Battalion in India. Somehow, he encouraged me when a great favorite of mine, a huge piper from the Western Isles, was listed as a deserter and caught trying to stow away on a tanker bound for Cardiff.

"Johnstone will be court-martialed," said Hawkins. "He is in cells now and wants you to defend him." Any man had the right to nominate any officer he wished to defend him before a court-martial. Flattered by this demonstration of respect but alarmed by his poorly developed sense of self-preservation, I hurried off to the military prison where Johnstone was incarcerated.

"Hoo mony days d'ye think I'll git, sorr?" demanded the prisoner before I was halfway in his cell.

"Well," I said, "I'll do everything I can to prove you intended to come back so they might make it 'absent without leave' instead of 'desertion,' but I'm afraid you'll get between sixty days an six months whichever way it goes."

"Naebody's goin' tae put me awa' in the glass hoos for six months," said Johnstone slowly and with that he put his left hand around the edge of the great iron door of the cell and with his right hand slammed it shut. All four fingers of his left hand were smashed and dangling like doll's.

A few weeks later, when he was back in a cell once more awaiting his court-martial, he asked to see me again. It is incredible that I fell into the trap.

"Hoo mony days will they put me awa' for noo, sorr?" he asked, but before I could answer, the door clanged shut and he was grinning triumphantly at the same mangled hand.

He never did go to prison. He was dismissed from the service as an undesirable character. He came to say good-bye before he left and was very worried that he would never be able to play the pipes again.

One sad day, Henry Hawkins, the subalterns' friend, was promoted to major, and, after several experiments, his place was permanently taken by "The Weasel."

The Weasel was a most unsavory piece of work. Yellow teeth protruded from beneath a small nicotine-stained mustache and a receding chin did nothing much to help a pair of shifty eyes that were pinned together like cuff links above a beaky nose. On his thin chest there were no medals for valor. He made a bad move early. He called Trubshawe in and informed him that he drank too much. Questioned as to how he could have arrived at such an outlandish conclusion, the Weasel announced that he had carefully checked Trubshawe's mess bill and would check all subalterns' mess bills each month in the future. Trubshawe quickly made arrangements with Mr. Gifford for a sizable proportion of his future alcoholic intake to be charged as "COD packages," but the Weasel's spy system was born that day and from then on none of us felt secure, least of all myself when he said to me, "I've been looking through your file, Niven—I wouldn't say that the Argylls have missed very much, would you?"

He was never openly hostile to me till one day when platoon training was at its height. I was given the task of attacking a small hill across a mile and a half of completely barren land. The colonel, accompanied by the second-in-command and several other senior officers, was on the top of the hill. He listened disinterestedly while the Weasel gave his orders.

"No. 3 Platoon will attack demonstrating the fullest possible use of cover: road and sea are your boundaries, both inclusive."

As we marched down the dusty road to our start point out of sight in a dip, "Ginger" Innes and I held a council of war. At all costs we must try to avoid cutting ourselves to pieces crawling in full view across a mile and a half of razor-sharp volcanic outcrop, but nobody in the platoon could swim unnoticed a mile and a half naked, let alone wearing full equipment. The road too was in full view and so dusty that the approach of a goat sent a cloud of telltale white puffs billowing into the sky. Salvation, however, in the shape of a half-empty bus stood waiting in the hollow as we descended below the line of vision of the group on the hill. Country women, wearing voluminous black national *faldetta* headdresses were already seated in the bus clasping on their knees baskets of chickens, fish and other goodies which they were taking to market.

"Road inclusive" had been the Weasel's orders, so blessing my good fortune, I judiciously scattered the platoon about the bus. Some lay on the floor with the goats and thus shielded from view by the black tentlike confections on the good ladies' heads, the whole platoon motored peacefully past the unsuspecting brass. Half a mile behind them was another dip in the road. There we debussed and with their backs toward us, our quarry were easy to stalk.

Thirty yards from the group, while our two Lewis guns happily opened up with their football rattles, the rest of us charged with fixed bayonets and blood curdling yells. Perhaps I overdid it a little on arrival by saying to a stunned Weasel, "Bang bang, you're dead!"

Not only did he give me a monumental bollocking in front of my own men, calling me among other things a "bloody boy scout," but he sent us, at the double, one and a half miles to our original start point and then made us crawl back across the volcanic razors. Far from holding this purgatory against me, the Jocks pretended to have enjoyed the whole day hugely and the episode was ever after referred to as The Desperate Battle of the Bus.

Trubshawe was not the Weasel's type of man at all, and his wonderful eccentricities were like a red rag to a bull. Trubshawe's steel helmet caused a certain strain on an important parade.

"Can't possibly wear the bloody thing, old man; it's too heavy and red hot to boot, so I've had this little number run up for the occasion."

He then placed on his head a papier-mâché replica that was as light as a feather and from three feet away was indistinguishable from the original.

"Can't go wrong, old man. I'll get one for you next time."

Throughout that increasingly sulfurous morning, I watched Trubshawe jealously as he strode about at the head of his platoon as fresh as a daisy with his helmet at rather a rakish angle like a yachting cap.

Just before the end of the parade, the threatening storm broke, and in the torrential downpour, Trubshawe's hat melted and began to close over his ears. An uncertain tittering came from the ranks behind him as the soldiers beheld their splendid officer transformed into something resembling a very lanky hirsute gnome at a pantomime with a bluebell on his head.

The Weasel confined Trubshawe to barracks for that, but Trubshawe hired a string quartet to play for him in the evenings in his room. As his quarters happened to be immediately above the Weasel's lair, he was soon released.

I don't believe that Trubshawe was ever a very serious soldier, although he was full of compassion for those who were. He was able to indulge this rather aloof, though never patronizing, attitude toward the military because, like many officers in the regiment, he had a private income which handsomely papered over the bare patches between a subaltern's pay and the financial facts of garrison life. I had no such cushion, but Trubshawe's generosity, which was boundless, made it possible for me to be constantly in his company without feeling as though I were a sponger.

I was two years on the island before the Weasel gave me an affirmative answer to my many requests for two months' leave and permission to spend them in the United Kingdom.

Overnight on a delapidated ferry boat, the *Knight of Malta,* found me in Tunis from whence a freighter took me to Marseilles, followed by a long train journey to Calais, Dover, Portsmouth and Bembridge.

Two years had wrought awful havoc with the beauty of my mother, and when Grizel told me that "Mum's pains" were more and more frequent, so selfishly occupied was I with my immediate pleasures that I only dimly realized how serious her illness had become. She herself was gay and vague and wonderful and pushed it all aside as something boring she had to live with.

Tommy was nowhere to be seen, and my brother, who was now busy growing bananas on Norfolk Island, was back from the South Pacific. Bembridge was in full swing and I had an unforgettable homecoming. I spent two weeks in London being scared to death by Glyn Mills about my overdraft and catching up on old friends in a whirl of parties, but there was a sadness.

Nessie had never been a great correspondent and her last letter had filled me with unease. It ended ominously: "I've a bit put by now, dear, and I've found a bloke who might suit very nicely, so I might say thanks ever so and piss off to America. He knows all about me and says it makes no difference. If I do decide, I hope you get back before I go so I can see you. I'll close now. Love, Nessie."

I never did see her again. When I arrived in London, I gathered from her friends and co-workers that she had left a month before to get married in Seattle. I felt jealous and jilted. She never wrote to me again.

7

After my leave, I pondered deeply about my military and, increasingly more pressingly, my financial future.

Brian Franks had been at Bembridge and was learning the hotel business. At the moment, he was working his way up through the kitchens of the Dorchester but was filled with enthusiasm and painted a glowing picture of his prospects.

Most of my other friends had, by now, left university and were launched on glamorous and seemingly profitable careers in business. I felt rather left out of the scheme of things, a feeling that was not helped by meeting two young officers on leave from the Argylls in Bermuda. Not only was their regiment soon heading for China, but in every way it sounded a far happier and more human situation than the one in which I found myself on my return to Malta.

For a start, Trubshawe had fallen in love and much of his time was taken up by a beautiful blonde called Margie MacDougall who was spending a few weeks with Celia Tower, the equally beautiful wife of a lieutenant commander in destroyers. Trubshawe in love was something to behold. He went about looking pale and interesting. I charged him with being off his feed, but he refuted this in a dazed way and mumbled that Margie was a Christian Scientist and that although he did not wholeheartedly agree with much of her indoctrination, he was prepared under certain conditions, to forgo a sizable percentage of his daily ration of bottled goods. Sinister cracks were appearing in the Trubshavian façade. "We should give up blood sports, old man. No more the chase, be it fox, stag or field mouse. Amateur theatricals—that's something for us."

In a day or two my bemused friend and I presented ourselves to Captain Hoskins of the Rifle Brigade who was

military secretary to the governor and the undisputed leading light of the Malta Amateur Dramatic Society. After
reading a few lines from Frederick Lonsdale's *The Last of
Mrs. Cheyney,* we would-be amateurs were dusted aside
with the classic, professional brush-off: "Nothing for you
at the moment but don't call us—we'll call you!"

We drowned our disappointments in a sea of gimlets in
the Snake Pit, the ladies' annex of the Union Club in Valletta, while Margie looked on with an apprehensive eye and
Celia with a twinkle.

"It's a plot, old man. We'd better get our own show together and break the monopoly."

So we resuscitated an old regimental concert party called
The Hornets and presented an abysmal confection for three
consecutive nights at the Coronado Canteen above the
dockyards.

As in all amateur dramatics, the performers had a wonderful time and went on far too long in front of a stoic and
partisan audience. We regaled ourselves, and spasmodically
our friends, with scenes stolen from the Co-Optimists, and
the Hulberts, interlarded with Highland dancing and Sau-
chiehall Street wit.

Trubshawe had designed the posters which announced
the forthcoming event in these terms: OFF LIKE A FLASH!!!
(AS THE NIGHT-LIGHT SAID TO THE NIGHTDRESS).

These posters were sent around to all the wardrooms and
gun rooms of the Mediterranean Fleet so the Weasel, in an
ugly scene in which he invoked regimental horror, ordered
us to visit every ship in turn, to apologize to the mess president of each one, and to retrieve the offending advertisements. Anthony Playdell-Bouverie and David Kelburn
came with us, and it was a miracle that we all didn't drown
in a sea of pink gin during our futile efforts to obtain the
surrender of documents which the Royal Navy had no intention of giving up. At least it had the beneficial result of
getting Trubshawe farther off the wagon—"Weasel's
orders, old man." Trubshawe and I had by now become the
focal point of the Weasel's oft-expressed distaste for young
officers, though not, it was rumored in the Snake Pit, for
young men. Hardly a week went by when we were not saluted by his orderly: "Adjutant's compliments, sorr, report
immediately to battalion orderly room," and off we'd trot
to collect another raspberry. So many did we collect at one

point, that when the whole shooting match marched out of barracks and went under canvas for summer maneuvers, we decided not to be outdone when it came to the decoration of our tents. The colonel had a little marker stuck in the ground at the entrance to his marked CO and there were others denoting the denizens of all the important tepees— 2ND I/C. ADJ. QM, RSM, etcetera—so Trubshawe and I persuaded the armorers' painter to install a couple for us. CHIEF RASPBERRY PICKER and ASST. RASPBERRY PICKER. The Jocks were delighted but the next day came the usual refrain: "Adjutant's compliments, sorr. . . ."

The summer maneuvers were something that Lady Baden-Powell would have been ashamed of if conducted by a group of Brownies, and I was still close enough to Sandhurst to be staggered by the fact that a long halt in the proceedings was always called at midday. While the Jocks sat in searing heat among the crickets and lizards devouring their "stew and duff" and swigging down their "gunfire," the officers repaired to a huge marquee where Mr. Gifford, in a white tropical suit and white shoes, aided by three mess waiters, presided over an Ascot-type meal of gargantuan proportion.

About this time, the Raspberry Pickers received a reinforcement—John Royal, a vast young man of phenomenal physical strength and an anarchist at heart. He appeared one day straight from Sandhurst, and I want to introduce him clearly because he will turn up again much later in this dull story and I don't want him, on his reappearance, to pass unnoticed.

His opening line was memorable. Trubshawe and I were sipping something cool on the balcony of the Sliema Club when a voice behind us said: "I've been looking all over Valletta for you two; that old pouf in the orderly room told me that I should avoid you at all costs!"

John was almost as tall as Trubshawe but built like a heavyweight fighter in his prime. A broken nose did nothing to dispel this impression.

He was extremely handsome in a dark, Celtic way and extremely hostile when drunk. Also, as Trubshawe succinctly put it, "The man puts in some very plucky work with the elbow."

Very soon after his arrival in Malta, John was posted to the Second Battalion and departed for India, but during the few weeks he was with us, he made an indelible impression.

He was devoted to animals and could not bear to see the Maltese drivers ill-treating their horses. On one occasion, when he saw one poor emaciated beast straining uphill with a huge load of sandstone blocks and being belabored with a heavy stick, he pulled the man off the shafts, put him across his knee, and gave him six of the best with his swagger cane.

John also introduced us to green beer.

Trubshawe and I had been ordered by the Weasel to make all the arrangements for the annual regimental party at the Marsa Polo Club. Knowing we were given this assignment in the hopes that a normally deadly supper dance might be infused with something perhaps a little unusual, we went to great lengths planning to decorate the place differently, and while Trubshawe spent days bashing some sort of rhythm into the Regimental Band, I busied myself with the catering aided by Mr. Gifford.

Three weeks before the regimental party, John told us about the green beer. It appeared that a brewer in Edinburgh had come up with this novelty and he quickly talked us into ordering it for the occasion. Cables were exchanged, and to obtain a decent price per crate, we ordered an enormous amount of the stuff. The shipment arrived at the docks just in time and the mule teams in the transport lines were hastily pressed into service to cart it to the Polo Club where Trubshawe and John and I were waiting to try it.

It tasted all right, but the color, far from being the joyous sparkling creme de menthe we had anticipated, was that of some loathsome opaque and polluted pond.

On the night of the party, acres of green bottles stood hopefully on the tables while the guests avoided them like the plague and drank everything else in sight.

The next day, the Weasel sent for the Raspberry Pickers and said that it was our responsibility to get rid of the green beer. We thought we might be able to con the sergeants' mess into buying some. So together with John Royal we organized, one Sunday, a sergeants' mess picnic, the idea being that if we gave the sergeants enough of it free and slipped them a lot of whiskey to help it down, they might overlook its horrendous color and relieve the officers' mess of a sizable portion of the stock.

It didn't work, of course. We took several carloads of *sergenti,* sandwiches, whiskey and crates and crates of beer to a remote bay and for hours a glorious time was had by all —swimming, singing, telling exaggerated regimental anecdotes, boasting and drinking. In an effort to get them hooked on the stuff, the three of us, while carefully leaving the whiskey out of our own mugs, dreamed up toast after toast, but as evening approached, wild Highland cries became fewer and the sound of snores and throwing up became the norm.

When finally we delivered our subdued charges back to the sergeants' mess, it was all too plain that we had overplayed our hand: To a man they swore they would never touch the stuff again.

I remember the end of that picnic very clearly because "Clachie" Chisholm, the pipe major, was so drunk that "Sixty" Smith and I had to put him to bed, and valiantly trying to get his kilt off while he was thrashing around and muttering obscenities in Gaelic, we suddenly unveiled an elderly pair of green regimental boxing shorts. There is always speculation about what a true Scot wears under the kilt; here was additional evidence that it is a very personal decision.

John Royal departed for India the same day that Trubshawe became engaged to Margie MacDougall; neither event ended well but John's problem came to a head first.

Soon after his arrival, the officers of the Second Battalion were invited to a ball given by the local maharaja, and John became sleepy, so after dinner, he lay down behind some potted palms and stole forty winks. He was awakened by a captain of a Cavalry Regiment who stirred him, none too gently, with his foot.

"Stand up," said the captain. John stood.

"You are drunk," said the captain.

"You are right," said John and flattened him with a left hook. He then composed himself once more behind the potted palms. Pretty soon he was awakened again, this time by a full colonel of artillery.

"Stand up," said the colonel. John stood.

"You are drunk," said the colonel and he collected a right cross.

John was court-martialed and insisted on conducting his own defense. He had been dropped on his head as a baby, he said, and this had the unfortunate effect of making him lash out at the first person he saw when he was woken from a deep sleep.

The prosecuting officer smiled faintly. "Perhaps you would tell the court what happens to your batman when he wakes you up in the morning?"

"Nothing," said John unmoved. "I have issued him with a fencing mask."

John left India and the Army and I did not see him again for ten years.

Margie MacDougall left Malta and Trubshawe was saddened. He was comforted by the beautiful Mrs. Tower and rallied strongly. Trubshawe had decided that perhaps the Weasel had a point when he hinted that there were other things that Trubshawe might do better than soldiering.

"When Margie and I marry, old man, we'll live in the depths of the country in some beautiful village. I'll run the cricket club and Margie can hand out pheasants to the tenants ... of course a lot depends on the local brewer."

He really tried hard to become a good soldier, but fate usually arranged to drop a banana peel for him to step on. Trubshawe once issued a command that went down in history. He and I were suffering through a hideous enterprise called a Regimental Sergeant Majors' Parade. This meant an hour of formation drill for the entire battalion with the parts of colonel and company commanders being played by the most junior officers.

I was performing as a company commander while Trubshawe, under the eagle eye of R. S. M. MacMillan, was going through his paces as commanding officer. We were on a large flat expanse on top of some cliffs and Trubshawe had us going along very nicely in close column just the way the Brigade of Guards do when trooping the Color. "Clachie" Chisholm and his boys were blowing their guts out, and it was all pretty inspiring one way and another till Trubshawe shouted some strange orders and the whole thing disintegrated. One minute several hundred Highland troops were swinging proudly along, the next they were a disorganized rabble heading for disaster like the Gadarene swine. Junior officers and company sergeant majors all competed with the R. S. M. in roaring out conflicting instructions; the Jocks became increasingly bewildered; and the brave music of the pipes turned into dying wails as the chanters fell from the lips of the horrified pipers. Suddenly above the din came a stentorian Trubshavian bellow: "Oh, Christ, FORM SQUARE." It hadn't happened since Waterloo, but it happened that day on top of the cliffs and the few goatherds who had gathered to watch us shook their heads in wonderment.

My twenty-first birthday came and went and I was still on that island. Every day it seemed to get smaller. Rumors were constantly flying that the battalion was to be reinforced and sent to Egypt, to China, or to Singapore, but nothing ever happened and after each flurry of excitement, the battalion settled further back into its torpor. Trubshawe was now determined to resign his commission within a year, so I asked officially to be seconded for service with the West African Frontier Force, a ploy that would have given me an exciting change of scenery and considerably more pay. The Weasel refused to recommend it.

My last year in Malta was enlivened by two things. First, I was made transport officer and, as such, spent my days in the stables with several dozen chargers, draft horses and mules. The mules were a belligerent lot; probably they had an inferiority complex because they did nothing except pull the company cookers. It was a splendid sight to see a company on the march. At the back and always falling farther and farther behind were a couple of mules hauling an immense black caldron on wheels. Inside this, depending on the time of day, was either boiling tea or boiling stew. Both tasted much the same, but at all times, behind the caldron, was the company cook enveloped in a cloud of steam and stirring the contents as he marched.

Sergeant Fensham, the transport sergeant, a bandy-legged little man with the broken-veined complexion that goes with the proximity of horses, was ready for every four-legged emergency. If the colonel's horse was too fresh before an important ceremonial parade, he would calm it down with a jab of tranquilizer. Once he gave it too much and we both watched apprehensively as, with rolling eyes, it tottered about with its precious cargo in front of several thousand onlookers.

Someone with a distinguished military background died in Sleima and a military funeral was arranged, so I was ordered to produce a team and gun carriage to bear the coffin. Sergeant Fensham paraded the six blackest draft horses we had, and towing the black gun carriage, we set off to pick up our cargo.

Somewhere in the middle of Valletta, one of the horses fell down and grazed its knee. Somehow it knocked off a divot of black hair and exposed a few square inches of hard chalky-white skin. This ruined our carefully arranged black ensemble but Fensham never missed a beat. He reached into his saddlebag, produced a box of black Cherry Blossom boot polish, and with the offending patch covered, we were on our way in less than a minute.

The other boredom reliever of those last twelve months was the Fancy-Dress Ball in the Opera House. It was a predictable show: Admirals dressed as Pierrots, their wives as Columbines. Bopeeps were plentiful and there was a sprinkling of Old Bills and Felix the Cats among the military. Parties took boxes in the lovely tiered building and everyone tried hard to pretend that it was every bit as abandoned as the Chelsea Arts Ball.

Trubshawe and I went as goats. First we put noisome rugs on our backs. Then horns on bands were affixed to our heads and, finally, between our legs, for the goat fittings, footballs swung with rubber gloves sewn onto them by the regimental cobbler. Half a pint of dry martinis apiece and we were ready for the fray.

We arrived just in time for the Grand March for the prize giving. The judges for the best costumes were on the stage, and around and around in front of them, two by two, like the animals going into the Ark, went the clowns with their red-hot pokers, the ballet dancers and the Mickey Mice. Rumblings of disapproval rose from the boxes as the two drunken goats joined in at the back of the parade.

"Trubshawe . . . Niven . . . goats! Bad show! Damn bad show!" Military mustaches and naval eyebrows bristled from every floor.

"I'm getting dizzy, old man," said the goat behind me after we had completed several circuits.

"Left wheel!"

Obediently, I turned out of the parade toward the empty center of the floor.

"Now squat!" commanded Trubshawe.

"What?" I asked, apprehensively.

"Squat, you bloody fool."

So there at the very hub of the wheel with a kaleido-
scope of color circling around us and the focus of hundreds
of disapproving eyes, I squatted. Trubshawe produced a
brown paper bag from the folds of his smelly rug and
sprinkled black olives on the floor directly behind me.

Except for the box that held David Kelburn and
Anthony Pleydell-Bouverie, this flourish was coldly received by the ticket holders, particularly by a party of Maltese students who had a very short fuse when they thought
that someone was mocking the local institutions. They jos-
tled and shoved us as we left the floor and made threatening noises.

"Better take off, old man," said the leader as he headed
for the exit and the last I saw of Trubshawe that night
he was pounding down the main street of Valletta toward
the sanctuary of the Union Club pursued by the hornet students and tripping over his "udders."

We were confined to barracks for that little adventure,
but the boredom of our incarceration was soon relieved by
the arrival of a whole new spate of rumors. This time they
had a ring of truth to them. The quartermaster was seen
checking the winter stores and, in the transport lines, Sergeant Fensham hinted darkly that he had heard we might
have to find buyers for some of our animals. The Weasel
was seen mincing around, obviously having tucked into a
sizable canary.

In fact the battalion had been ordered home to the British Isles—to the Citadel Barracks, Dover. It was like some
gloriously prolonged "end of term," and when the evacuation order was finally given, the whole battalion set about its
allotted tasks with a willingness I had not hitherto seen.

"Sixty" Smith, who had become my friend and adviser,
was ill in hospital. It had started with sandfly fever, then
complications and now he was much more sick than anybody realized. Pleurisy had set in and there was no question of his sailing home with the rest of us. I went to see
him the day before we embarked on the troopship and was
shocked by his appearance.

"Would you ask the colonel a favor for me, sorr? Would
ye ask if the battalion could march a wee bit oot the road
on their way tae the docks so I can hear the pipes fer the
last time—it's nae far . . . aboot five minutes."

I suddenly felt chilly in the warm little room. "What the hell are you talking about, 'Sixty' . . . hearing the pipes for the last time . . . ?"

"Becos I'm gonna dee," "Sixty" replied quietly and I found it impossible to look into his clouded eyes.

The Weasel was oddly sympathetic to the request, and when he gave me the answer, he told me the colonel had added that he would like me to be with the old man when the troops passed the hospital the following day.

It was late afternoon when they passed and the sun was golden on the church spires that "Sixty" could see from his bed. In the distance he could hear the swinging march: "Wi a hundred pipers . . ." and he asked me to prop him up in his bed. Nearer and nearer čame the battalion and as he lifted his head to listen, he must have been thinking of a whole lifetime in the regiment he had joined as a boy. Just before the column reached the hospital, the tune changed: changed to the regimental march, "Scotland the brave," and tears of pride slid down his granite cheeks. He sat bolt upright till the last stirring notes faded away into the distance, then he slid down into his bed and turned his face to the wall.

That night "Sixty" died.

The troopship was a hell ship of about 11,000 tons and bursting at the seams with men from every regiment on their way home from various parts of the empire. For four days she was hove to in the Bay of Biscay in a storm of Wagnerian proportions. Life in the troop decks in the bowels of the ship was unbelievably awful, but the Jocks rose above the overcrowding and the smell of vomit by keeping their minds on the fact that at least they were off the island of Malta and headed in the right direction.

We arrived in the Citadel Barracks, Dover, a few days before Christmas. It was a place of undiluted gloom. A grass-covered fortress, high in the mist above the slate-roof Victorian horror of the town below; but as we marched into the barracks, on that drizzly December evening, there was not a man among us who did not rejoice.

The Weasel sent practically everyone in the battalion home on leave, leaving behind a skeleton party of caretakers, and as we were still under the cloud caused by the goat episode, the two officer skeletons were Trubshawe and myself. It was really quite enjoyable and a great relief to be de-Weaseled for a while.

Hogmanay at the turn of the year was not as boisterous an affair as usual, but over at the canteen, Cook Sergeant Winters gave the fifty members of the caretaker party a splendid spread of haggis and all the trimmings and following regimental tradition, the officers waited on the men. It was a riotous day with Trubshawe at his very best belting out an endless stream of songs on the tinny canteen piano while toasts were offered and accepted.

The following day was a day of shock for the Raspberry Pickers. We rose late and were gloomily gazing out of the window of the officers' mess from whence far below it was sometimes possible to see the English Channel through the murk. After the sauna-bath climate of Malta, the penetrating damp of the Dover heights could only be combated by a concoction of Trubshawe's—port and brandy mixed. We were doing our best to get warm when the door behind us opened and the solitary mess waiter stood there making spastic movements of the head and shoulders, rolling his eyes and jerking his thumb over his shoulder. When he stepped aside, the reason for his alarm became clear. Behind him was a real live major general—the first we had ever seen. A lean and very formidable figure, he walked briskly into the room; the red band on his hat and red tabs on his collar sowed instant alarm in our breasts; and this was not diluted by the sight of general staff armbands on the major and captain immediately behind him.

"Where is your commanding officer?"

"On leave, sir," said Trubshawe.

"Adjutant?"

"On leave, sir," said I.

"Who is the senior officer present?"

"I am, sir," said Trubshawe.

"I don't mean in this room," snapped the general. "In the barracks."

"Still me, sir," said Trubshawe and tried a misguided smile of welcome. "Can we offer you a little something to keep out the cold?"

There was an ominous silence while the man treated us to a long-penetrating stare. Then he turned and held some sort of low-keyed, high-level military discussion with his staff. The major and the captain noticeably changed color and we got the distinct impression that someone had blundered.

"All right . . . then you show me around," said the general.

"Well," began Trubshawe like some obsequious house agent with a prospective client, "this is the anteroom and the dining room is up these steps to the right, the kitchen is below and the bedrooms, such as they are . . . ," he trailed off as the general looked at him speculatively for a long time, tapping his highly polished riding boot with his swagger cane.

"Show me around the barracks," said the general in a controlled voice, "that is, if it's not too much trouble."

"Pray follow me, sir," said Trubshawe (greasy-head-waiter routine now leading way to a bad table). "Come, Mr. Niven," he added over his shoulder as an afterthought.

The grisly little procession wound across the almost-deserted barrack square; a few bedraggled and hungover Jocks looked up apprehensively from whitewashing some stones around the guardroom.

"Fatigue party, 'shun," yelled a corporal rising from behind a sporting paper. Unfortunately, his snappy salute was ruined by the fact that he omitted to take a cigarette out of his mouth.

"Mr. Niven! Take that corporal's name," roared Trubshawe, all military efficiency now and pulling the big switch.

"Sir!" I yelled back and rushed over to the offending man. "For Christ's sake," I hissed at him, "it's a general doing a surprise inspection—get the word around quick—get everybody looking busy."

I rejoined the group just in time to see the general point his swagger cane toward a squat building.

"What's that?" he demanded.

Now we must pause to remember that Trubshawe and I had been under no pressure during the past week or so to make a detailed reconnaissance of the dreary precincts of the Citadel and, consequently, had a somewhat sketchy idea of the layout of the place, but it still came as a rude shock when I realized that the Chief Raspberry Picker was shamelessly passing the buck to his trusted lieutenant.

"Mr. Niven," he said sweetly, "what's that?"

"Er . . . the library, sir," I faltered, hazarding a guess.

Trubshawe must have misheard me. "The lavatory, sir," he said. We went inside what was quite evidently the band practice room. In the far corner was "Clachie" Chisholm, who hated going on leave, frantically beating life into the bag of his pipes while his trembling fingers groped for the first plaintive notes of "The Flowers of the Forest."

The inspection of the barracks proceeded on its nightmare course. Trubshawe heard my whispered cue of "Latrines," headed in the indicated direction, took one look at several pairs of protruding white spats belonging to Jocks who had decided to seek sanctuary there, lost his head, and made the sort of noises reserved for orderly officers in the dining hall at mealtimes. "Any complaints?" he asked.

Bewildered and aggrieved Scotsmen rose from their individual thrones: "No complaints, sorr," they mumbled.

We ricocheted off the cookhouse, which we recognized only because Cook Sergeant Winters, in a white apron, was standing outside it beckoning with heavy-handed helpfulness with a ladle, and we correctly identified the regimental canteen—not too difficult either as we had only left the place a few hours before.

By now we had received some timely reinforcements in the shape of Ginger Innes wearing the red sash of orderly sergeant and a smart-looking corporal from Trubshawe's platoon called MacQuire. Our morale rose as, with their whispered help, we successfully fielded searching questions in the quartermaster's stores, the miniature range and the domain of the pioneer sergeant.

By now the full complement of fifty caretakers had been mobilized by bush telegraph and wherever we went there were small groups of men momentarily springing to attention and ceasing their cleaning, polishing, leaf sweeping and wheelbarrowing.

Trubshawe, as we headed for the general's car, felt that victory was within his grasp. He relaxed and was in an expansive mood when the general fired his last inquiry. "What's in there?" he asked, indicating a large garage-shaped building with red double doors and FIREHOUSE written above them.

Almost smugly Trubshawe said, "Why, the fire engine, sir."

"Get it out," said the general.

"Yes, sir," said Trubshawe who looked for a long moment as though he had been hit with a halibut. Then he turned, almost apologetically to me. "Mr. Niven, get the engine out, please."

"Very good, sir," I said, giving him a real killer look.

"Sergeant Innes, get the engine out."

"Sir! Corporal MacQuire, th'engin—git it oot."

The buck was now passing with great rapidity.

"Lance Corporal Bruce, git th'engine oot. . . ."

"Private Dool, git th'engin oot."

The cry echoed around the Citadel.

The general had started once more on that ominous metronome bit with the swagger cane and the riding boots.

"What sort of engine is it?" he asked quietly.

"Oh, a beauty," said Trubshawe.

"Merryweather," I piped up from the back.

"Yes," said Trubshawe, "made by Merryweather & Company and it has a lot of brasswork and coils and coils of hose."

"Get it *OUT!*" said the general, much louder now.

Trubshawe seemed almost on the point of surrender; then like a lookout of Mafeking seeing relief approaching, he let out a long sigh. A soldier bearing a huge key was approaching at the double from the direction of the guardroom but I could hardly believe my ears when I heard Trubshawe pressing his luck. "Many's the night, sir, when this trusty engine has been called out to help the honest burghers of Dover."

"GET IT OUT!!"

At last the key was inserted in the lock, and with the flourish of a guide at Hampton Court opening the door of Henry VIII's bedchamber, Trubshawe pushed open the double doors.

Inside, against the far wall stood two women's bicycles; a dead Christmas tree from another era lay in the center of the floor; and in the foreground was a bucket of hard and cracked whitewash from a bygone cricket season.

The general turned and stalked to his car without a word. The staff officers gave us pitying glances before they followed him. In silence they all drove away, and in silence Trubshawe and I returned to the officers' mess.

In the next few months a tremendous upheaval took place in the battalion. We received a new commanding officer, and there was a change of adjutant.

The new colonel, Alec Telfer-Smollett, DSO, MC, was nothing short of a miracle. In no time at all he shook the battalion out of its warm-climate-garrison complex. The whole atmosphere became charged with a sense of purpose. It became possible to perform the dullest chores and at the same time to feel one was doing so for a good reason.

Telfer-Smollet was patience itself with me; in fact he took special pains with all the junior officers to make them feel at home and I use that word advisedly because he was a firm believer in an ancient concept of a regiment—that it should be a family.

I found myself often dining alone with the colonel and his wife, and, unbelievably, at least twice a week I was invited to play golf with him. He laughed at my poor local anecdotes, nurtured my flagging military ambitions, sympathized with my permanent financial straits and cheated blatantly in the scoring.

He was a wonderfully warm and understanding human being and he came within an ace of persuading me to become once more a serious soldier, but this was quite unwittingly sabotaged by a petite snub-nosed blond, very pretty American girl with the smallest feet I had ever seen—Barbara Hutton.

In the spring of that fateful year, my French grandmother died. For years she had lived in rooms in Bournemouth, and as children, my sister, Grizel, and I had paid her annual visits, traveling from the Isle of Wight on a paddle steamer as day trippers. I remember her as a very beautiful old lady with a cloud of carefully coiffed white hair and a little lace choker at her throat kept high under the chin with bones. She had very pale and strangely lifeless skin on her cheeks, which I always tried to avoid kissing. She left me two hundred pounds in her will.

I immediately invested about half of this windfall in a secondhand Morris Cowley and gleefully entered the London social scene.

Soon I found myself on the Mayfair hostesses' lists—as usual they were desperately short of available young men— and every post brought its quota of invitations to debutantes' parties or weekends in smart country houses. Dover being near to London and weekend leave being plentiful, I indulged myself to the hilt with the minimum of outlay and became a crashing title snob in the process. For a short while I really believed that dukes and baronets were automatically important.

One evening at a dance I met Barbara. She was spending a few weeks in London with her uncle Frank and at the time she was engaged to Alex Mdvani, a Georgian prince who was to be her first husband. A gay and sparkling creature, full of life and laughter, she became a great ally at some of the more pompous functions. When she left London, she made me promise to come to New York for Christmas, an invitation as lightly made as it was lightly taken.

During the year I spent a few short leaves at Bembridge and was sad but not unduly worried to learn that "Mum's pains" had become a very much more frequent occurrence. She spent a lot of time in bed and suffered considerably from what the local doctor diagnosed as colitis. In November I was sent on a physical training course for several weeks at Aldershot. One night I was called to the telephone and found myself talking to Tommy, whom I had not seen since I left England more than three years before.

"Your mother is very ill," he said. "She is in a nursing home in London and you should come and see her immediately." He gave me very little further information except the address.

I quickly obtained leave and rushed to Queen's Gate. Although I had seen her only a few weeks before, she was so ravaged by cancer that I was utterly and completely horrified by what I saw. She did not recognize me and she died the next day.

I went back to Aldershot and completed my course in a sort of daze. I simply could not comprehend what had happened. I had never had to cope with a loss of this magnitude, and I endlessly chastised myself for always taking her presence for granted, for not doing much, much more to make her happy and for not spending more time with her when I could so easily have done so.

Alec Telfer-Smollett was a father figure, and when I got back to Dover he helped me with great wisdom and infinite patience to get over the worst part. With Christmas approaching and with four weeks' leave coming to me, he suggested that I should go far away somewhere and be with people who could not remind me of what he knew well was a gnawing feeling of guilt.

It was then that I remembered Barbara Hutton's invitation. In reply to my cable asking if she had really meant it, I received one which said: "Come at once, Love, Barbara."

I flogged the Morris Cowley, borrowed a little money from the bank and a little more from Grizel, who had become a very clever sculptress and was now installed in a tiny house in Chelsea, and ten days before Christmas, I embarked on the one-class liner SS *Georgic* and throbbed my way to New York.

"Throbbed" was the word; I had the cheapest berth in the ship—directly above the propellers.

8

The trip from Southampton to New York should have taken eight days, but we met a gale head on, so it took ten.

My little throbbing box of a cabin I shared with an enchanting middle-aged American who had been making his first-ever visit to Europe on the strength of having sold his clothing store in Milwaukee. He was much exercised by the thought of going home to face, once more, the rigors of Prohibition, and during the trip he proceeded to make up for the lean times ahead. He was none too fussy either about mixing his intake.

"Dave," he said one evening. "I've gotta great idea . . . tonight you and me are gonna drink by colors."

We settled ourselves at the bar, and he decided to drink the colors of the national flags of all the countries he had visited on his trip—Stars and Stripes first of course. Red was easy—port. White was simple—gin—but blue was a real hazard till the barman unveiled a vicious Swiss liqueur called Gentiane.

The French and British flags fell easily into place, but a horrible snag was placed in our path by the Belgians. Black, yellow and red. Black beer was used to lay a foundation for yellow chartreuse and more port, but it was the green crème de menthe of the Italian flag that caused me to retire, leaving my newfound friend the undisputed champion.

The crossing was my first confrontation with Americans en masse and I found it a delightful experience. Their openhanded generosity and genuine curiosity about others came as something of a shock at first. What a change, though, to be asked the most searching personal questions in the first few minutes of contact or to be treated to a point-by-point replay of the private life of a total stranger. What a difference as an unknown foreigner to be invited to sit at a table of friends or to join a family. I suppose it is the fact that we have fifty-odd million people crammed onto an island the size of Idaho and are unable ever to get more than eighty miles from the sea that makes us so defensive. Who else but the British would spread hats, handbags, umbrellas and paper bags on the seats of railway carriages and then glower furiously through the windows at anyone who shows signs of entering and ruining the privacy?

I had my first brush with the American language in that ship. For a partner in the ping-pong doubles championship, I had snagged a delicious lady from Sioux City. "Now we have a practice tomorrow," I warned her. "If you're not on deck by eleven o'clock, I'll come down to your cabin and knock you up." She put me straight.

On the last night and under the lee of the American continent, I packed my few belongings and wondered what the hell was going to happen the next day. After a sleepless night, I went on deck to find out.

I do not, with my poor pen, have the impertinence to try to describe a first impression of the New York skyline because no one I have ever read has done it justice so far, but that forest of gleaming white set against an ice-blue sky is something I will never forget.

Barbara had cabled that she would meet me at the dock, so as the Moran tug company's fussy little workhorses pushed and tooted us into our berth on the Hudson River, I went below and gathered together my hand baggage.

My Milwaukee friend was there, having fitted himself into a strange forerunner of today's space suits. Inside and beneath the armpits were cavernous pockets which concealed large aluminum tanks, each capable of holding about two and a half gallons of scotch whisky. He was in the process of being topped up by the steward.

He pressed speakeasy cards on me, telephone numbers of friends in New York and issued a permanent invitation to visit with him at his home and meet some lovely people.

"Goddamned Prohibition," he muttered as I left, "takes a man's balls off."

I walked down the gangplank and looked back at the good ship *Georgic*. A few years later she was sunk by the Germans. Barbara was waiting for me at the dock and had brought two or three carloads of friends to welcome this

strange young man with the funny voice. I was a bit of a
freak in the United States in those days as the vast majority
of people had still never met a Briton nor heard an "English accent." Nobody went to see English movies because
he couldn't understand them.

They gave me a rousing reception, and I am happy to
think that several of those I met on that Christmas Eve are
still my friends today.

Barbara's family lived on Long Island, but for a town
house they utilized several suites in the Hotel Pierre. I was
to be installed there, and on the way—it was now growing
dark—I beheld a breathtaking sight. The limousine swept
around the corner of the Grand Central building and
stopped. In the frosty evening, there stretched before me,
as far as the eye could see, a straight line of enormous illuminated Christmas trees. Also, as far as the eye could see,
on the right-hand side of the trees was a necklace of red
lights. Suddenly, these lights changed to green and we shot
forward. At that time, traffic lights were only being experi-
mented with in London, so I could be forgiven if I was unduly impressed by New York's Christmas decorations.

I was given a very nice room at the Hotel Pierre, and
Barbara, the perfect hostess, made it clear that she hoped I
would spend as long as I liked there but to feel perfectly free
to come and go as I wished and not to feel bound to her or
her family.

That night, she gave a party at the Central Park Casino.
The incomparable Eddy Duchin was at the piano leading
his orchestra, and a very attractive couple of young
ballroom dancers were the stars of the B Cabaret—George
and Julie Murphy. (George became an able Senator from
California.)

It may have been Prohibition, but so far I had not noticed it. A vague pretense was certainly made to keep bottles out of sight, and many people made extra trips to the
lavatory or to their cars there to uncork a flask, but otherwise it was business as usual.

Christmas Day with Barbara's family and presents for
the unknown young man of hair-raising generosity. Next a
visit to Princeton to watch the annual football battle with
Yale. The trip to Princeton was organized by a cousin of
Barbara's, Woolworth Donahue, and for the occasion, for

our comfort and refreshment, he thoughtfully provided a special coach on the train.

The three-hour ride passed in a flash. The men all were about my own age, and the girls were the result of their very competitive selection for this high point of the college year.

The result was spectacular. I had never seen such beautiful girls in my life and there were more to come. Jack and Marshall Hemminway were our hosts at Princeton, and there the train group joined about forty more for a colossal spread before the game. Finally, we set off for the stadium with our Princeton pennants, our rosettes, our bottles of bourbon and our wonderful, wonderful girls. Coonskin and camel-hair coats were very much in evidence.

I didn't see very much of the game. Once the college bands and the team mascots had left the pitch to the players, excitement was at such boiling point that the moment anything important happened, everyone leaped to his feet, thereby obscuring my view. I did not have the same built-in springs in my knees as the others and was trained in the Twickenham school of indulging in a little polite hand clapping while seated, my most exciting moments were blanketed by vast expanses of coonskin and camel hair . . . but no matter, I had a wonderful day and have since become an *aficionado* of American football.

The days in New York passed in a blaze of parties, speakeasies and nightclubs with daytime forays to visit people on Long Island, sometimes in specially chartered and bar-equipped motor buses. There were also boxing matches and ice hockey games to see at Madison Square Garden, big Broadway musicals to visit, great bands and singers to listen to.

The headquarters of the group I was adopted by was Jack & Charlie's 21 Club—the best speakeasy in New York, run by good-looking Jack Kriendler and the amiable, rotund and folksy Charlie Berns. The doorman was named Red, and Jim was the watchdog peering through the big bulletproof door. If an alarm was given of an impending raid by the law, the first thought was to protect the customers—no one would be caught drinking—so waiters were trained to seize all bottles and glasses from the tables and put them on the bar where Gus, the barman, was in position to throw a switch; the whole bar then tilted up and the offending evidence slid down a chute to the cellar.

No evening was complete without ending up in some dive in Harlem. I don't think I'll try that today.

The price of New York was bloodcurdling, but such was the generosity of my newfound friends that it was just taken for granted that I was never to be allowed to pay for anything. It was even made clear that if I attempted to do so, I would no longer be invited. I didn't feel too bad about this arrangement because there were one or two members of the group who were also financially embarrassed at the time and they, too, were carried by those in funds. One was a struggling reporter on the *Sun,* a huge teddy bear of a man named John McClain, destined to become my friend for life. McClain used to point to a slightly older man on the periphery of the group, always with the prettiest girl, a tall, shy, silent, slightly deaf, and compared to the rest of us, very serious-minded citizen. "Let that son of a bitch pay for once," McClain would rumble. The tall man's name was Howard Hughes.

Phil Ammidown had a Pierce-Arrow convertible and was leaving for Florida. "Come with me, Dave," he said. "I have a home in St. Augustine. We can spend a couple of days there, take in a party at the girls' college in Tallahassee, then go on down to Palm Beach."

The night before we set off, A. C. Blumenthal, the diminutive financial genius, gave a party, just six of us: Blumenthal's wife, Peggy Fears, and two other glamorous members of the Hollywood scene, Mary Duncan and Bubbles Haynes, Ammidown and myself. Blumenthal arrived bearing a suitcase almost as big as himself, a glorified model of Trubshawe's Dipsomaniac's Delight of beloved memory. The farewell party went on at various places all over town till Phil and I were waved away in the Pierce-Arrow en route for Florida.

First stop, Richmond, Virginia, and my eyes now gummed together with tiredness snapped open with amazement when, just as I was signing the hotel register, I noticed a full-sized alligator in a small pool about six feet from the reception desk.

Phil was a demon driver and the Pierce-Arrow was a very fast car—a combination that provoked a movie-style chase by a speed cop from the state highway patrol who was gaining on us with siren blaring when we shot across the state line into Florida and safety.

St. Augustine is the oldest town in the United States; indeed the oldest house in the country is still standing there. Phil's house nestled peacefully in lush woods just outside, and for two or three days I was able to charge up my batteries after the hectic days of New York. I reveled in the peace and charm of the place, and after the frenetic pace of the big city I sniffed the warm magnolia-scented air, stared at the hibiscus, listened to the cicadas and the lazy drawling voices of the inhabitants, and found it hard to believe I was in the same country. The Citadel Barracks, Dover, were every minute receding farther and farther into their clammy and depressing gray mists.

The party at the girls' college was well worth taking in and here literally nobody had heard an "English accent." I was kept talking endlessly and never have I had a more surefire audience.

The party took place just before the end of the year. The girls of the college had a tradition that during Leap Year they had the right to ask the men to dance and also to cut in on them. I had witnessed this rather barbaric tribal ritual of cutting in at parties in New York and had many times been highly frustrated, having cut in on a beauty only to feel, as she melted into my arms, an ominous pat on the back from the next customer from the stag line, watching and choosing his moment from the middle of the floor. I had also suffered, once or twice, by getting stuck with a comparatively unattractive girl and not receiving that now-welcome and relieving tap on the shoulder, but I had never sunk so low as to dance around with some poor unprepossessing creature in my arms and hold a ten-dollar bill behind her back as a bribery to a rescuer. However, having sweated out my first invitation to dance, I thereafter kept my ears pricked for the rustling of currency behind my head.

Through forest and swamp, the arrow-straight U.S. Highway 1 connects Jacksonville with St. Augustine, and halfway between the two, Phil and I nearly died. Five o'clock in the morning and traveling fast, we could see the lights of a car coming toward us at least ten miles away. As we shot past the other headlights and into the dark beyond, there was an almighty crash. We were both knocked unconscious. When we came to, we were in the swamp on the left-hand side of the road, incredibly, the car was right side up, and we were sitting in it pinned against the high back of the seat by the bronze frame of the now-glassless windshield bent hard against our chests. The front of the car had been completely demolished. Water and mud were up to the floorboards and we knew we were covered in warm blood. From the swamp beside us came a terrible grunting and splashing.

"Alligators," whispered Phil. "Don't make a sound."

As we sat, cowering and waiting for the foul slavering jaws to come snapping at us through the nonexistent front of the car, we felt ourselves all over. The blood could not have come from us, we were unscratched.

"We didn't hit the other car," I whispered. "We were past it when it happened."

The awesome noises continued for a long time, then just as the first gray light of dawn was beginning to silhouette the moss-festooned trees, they stopped. The light grew stronger and we saw what had happened.

In that split second when we were blinded by the too-quickly turned-up headlights of the other car, two huge black mules had emerged from the swamp and we had hit them broadside. Poor brutes, one must have been flung up in the air and over our heads. Its body had bashed us against the high soft seat back, knocking us out, but, by a miracle, not breaking our necks. The noises had come from the wretched animals dying in the swamp. The Sun Life Insurance Company used a photograph of what was left of the car as a warning and reminder.

Phil Ammidown, if not a man of great means, was certainly a man of style. He bought a new car that same day, and in the afternoon we continued south to Palm Beach.

Phil found us rooms in a small hotel and got busy on the telephone. Soon the days were flying by, girls everywhere, glorious golden ones, and golf, tennis, fishing in the blue Gulf Stream for marlin, dancing in roofless restaurants—"How deep is the ocean? How high is the sky?" Parties, lovemaking, kindness and overwhelming generosity on all sides. Lili Damita, a gorgeous French actress, paraded about with a leopard on a leash and Winston Guest put a shark in his mother's swimming pool. I hoped it would never end, but, suddenly, it was Pumpkin Time.

Somebody sidetracked me and I missed the last train that would carry me north to catch my ship for home. I dispatched a cable to Colonel Telfer-Smollett: "DEAR COLONEL MAGNIFICENT OPPORTUNITY BIG GAME HUNTING WHALE FISHING FLORIDA REQUEST ONE WEEK EXTENDED LEAVE." This would give me ample time to catch the German ship *Europa*, but if permission was not granted, I would be in deep trouble for overstaying my leave.

The answer came back: "NO WHALES OR BIG GAME WITHIN A THOUSAND MILES STOP TAKE TWO SMOLLETT."

A last-minute party caused me to miss yet another train, but "Woolly" Donahue gave me a going-away present of an airline ticket, and deafened and petrified by flying for fourteen hours in a nonsoundproof Tri-Motor Ford through the most hideous weather, I crawled on board the *Europa* and made for another rabbit hutch of a cabin in the bowels of the ship. As I unpacked, I realized with a tinge of guilt that I had hardly thought about my mother. . . . Oh, the callousness of youth!

The Great American Kindness went on all the way across the Atlantic. The little cabin was full of good-bye telegrams, and Barbara had arranged for a most welcome delivery of champagne. McClain had alerted a friend of his that I was on board so one night I was invited to a dinner party in the first class given by "Jock" Whitney, a wonderfully intelligent and witty man who can light up a room and who quite lately was one of the most popular and successful U.S. ambassadors to the Court of St. James's.

On another occasion, I was asked to dine in the first class, and my host insisted, after dinner, in cutting me in on his syndicate that was bidding for a number in the ship's sweep. (The captain would give his estimate of the day's run from noon to noon, and ten numbers on either side of that, with a high field and a low field, could be bid for—sometimes thousands of pounds went to the winner.)

My contribution was minimal, a fiver, I think, all I could afford anyway. I don't know how my host arrived at the result, but when his number won, he told me my share was £160.

Thanks to this wonderful and, I am ashamed to say, now-nameless man, I arrived back at the Citadel Barracks with more money than when I had left. I had tasted the fleshpots; in fact I had stuck all my trotters in the trough and had gorged myself. It had all been too rich for my blood. and in a welter of false values I knew that one day, somehow, I would go back to America.

Trubshawe was on his last legs militarily. "Can't go on much longer, old man. It's all getting too much like the Army . . . it's hunting four days a week and checking on the young pheasants for me."

I soon noticed the change myself. Telfer-Smollett was determined to shake the battalion out of its Maltese malaise and bring it to a peak of efficiency, and this meant first of all a great sharpening up of the officers.

The colonel was wonderful to me and the off-duty golf games were as frequent as ever. There was nothing I could not discuss with him. His good advice was boundless. He understood perfectly the itchy feet I had contracted during my flying visit to the United States. He also saw the limited possibilities in the Army for an impatient young man of very slender means. We discussed the possibility of my following Trubshawe's example and resigning my commission, and he counseled caution. "Give it a few more months," he said. "Don't rush it." I could become a good soldier, but I had seen that grass on the other side of the fence and it was green! green! green!

Trubshawe helped me find an old car. "A man must have wheels." We settled for a 1927 3½-liter sports Bentley. It had done more than a hundred and twenty thousand miles, had a strap over the hood, a hand brake outside, a compass, an altimeter, and a pressure pump on the dashboard, a cutout that made the exhaust roar like an airplane, and a three-tone horn. With a car like that one could only wear a checkered cap. It was the complete cad's car. It was cheap because it was about to fall apart. and the terms of payment were long. When I had handed over the down payment, I didn't have enough to pay for the license—twenty-five pounds. Luckily the color of the license for 1932 was a light fawn, so it was a simple matter to put a Guinness label in the license holder. Guinness labels at that time were numbered, and from five yards. my homemade license was indistinguishable from the real McCoy.

Although I kept my promise to Telfer-Smollett and worked hard, I also used my wheels to good effect and London saw almost as much of me as Dover.

Ann Todd's career was booming, and because of my

friendship with her I began to get a little stagestruck. She introduced me to a strikingly good-looking young actor who was even then electric on the stage. Since then, he has two major claims to fame: He is godfather to one of my children and has become the first in his profession to be made a baron . . . Laurence Olivier.

I became deeply attached to a lovely girl, a divorcée with a flat in Kent Terrace and a horrible dachshund called Axel. Betty was half in the theater and half in the society world and everyone was chasing her. She made me jealous.

With my wheels I was able to see a lot of her in London, but when she moved to Dover, Telfer-Smollett gave me a lecture.

Betty and a couple of friends of hers were given walk-on jobs as show girls in a musical, and I drove to Manchester one weekend to see her. I arrived in time for the Saturday matinee and sat in the Dress Circle waiting with bated breath for the appearance of my loved one. Next to me slumped a drunken mumbling man, and beyond him, sitting bolt upright, staring straight ahead, lips pursed and sporting a hat like a fruit basket, was his wife.

When the show girls came on the man stirred and said to his wife, "Wot a lot of luvly girls." No answer.

" 'Ere"—he nudged and spoke louder—"wot a lot of luvly girls." Still no answer, just a tightening of those lips.

"I said," he shouted, "wot a LOT OF LUVLY GIRLS!"

The wife turned to him, fixed him with a baleful stare, then equally loudly she said, "YOUR BREATH!!"

My car also led to my becoming a devotee of the country house weekend, and my batman, Private McEwan, was becoming quite proficient at packing for me when I left on my social safaris. He had an exaggerated if flattering idea of my sexual prowess, and once when I was invited to a ducal mansion, he obtained two-dozen condoms from the medical orderly and stowed them away in my suitcase.

I was going up to dress for dinner on the first evening when I encountered an elderly maid on the main staircase. She dropped me a little curtsy and said, "I've laid out your dinner jacket, sir, and you'll find your balloons on the dressing table."

*   *   *

That spring was a jolting one for me. The first surprise was a letter from Tommy. I had not seen him since my mother died. He suggested a Sunday luncheon at the Carlton Club, and thinking that perhaps we were about to find some kind of rapprochement after years of hostility, I went.

I gave my name to the porter and was led through several gloomy rooms. My stepfather rose from a chair, ignored my outstretched hand, and said, "The solicitors tell me that so far, you have paid nothing toward the grave." I did not stay for luncheon and I never saw him again.

The next I heard that Trubshawe had decided to leave the Army and get married. Although I had been given plenty of warning of this impending, as it turned out, disaster, I was shattered by the news.

"I'll wait for the levee and the Caledonian Ball, old man, but I've come to the end of the tartan trail."

The thought of soldiering on without my friend was horrendous and my thoughts turned even more toward taking the plunge into the unknown of civilian life.

The levee took place at St. James's Palace in June. Officers of all arms holding the king's commissions were supposed to present themselves to their sovereign once or twice during their careers. Many people in the battalion were due for this ceremony and Telfer-Smollett entered wholeheartedly into the arrangements. The biggest problem was that of regimental full dress and where to find it. Some of the older officers had their own, but the rest of us, with few exceptions, having received only £50 from a grateful government at the commencement of our service with which to outfit ourselves completely, had no wish to go a further £150 into the hole for one morning of peacock glory.

About ten of us attended the levee, and everyone seemed to have everything on and everything on right. We dressed in rooms at somebody's club and the outfits were privately owned, borrowed or hired from Moss Bros. The smell of mothballs made our eyes water, but we made, I thought, quite an imposing sight as we strode down St. James's Street in the June sunshine, shakos on our heads, McKenzie tartan plaids over our silver-buttoned scarlet doublets, claymores, dirks at our sides and dress trews. Sir Arthur Balfour was the colo-

nel of the regiment, and as we followed in his wake, for
he was technically there to present us to the king, Trubshawe remarked that we looked like "a gaggle of Highland postmen." (see photo.)

Inside St. James's Palace was most impressive; two
large anterooms were filled with several hundred officers from all branches of the three services. It was a
blaze of color: Highlanders, Hussars, Greenjackets,
gentlemen-at-arms, Indian Cavalry officers in turbans,
Gurkhas and maharajas. There was a suppressed bon-
homie in the first anteroom and many old friends were
recognized, some from Sandhurst days. The second anteroom, into which we finally filtered, was quiet, and
one sensed a certain nervousness. In all it took about
two hours to percolate through the two anterooms and
into the Throne Room where we were to pay our re-
spects to King George V.

Finally, my turn came. I was ushered through the
door, and remembering my minute instructions from
Colonel Balfour, I handed my calling card to the gentle-
man-at-arms just inside on the left. Ahead of me was a
slowly moving single line of officers, inching forward toward the dais at the end of the long beautiful room.
About twelve men were in front of me, and as I, in turn,
began to move forward, I had plenty of time to take in
the scene.

On the dais and standing at the back were about
forty very impressive gentlemen—the most senior in the
Royal Household and Services. They stared out impas-
sively from beneath beetling brows. At the center, on a
gold throne, sat the king in field marshal's uniform, and
standing immediately behind him to right and left, his
four sons. The Prince of Wales in the uniform of the
Welsh Guards, the Duke of York in naval uniform, the
Duke of Gloucester in his Hussar uniform and the Duke
of Kent in the sky blue of the Royal Air Force.

I found myself filled with great emotion. When I
reached the end of the line, my calling card had miraculously arrived at the same instant and was being handed
to a senior official who glanced at it and announced,
"Mr. David Niven—the Highland Light Infantry." I
turned to the right, my shako under my arm, praying I
would not trip over my claymore, and marched the reg-

ulation number of steps that would bring me opposite the king, then a smart left turn and I was face-to-face with my monarch. I bowed. He acknowledged me with a slight inclination of the head. A smart right turn and I marched out into another anteroom. It had been an unexpectedly moving experience for me and for the others too. We gathered in silence till Sir Arthur Balfour joined us and told us that the colonel in chief of our regiment, the elderly uncle of the king, the Duke of Connaught, wished to receive us in his apartments behind the palace.

During the short walk I was brought down to earth by Trubshawe, who said, "I hope the poor old sod doesn't get gassed by all this camphor." Standing in a line in his dining room, we were presented to the duke. He seemed a very old man and his German accent was most pronounced.

"It's good to see the old uniform again," he intoned, peering at us over a white mustache and a huge beak of a nose.

"Jesus!" whispered Trubshawe, standing next to me. "Somebody's got one of his old ones on."

The next night was the Caledonian Ball held at Grosvenor House and another splendid spectacle awaited us. Scots from all over the world were present in full regalia and the *pièce de résistance* was always the set reels. The huge ballroom was cleared, and in the middle the Duke of Atholl's private sixteensome took up position, then around it were placed the eightsomes of the six Highland regiments: the Black Watch, ourselves, the Gordons, the Camerons, the Seaforths and the Argylls.

Trubshawe and I with, luckily, two very special friends, Keith Swettenham and Michael Bell, were the four subalterns selected by Telfer-Smollett to represent the Highland Light Infantry. The four girls we were to partner wore the sashes of their clans and had been carefully selected by the Ball Committee for their territorial connections with the regiment and not, we noticed, with some alarm, for their good looks. However, we had just arrived from a riotous dinner in a private room at the Mayfair Hotel, which Brian Franks had arranged, so we were not too unnerved when introduced to these horse-faced partners from faraway glens. Also,

the dinner party was there to cheer us on, headed by
Margie MacDougall, Celia Tower, David Kelburn,
Anthony Pleydell-Bouverie and Brian Franks.

"Clachie" Chisholm, the pipe major, had been polishing
up our dancing for days before the big night, so, all in all,
we were quietly confident of holding up the good name of
the regiment in front of hundreds of pairs of critical eyes.

Now, in an eightsome reel, it doesn't matter how well
the individuals dance the steps if the whole eightsome fails
to stay in its allotted position.

The unknown girls were expert dancers, and it was the
dawning look of horror on their faces that alerted me to a
very nasty situation: Somehow our entire eightsome, performing perhaps with too much verve and abandon, had
started to creep slowly down the ballroom floor toward the
Gordons. A crash was imminent. The Gordons turned
rather nasty, and hissed oaths came our way. In a body we
recoiled and began traveling inexorably in the direction of
the Camerons, who tried to avoid us and got into a really
horrible mix-up with the Seaforths. Having started the rot
and having cleared a large portion of the floor for our own
use, our eightsome settled down beautifully and never
moved again. The other eightsomes were left cannoning
into each other and generally behaving like goods trains at
Clapham Junction gone mad, ricocheting off the Duke of
Atholl's sixteensome in the center. Trubshawe observed the
Argylls trying to ignore a couple from the Black Watch,
who were now dancing dazedly in their midst, and summed
up things: "Bit of a fuck-up at the other end of the room,
old man."

Trubshawe adhered to his timetable and by midsummer
he had left the regiment and married Margie MacDougall.

The junior officers, noncommissioned officers and men
of the battalion were sad to see him go. The senior officers
had mixed feelings. For me it was disaster.

I took Telfer-Smollett's hint that it might still not be too
late to become a good soldier and worked like a beaver
with my platoon. When the interplatoon competitions
came, we swept the board. Almost immediately more than
half my men were drafted to India. I was sent on a course
to the Machine Gun School at Netheravon, and once more
gloom descended on me like a blanket.

I was befriended around this time by the family Weigall

who lived in a large white Georgian house in Ascot. Sir
Archibald was tall, charming, good looking, pink faced and
vague. Lady Weigall, permanently in a wheelchair, wearing
a blond wig with a blue bow in it, was plump, vivacious, a
tremendous gourmet, who loved laughing and being
shocked. She was attended by two resident doctors, a
youngish male social secretary and a mysterious old gentleman called C. J. who read *Horse & Hound* all day long
and who was rumored to have been Lady Weigall's boyfriend before Sir Archibald showed up. Priscilla, the only
child, was a flashing brunette with a delicious sense of
humor who was correctly considered "Deb of the Year."

I spent many happy weekends at Ascot and the Weigalls
took a great interest in my future. Sir Archie and Lady
Weigall thought it fitting that I should go to Australia as
ADC to the governor general. Priscilla had other ideas.

"You should be a movie actor," she declared flatly and
promptly went to work to promote the idea. First, she introduced me to my boyhood hero, the great Douglas Fairbanks. A chronic Anglophile, Fairbanks was enjoying a
period of playing the country squire and had rented
Mimms, a lovely Queen Anne house in Hertfordshire.

Fairbanks invited me to play golf with him at Sunningdale, which I did and basked happily for eighteen holes in
his reflected glory. I was so impressed by the gaiety and
simplicity of the great man, I never dared mention Priscilla's project.

Undeterred by my cowardice, she next presented me to
Bunty Watts, a producer at Sound City, a minute studio
nearby, and one Sunday I appeared in front of the cameras
as an extra in a racing film, *All the Winners,* with Allan
Jeayes as its star. Greatly to Priscilla's disappointment, I
was not immediately signed to £1,000,000 contract and I
returned to Netheravon in time for parade on Monday
morning.

My loathing of the Machine Gun School was only
equaled by my pathological hatred of the Vickers Mark IV
Machine Gun, a foul piece of machinery of such abysmal
design that it was subject to countless stoppages, all of
which we were supposed to be able to diagnose and rectify
at a moment's notice. There were about a hundred officers
on the course drawn from every conceivable regiment.

Henry Clowes of the Scots Guards was my constant companion, and although I nearly killed him one day, when the vintage Bentley skidded and somersaulted on Salisbury Plain, pinning us underneath it, he forgave me and did all he could to help me through the hot mornings when I arrived, sleepless, from London just in time to grab a piece of machine gun and rush onto parade.

One such morning was the harbinger of military doom. I had escorted Priscilla to a dance and a nightclub, and I screeched up in the Bentley only just in time to take off my tailcoat, jump into my brown-canvas overalls, cram my Glengarry on my head, and relieve Henry of a hideously heavy tripod before my name was called on the early parade.

"Present, sir," I puffed.

All morning we labored, putting that damn gun together, then taking it to pieces again.

"All right, gentlemen," said the chief instructor, a full colonel, "it's a very warm day. You may remove your overalls, jackets and work stripped to the waist."

Sighs of relief all around as the officers peeled off.

"Mr. Niven, you may remove your overalls," said the chief instructor.

"No, thank you, sir, I have a sniffle."

"Remove your overalls, Mr. Niven," ordered the colonel grimly.

"Yes, sir."

I stood in the middle of Salisbury Plain unveiled in white tie, stiff collar, shirt and white waistcoat . . . Glengarry still on my head.

After that I was a marked man.

The end, militarily speaking, came for me on another stiflingly hot day during the last week of the course. I had a much-looked-forward-to assignment with Betty in London and my timetable was in grave danger of being ruined by a long-winded address being delivered by a visiting major general. In the hot tin-roofed lecture hut he was droning on about fields of fire, close support and trajectors. Bluebottles were buzzing about and my head was nodding. Finally he closed his notes.

"Any questions, gentlemen?"

My hand went up. I will never know what prompted me

to do it—four years of frustration, I suppose—but I
opened my mouth and heard myself say, "Could you tell
me the time, sir? I have to catch a train."

"Stand up that officer." I stood. "Your name?" I told
him. "Go to your quarters and remain there." I departed.

Soon an officer of the Seaforths of the same rank as myself joined me in my room; ominously he was wearing a
sword. He was very embarrassed. "I'm afraid I have been
told to . . . er . . . stay with you," he said.

"Close arrest?" I asked.

"Looks like it," he said.

The embarrassment deepened as we sat staring at each
other in the hot little room, he in the leather chair, me on
the bed. After about an hour, with exasperated flourish, he
took off his sword.

"This is bloody ridiculous," he said. "Let's have a drink."

I agreed eagerly and summoned the room orderly, who
was lurking suspiciously close, determined not to miss a
moment of this juicy situation. A bottle of whiskey arrived
from the mess, and almost in silence the Seaforth Highlander and I drank it, and when I say "it," we drank the
whole bottle.

"I've a suggestion," said the Seaforth as the last dram
was drained, and he said it slowly and with great delibera-
tion. "I'll go to the lavatory, which I badly need to do, and
you escape."

The beauty and simplicity of this plan would have
shamed Field Marshal Montgomery's famous "Left Hook"
at El Alamein.

The Seaforth, with brimming eyes, then clasped both my
hands in his, shook his head mournfully, and tottered off in
the general direction of the latrines. I climbed hurriedly out
of the window, closed my eyes, and leaped into space.
Luckily my room was on the ground floor so I found myself in no time up to my chin in exhausted and dusty rhododendron bushes.

I ran to the Bentley and drove rapidly, and luckily without incident, to London.

Betty I never saw again. I arrived comparatively sober
and utterly appalled by what I had done. I rounded up two
friends, older friends whom I admired, Victor Gordon-
Lennox, an ex-major of the Grenadier Guards, then the
Washington correspondent of the *Daily Telegraph;* and

Philip Astley who, as adjutant of the Life Guards, had just been asked to resign his commission for committing a heinous crime: He had married an actress, the gorgeous Madeleine Carroll.

The three of us dined at White's; outside, Guiness label gleaming, stood the Bentley. The two ex-Guards officers listened attentively while I told them what had happened. After dinner came the inquest.

"How much do you like the Army?" asked Victor.

"I hate it," I answered.

"You're bound to be court-martialed. Why don't you pack up before you're thrown out?"

"Because I'm broke," I said.

"Do you have any money at all?" asked Victor.

"A few pounds and about half that old Bentley outside."

They left me nursing a large glass of vintage port while they murmured together in a bay window overlooking St. James's Street. I tried to avoid the eyes of an ex-member of White's who stared at me disapprovingly from a large gilt frame—the Duke of Wellington.

Finally the jury returned to their seats.

"There is no question that you are through in the Army," said Philip, "but Victor has a possible solution."

Victor, lately married to a Canadian girl, then spoke: "I am sailing on the *Empress of Britain* tomorrow to pick up Diana from her parents' island in the Rideau lakes, then I'm off to Washington. Give me the Bentley or the part you have paid for and I'll give you a return-trip ticket to Quebec. Come and stay on the island for a week or two and you can decide what to do next."

I was stunned by my good fortune.

"Now we'll go downstairs," said Philip, "and you can write your colonel your resignation. I'll help you—I've done it."

Below, by the porter's desk—the only place in White's where guests can use the club stationery—I wrote out a cable to Alec Telfer-Smollett at the Citadel Barracks, Dover:

DEAR COLONEL
REQUEST PERMISSION RESIGN COMMISSION.

I sailed for Canada in the morning.

9

The *Empress of Britain,* like my earlier trans-atlantic carrier, the *Georgic,* was also sunk a few years later by the Germans. She was a beautiful ship and the September crossing
was perfect. We ran into fog only once about one day out
of the Gulf of St. Lawrence. Suddenly, it got much colder
and we reduced speed. I remarked on this to a steward.

"Icebergs about," he said.

"How do you know?" I asked.

"We smell 'em," he replied.

As yet there was no radar in passenger ships and the
steward gave it as his considered opinion that the captain
wetted his pants every time they entered those particular
waters.

The fog lifted and everyone was pointing. A mile or so
away was a gigantic fortress sailing majestically along. Pale
pink in the setting sun on one side and blue-green on the
other. It towered out of the water, and with nine-tenths out
of sight below the surface, imagination boggled at the size
of the whole.

Diana Kingsmill Gordon-Lennox was a rarity—a genuine Canadian eccentric. Dark, with beautiful teeth and a
lovely smile, she was highly intelligent, smoked small cigars
and wore a monocle. She met us in Quebec and we drove
and drove to Portland, Ontario. Diana seemed not at all
put out that Victor had arrived with an unknown friend;
she intimated that her father and mother were looking forward to having me on the island and was delighted when I
told her I loved fishing. "Then Daddy will have a play-
mate," she said.

We had a long motorboat ride from Portland, Ontario,
and finally arrived at the Kingsmills' island in the Rideau
lakes. The maples were turning and I had never seen such
blazing beauty; great splashes of red, brown, yellow and

gold were reflected in the still water and behind rose the
foothills of the Gatineau mountains all clothed in the same
breathtaking colors.

The island was of about five acres. The main house was
surrounded by perhaps four guest cabins; all were of wood.
Admiral Kingsmill and his wife were walking down to the
boathouse as we arrived. The admiral was a famous old
Canadian sea dog and with his forthright manner, pointed
white beard and ramrod carriage, he certainly looked the
part. Diana had heard my story on the long drive from
Quebec and had said it would be better to forget my true
exit from the British Army. "Just settle for a straight resigning of the commission when talking to the old man,"
she said cautiously.

Lady Kingsmill was a gentle motherly creature and I was
immediately made welcome.

The days slid by. People came from other islands to visit
the admiral and I endlessly went fishing for the big green
bass, the fighting, jumping, black bass, the giant pike, and
the ferocious muskellunge.

Victor and Diana took me on excursions into the back
country and we endlessly discussed my future. Return to
England? Hardly. Immigration to Canada was ruled out
because of my lack of training in any useful profession,
and, anyway, I had a strong urge to go down to New York
where at least I had some contacts.

I was alone in a canoe one evening at sunset, cogitating
and well muffled up against the early autumn chill that had
been increasing daily and the loons were serenading me
with their plaintive cries when I saw what I took to be a
man swimming near a small uninhabited island. The water
was very cold, so out of curiosity that anyone could be that
far from home at that time of day, I paddled over to investigate and found a large bear peering at me from behind a
floating log. I gave it a wide berth.

I loved those lakes, but the time had come to move on
and Victor had to go back to his desk in Washington. I
made up my mind to cash in my return-trip ticket to England and cast my lot in New York.

The next day I had an agonizingly sore throat which got
progressively worse. I didn't say anything about it because
they might have felt they were getting stuck with a permanent guest, so when Victor and Diana left for Washington,

I accompanied them as far as Ottawa, ostensibly to visit the Canadian Pacific Steamship Company and collect a little hard cash for my return ticket. Once there, I said good-bye to my savior and his wife and visited a doctor who said I had chronically infected tonsils which should immediately come out. I imagine he must have done something about the infection first, but anyway he stuffed me into Ottawa General Hospital. Sodium pentothal not having yet come on the market, the operation was carried out after I had first been rendered unconscious by a mixture of gas and ether being pumped into a rubber mask over my face. After the operation, I lay for days with a throat of greatly increased soreness, and to take my mind off my misery, I am afraid I indulged in a little gentle plagiarism.

I hope that the statute of limitations applies in this case and that the Mounties will not be sent to pull me in, and if it will help at all, I offer my belated apologies to the author. Thyrett Drake, a Buckinghamshire master of foxhounds. He had long before written a book called *Fox Hunting in Canada*. I found it in the hospital library, assiduously copied some of it, and sold four articles to the local newspaper under the title "Hunting of the Canadian Fox." It paid the doctor's bill.

I had met some friends of the Kingsmills, Pete and Ginny Bate, and one day they appeared at my bedside.

"We've talked to the doctor," they said, "and he has agreed that we can take you home with us. There's a room at the top of the house you can have while you are convalescing and it'll be much more comfy for you. Besides, we would love to have you."

I was overwhelmed by such a wonderfully warmhearted gesture by the slightest of acquaintances, though it is typical of Canadians as a whole.

I had at least a week more to spend in bed—apparently it had been an operation with "complications"—so I jumped at the idea and, swathed in blankets, was removed to 32 Range Road and installed, as promised, in a bright chintzy room at the top of the house.

On a Sunday night Ginny and Pete came up to see me. "We're going over to Pete's mother's for supper, but we'll be back before eleven. Do you mind being left alone?"

Of course I didn't. I was feeling better and due to get up in a day or so. They left me with a radio and departed.

I went to sleep about ten and woke up sometime later literally drowning in my own blood. I had had a terrible hemorrhage in the throat, and when I turned on my side, it poured out like a tap onto the floor. The bright chintzy room looked like an abattoir. I had not the faintest idea where the telephone was or what was the doctor's number, but I had a vague idea that the operator could somehow help me.

I collapsed at the top of the stairs, where the poor Bates found me mercifully a short while later.

Back to hospital and blood transfusions but finally I made it by train to New York. It was now mid-October and becoming exceedingly cold. I found a room in a cheap hotel on Lexington Avenue—the Montclair—and for a week I lay in bed without the energy to pick up the telephone to try to find some of last year's companions.

Finally, I began to make contact with the old group, and although they went through the motions of being pleased to see me, I soon realized that there was a big difference between an irresponsible young man over for a short holiday and an anxious young man badly in need of a job. The background was not too welcoming for a foreigner either; the United States was still in the grip of the Depression, and there were millions of United States citizens unemployed. . . . I could not have chosen a worse time for my arrival.

However, good health can overcome the gloomiest thoughts, and as my strength returned, my morale improved. I registered with an employment agency and picked up a few dollars here and there working at night for catering companies that handled cocktail parties. It was not a very technical job. The host produced the booze via his bootlegger and the caterers provided the hors d'oeuvres, the barman, the glasses and the waiters. I invested in a white jacket and took great care to check the addresses I was sent to, only accepting jobs where it was very unlikely I would be seen by any of my acquaintances.

John McClain, the reporter, was doing better. He had just been given a daily column to write for the *Sun*, "Up the Gangplank." This meant that he had to meet and interview all interesting arrivals on the ocean liners. It was hard on him physically because the ships usually arrived in quarantine about four or five A.M. and there picked up the customs.

McClain made it a habit to go out on the customs cutter and cornered his quarry between their waking and their disembarkation. The time till the customs cutter sailed hung heavy on his hands, so he frequently found himself spending it in speakeasies and nightclubs. Some of his sleepless interviews were classics. One night early in November, I was sitting up with him. I had been handing around drinks at a long dull party over on the West Side and we met for supper at "Jack and Charlie's." McClain had a brainwave. . . .

"Look," he said, "Prohibition was repealed in April and it's due to be ratified in a few days and that will make all booze legal. Jack and Charlie are going to become wine merchants—maybe they'll give you a job. I'll have a word with them."

The next day I had a meeting with Jack Kriendler and found myself employed on a forty-dollars-a-week retainer against 10 percent of what I brought in in the way of orders. Jack explained that Frank Hunter of the World Champion Doubles Team of Tilden and Hunter would be president of the company and my immediate boss.

The houses on either side of 21 West Fifty-second Street had been bought—one was being converted into offices and storerooms. There Frank Hunter, a man of great charm and humor, introduced me to my co-worker, a tough professional salesman named Harry Rantzman.

During the months I held my job, I hardly ever topped four hundred dollars a week in sales which would have "augmented" my "retainer." Harry Rantzman ended up owning several apartment buildings in the Bronx.

The first day of work Kriendler sent me to FBI headquarters to have my fingerprints taken and to be photographed with a number around my neck, and to this day at 21 is that picture of me. Underneath is written:

OUR FIRST AND WORST SALESMAN

The products we had to sell were Justerini & Brooks (whole line), Ballantine's scotch, George Goulet champagne and a peculiar brandy called Jules Robin.

"Go out now and get the orders," said Charlie Berns airily. They gave me a price list and told me my beat. "East of Lexington over to the river and between Forty-second

Street and Ninetieth Street, that's for the professional buyers—the private customers you pick up anywhere you can."

I made my first sale the day before Prohibition was finally repealed—a case of champagne to "Woolly" Donahue. He needed it at once, Gus the barman gave me the case out of stock and Red the doorman and I delivered it in a Yellow Cab just before midnight on December 4. 21 Brands, Inc., was in business.

In the days that followed, two things became apparent. The first was that with all the ex-bootleggers and gangsters leaping into the legitimate wine and spirits trade, I was in for a rough time in the very rough sector of the city that had been allotted to me.

Secondly, Prohibition having only been in effect for thirteen years, many old-time wine merchants opening their doors once more were remembered and most private customers in a sudden wave of self-righteousness preferred to deal with them and rather looked down their noses at the upstarts who had erupted from the gangster-ridden world of speakeasies. This was an excuse I preferred not to make to Jack and Charlie when my shortcomings as a salesman came up for periodic review.

And thirdly, I found it almost impossible to try to sell to friends and acquaintances. I just could not bring myself to say, "Thank you so much for having me to dinner. Now, how about buying a case of scotch?"

The Montclair Hotel was pretty awful and the steam heat in my tiny room was suffocating, but it was cheap and right on the edge of my "territory." The front door of the Montclair was on Lexington Avenue, exactly opposite the back door of the Waldorf-Astoria, so during that miserable cold winter, I made it a point to come out each morning from the Montclair, carrying my bag of samples, cross Lexington, climb the long stairs at the rear entrance to the Waldorf, wend my way through the vast gilded lobbies of the most luxurious hotel in New York, descend the steps to the front entrance, pass through the revolving doors, and issue onto Park Avenue to start my day. . . .

"Good morning, Mr. Niven," said the doorman, saluting deferentially.

"Morning, Charles."

Very good for the morale. Then I turned right at the first corner heading for the sleazy restaurants and bars of my domain, and making the most of the warmth from the exhausts of the heating plants coming up through grilles in the sidewalks, I started my dreary rounds.

"Stand over there and wait your turn. Okay, jerk, let's see your list. What's this crap? Never heard of it. Git yer ass outta here."

Fourteen degrees below zero outside and stamping into stifling sandwich counters for lunch, then off again to try to corner restaurant owners sitting hunched over their own meals while waiters in filthy aprons wiped off tables and removed the debris of departed customers.

"Wait till I finish eating, for Chrissake. Okay, let's look at the list. . . . Who expects to get these goddamned prices anyway? 21 Brands, never heard of 'em. . . . Take off twenty percent and maybe I'll talk to you. Now beat it."

Back at the end of the day with little success.

"Good evening, Mr. Niven."

"Evening, Charles."

Up the front stairs, through the warm rich-people-fragrant lobbies of the Waldorf, down the back stairs, across Lexington, avoiding skidding taxis and clanging streetcars, and then going to ground like a bedraggled fox in my lair in the Montclair.

On one particularly depressing evening I had failed to sell anything all day and had just been pushed hard in the chest by a fat Irish barman who said that the case of Robin brandy I had sold him was undrinkable.

"Goddamned varnish remover, that's what it is. You come back in here again, son, and I'll stick it up your ass."

I had been slipping and sliding my way back to the hotel; it had snowed, then thawed; now it was freezing and the brown slush was treacherous. I was thoroughly dispirited as I contemplated the evening before me. With the exception of John McClain and Jack Hemminway, I had largely stopped seeking out the old group of a year before. They hadn't changed—I had—and I had come to realize that the vast majority of them were very rich and I was very poor indeed and the two just simply don't mix for too long.

At the Montclair the fairy desk clerk with a quiff of golden hair asked me for the umpteenth time if I was busy for dinner, and when I said yes, he twitched his left shoulder, made a little face, handed me my key, and said bitchily, "Nobody called you all day."

I toyed with a hamburger of sorts and a bottle of beer in my room and went to bed. In the middle of the night I woke up with a high fever and teeth chattering like castanets. The bout of flu ran its course in about a week. Christmas came and went without my noticing it. Big cities can be the loneliest places in the world.

New Year's Eve I felt well enough to face the world again. I took in the show at the Radio City Music Hall (personal appearance of Jimmy Durante) and stood myself a decent supper in a bar-grill off Broadway. There I met, or rather picked up, a showgirl from the "Ziegfeld Follies" who had been stood up by her date. We had a few drinks and she asked me to take her to see the marathon dancers. The Depression had produced some desperate people, but none could have sunk to greater depths of degradation than those poor creatures. Teen-agers and couples in their early twenties shuffling around and around the dusty floor of a central arena at three o'clock in the morning, taking it in turns to sleep in each other's arms. Shuffling around twenty-four hours a day for days on end. Zombies with exhausted pinched faces competing for a few hundred dollars in purse money and for the sadistic pleasure of jaded onlookers like my Ziegfeld pickup. She lived in a gaudy apartment on the West Side. A large number of vacuous satin-clad dolls were propped up on her bed. She was attractive in a brassy but curiously vulnerable way.

The next day, I got a call from Jack Kriendler. He must have got the news with his breakfast, he was very highly strung. "Jesus, kid, you gotta watch your step . . . you outta your mind or something? You wanna get rubbed out? . . . Lay off that dame you had last night, for Chrissake . . . she's dynamite!"

He told me the name of the man who had stood her up. It didn't mean anything to me, but McClain whistled when he heard it.

"Jack's right," he said, "forget it unless you want to wind up at the bottom of the East River in a barrel of cement."

An awful lot happened in 1934, and I had a funny feeling that things might be going to get better when one evening in early January, passing homeward through the Waldorf, I ran into Tommy Phipps, an old friend from England. There were three famous Langhorne sisters from Virginia—all very beautiful. One married Charles Dana

Gibson, the artist, and became the prototype of the Gibson girls; another, Nancy, married Lord Astor and became Britain's famous female Member of Parliament representing Plymouth from 1919 to 1945 and was presiding at the very time I met Tommy over the much-publicized "Cliveden Set." The third, Norah, the youngest, gayest and by far the most eccentric, married an English Army officer, Paul Phipps. Tommy, the result of this union, had been sent to Eton and now a few years later had come to America to live with his mother and a newly acquired stepfather.

Tommy insisted that I leave with him that moment to spend the weekend with his family in Greenwich, Connecticut. While I was flinging a few things into a bag, Tommy filled me in on the details.

"Lefty" Flynn had been one of the most famous Yale athletes. Fullback and all-American, he had also created impossible records in track, winning everything except the high jump, and he failed to win that, according to Tommy, only because he was busy winning the mile which took place at the same time.

He became a leading light in the Yale Glee Club and toured with it all over the country. When they were performing in Los Angeles, his monumental physique and good looks caught the eye of William Wellman, the director, and almost overnight Lefty was starring in cowboy pictures.

His instantaneous success had made him, at first, unreliable, to put it mildly, and during his third and last film, he had asked one day to be excused in the middle of shooting to go to the lavatory. Eight days later he had been located by distraught studio executives, in a hotel in Olahoma City, sitting up in bed playing a guitar and painted bright blue from head to foot. In the room playing with him was a six-piece Hawaiian orchestra which he had picked up en route in San Francisco.

Somewhere during his travels he had met Tommy's mother and the resulting *coup de foudre* had only lately resolved itself and resulted in a new home life for Tommy.

Lefty came to pick us up in an open red two-seater air-cooled Franklin.

In all the years I was to know him, he really never changed; fortyish then, I suppose, he was already bald on top but his body and movements were still those of a great athlete. He had a beautiful head with a high-bridged finely chiseled nose and magnificently set large deep-blue eyes. His voice was resonant and his laughter easily triggered and hugely infectious. His completely unforced charm was irresistible, and it was easy to understand why Norah had left home in the middle of the night, carrying nothing but a tennis racket. They had little money but they lived in com- fort in a pretty shady white frame house flanked by stock- brokers; lived like two newly married college kids, deeply and touchingly in love, happiest when singing together with Lefty playing his guitar and surrounded by a few friends— Norah the perfect complement with sparkling blue eyes and reminding one constantly of old Virginia and magnolia trees, crinolines and flirting behind fans. It would not have been human if Tommy had not felt a certain resentment against the man who had upset his quietly ordered family, but for his mother's sake, he masked it.

For me, it was easy to love them both immediately and deeply and I am forever grateful to them and to Tommy for the home they gave me from that weekend on. Not a frame-house home—though that was available to me at any time—something much more important: a home inside myself from which I felt safe to venture and do battle.

Norah and Lefty did not go to parties in New York, pre- ferring the simple life in Greenwich, but they had a very soft spot for that inveterate international party giver, Elsa Maxwell. One evening they waited for me at the end of my day's work and took me to tea with this legendary figure in her apartment in the Waldorf Towers.

Rumors abounded as to how Elsa managed to pay for all the extravaganzas she presided over. Some said she was backed by the nouveaux riches who picked up the tab in exchange for being launched, surrounded by Elsa's formi- dable list of the socially desired; others, less generous, hint- ed that she made a good living out of the by-products of these parties, and having talked someone into paying for one, she then collected a handsome percentage from the caterers, orchestras and decorators involved. The fact re- mains that she was personally enormously generous and died leaving very little money. I liked her the moment I saw her.

A small, dumpy figure of sixty-odd in a sacklike garment relieved by not a single bauble, she dispensed tea and

dropped names with great expertise. She reminded me
somewhat of Lady Weigall, so it didn't surprise me when
she said, "Selling liquor . . . that's no good, no good at all
. . . get you nowhere . . . you should go to Hollywood . . .
nobody out there knows how to speak except Ronald Colman."

Norah and Lefty made encouraging noises, so she went
on, "Next week I'm giving a party for Ernst Lubitsch . . .
just a small dinner up here for about forty . . . plenty of
people are dropping in after the theater, so you be here
about twelve and I'll introduce you to Ernst and tell him to
do something about it."

The following week, I showed up at the appointed hour
to find about a hundred and fifty people milling around, all
with the indelible stamp of self-assurance and wealth. "If I
could only sell each one of them a bottle of scotch," I
thought. Instead of trying, I grabbed a glass for myself and
looked around for Elsa Maxwell. She was sitting on a sofa
at the far end of the room, surrounded by admirers, and
didn't seem to show too much enthusiasm when she caught
my eye, just lifted a hand in greeting, so I decided to get on
with the job myself.

Beside me stood a little dark man with a pale face,
slicked-down black hair and a huge cigar. He was regard-
ing the social scene with evident distaste.

"Which is Lubitsch?" I asked.

"I am," he said and moved away.

A few days later, Elsa called me at the Montclair and
said, "I talked to Ernst about you, but he says this is not a
good moment to start in pictures, so I've thought of something else for you—you should marry a rich wife."

"How do I do that?"

"Become the most popular man in New York, of
course."

"On forty dollars a week?" I thought, but I kept my
mouth shut while Elsa went on issuing instructions like a
demented field marshal.

"I'm giving the party of the year for the Milk Fund. It
will be at the Casino de Paris. I shall have all the most eli-
gible bachelors in New York as professional dancing
partners at a hundred dollars a dance for the fund, and afterward there will be a big auction and people will vote
with dollars for the most popular man in New York. I want

you to be one of the men. You will all wear green carnations. . . . Good-bye," and she hung up.

The Casino de Paris was filled with the brightest, the most beautiful and the richest in New York. I had dusted off my aging dinner jacket and reported for duty as ordered. Elsa gave me my badge of office—the green carnation—and stood me in line with about twenty other fellows. I was probably the youngest. I was certainly the worst dancer.

A number of people bought dances from me and I was able to hand over a considerable sum to the lady treasurer, but I was ill prepared for the shame of the auction.

After a midnight show featuring that classic mime, Jimmy Savo, a huge imitation section of the big board on the New York Stock Exchange was wheeled onto the stage.

There were twenty names on it. I remember only five of them: Jock Whitney, Sonny Whitney, Lytel Hull, William Rhinelander Stewart and Clifton Webb, the current rage of Broadway. My name, spelled "David Nevins," was at the bottom of the list. As I watched the auction progressing, a cold sweat of embarrassment broke out all over me. Blocks of shares worth thousands of dollars were bought and the amount registered in lights beside the name after each sale. For a while I had hopes that people would think I was the maker of the machine or something, and in fact "Nevins" might have gone unnoticed if Fifi and Dorothy Fell had not felt sorry for me and bought a hundred dollars' worth of stock between them. My value and my shame remained there for all to see. The winner, Jock Whitney, notched up a colossal sum for the fund. Everyone, with one exception, was highly delighted with the evening.

I couldn't take the Montclair any longer. As a matter of fact, it was mutual because on the coldest night of the year I managed to loosen enough layers of cracked and grimy paint around the window to open it about four inches at the bottom. When I woke up, my radiator was frozen solid and the heating system for an entire floor had ceased to function.

I found a basement room on Second Avenue. My view was of feet hurrying by, and up beyond them, silhouetted against the sky, the rattling, banging elevated railway.

McClain, Tommy, Jack Hemminway and assorted girls came and, shouting against the din, drank the gin which

Gus had thoughtfully donated from 21 for the housewarming. It was the first place I had ever been able to call my own.

The freezing winter seemed endless. Lefty took me skating—something I had never tried before. On a pond near Greenwich I got out of control and charged a girl who was figure-skating around an orange. I cut the orange in half and knocked the girl over. Not the best way to start a romance, but this was no ordinary girl as I noticed while she was helping me to my feet. She was small, almost tiny, with a wonderfully alive and pretty face. Huge brown eyes, a cloud of auburn hair pushed out from beneath a woolly skating bonnet. We had hot chocolate together and I asked where she lived.

"May I call you when I come back to New York?"

"Sure, if you want to. My name is Hudson and you can find it in the book. My father's a doctor and we live at 750 Park. . . . Donald Hudson."

A few days later I called her. "May I speak to Miss Hudson, please?"

"This is she."

"Oh, well, this is David Niven—you said I might call you."

"Who is this?"

"David Niven."

"I'm sorry . . . I don't know the name."

"Don't you remember me . . . cutting your orange in half?"

"I *beg* your pardon."

"Last weekend . . . skating at Greenwich . . . don't you remember? I knocked you over?"

"You must be mistaken . . . I've never been to Greenwich in my life and I never go skating."

"You are Miss Hudson?"

"*Mrs.* Hudson."

"Oh, I'm terribly sorry. You see the Miss Hudson I thought I was calling said that her father was a doctor—Donald Hudson—living at 750 Park . . . I looked him up and—"

She interrupted, "Well, you found my husband's number and he's a lawyer, Dennis Hudson, and his address is 250 Park." She didn't say this unkindly at all and she had a

most attractive voice; also, I was safe at the end of the telephone, so I decided to press on.

"How is he anyway?"

"Who?"

"Your husband, Dennis."

"Very well, thank you."

"Is he a *good* lawyer?"

There was a tiny intake of breath, but I sensed that she
had missed the logical moment to put down the receiver.

"Very good, thank you."

"Where does he work?"

"Downtown."

"Well, then, how about meeting me for lunch somewhere
uptown?"

She still didn't cut me off.

"Certainly not, I don't have lunch with total strangers."

"That's the trouble with all you middle-aged American
women—no sense of adventure. . . ."

"I'm not middle-aged. I'm twenty-two."

I settled smugly on my dungeon bed.

"Then that's really awful. I suppose you go off and have
one of those terrible hen parties, nibbling on a salad and
gossiping?"

"Would you please not bother me anymore? I'm not
going to have lunch with you."

I said nothing . . . just waited.

"I mean, how do I know that you're not a murderer or a
kidnapper or something?"

"I tell you what I'll do," I said. "I'll wear a blue-and-
white spotted scarf and a red carnation and I'll stand on
any street corner you name at one o'clock. Then you can
walk or drive by and you'll know me but I won't know you.
You can take a good look, and if what you see seems all
right and not like a murderer or a kidnapper, then we'll
have lunch uptown. How about that?"

A long, long pause. Finally she said, "Madison and
Sixty-first Street, one o'clock," and hung up.

During the two hours before my blind date, I managed
to sell a mixed case of gin and whiskey and a sample case
of wine. I was well pleased with myself when I bought a
dozen roses for Mrs. Hudson and a few minutes before one
o'clock took up my position outside some bank or public

building on Madison at Sixty-first Street, around my neck my blue-and-white scarf, in my buttonhole my red carnation.

Keep moving in subzero weather, whatever happens. Don't stand on windy street corners. By one thirty I was shivering and blue. By a quarter to two I couldn't feel the end of my nose and the roses were turning black. I was beginning to feel pretty stupid.

Just before two o'clock, a girl walked by and smiled sweetly. "Good afternoon, Mr. Niven," she said. I took off my hat but she kept walking. Then a girl approached from the opposite direction. "Good afternoon, Mr. Niven." Off came the hat . . . she kept going. Next, three came by, arm in arm. "Good afternoon, Mr. Niven," they chorused.

Two went by on bicycles and four more in a taxi. She must have been awfully busy rounding up her friends, but her masterstroke was the singing group from Western Union.

"Mr. Niven?"

"Yes."

"We have a message for you, sir. One! Two! Three! Happy lunchtime to you . . . happy lunchtime to you . . . happy lunchtime, dear David . . . happy lunchtime to you."

I wish I could report a romantic aftermath to this episode, but there was none. And by a strange coincidence, the Miss Hudson I thought she was married Phil Ammidown a year later.

In March I dropped in at a bar on Fifty-eighth Street hoping to pull off a big sale. I didn't and was soon sipping a consoling drink and staring at the back view of the first cowboy I had ever seen. He sported a black ten-gallon hat, black shirt with white buttons, a white kerchief at his throat and black levis tucked inside heavily worked high-heeled boots. He also wore a large pair of spurs. From the back, he didn't look much like the traditional tall, lean, leathery man of the saddle. There was a white pudginess about his neck and a very definite bulge at his waistline. He stood no more than five feet four inches.

He finally got his drink and turned away from the bar, a bad move because his spurs became locked together, his drink went flying and he fell into my arms.

Doug Hertz, for as such he introduced himself, had a round white face, small black eyes and a little black pencil mustache. It seemed doubtful that he could ever have been west of Brooklyn. The stories he told later of his childhood were conflicting, but I am sure I detected in his accent a mixture of the Mersey and Whitechapel somewhere under the other layers.

"Sorry, pardner," he said, "some dude gave me the elbow."

Doug Hertz was a promoter of extravaganzas and sporting events. As the evening wore on, it appeared that he had gone down with the *Lusitania*, bobbed up again, and had the top of his head blown off in the Argonne.

"Under this," he said, rapping two knuckles on a thick, black thatch of curly hair, "you'll find a steel plate. . . . Hair grows like moss . . . pull it out tonight and it's back in the morning."

He had, also, it seemed, worked as ranch hand, circus roustabout, oil rigger, bouncer and strikebreaker. Looking at his small, soft hands, I was doubtful.

"You got any dough, son?"

"None, I earn forty bucks a week."

"That's tough. Find me forty grand and I'll make you a million."

The scheme he uncorked was wondrous.

"You've seen a rodeo, son, and you've seen a horse race. I'm gonna combine the two. Races that will last fifteen minutes." He leaned forward, conspiratorially. "IN-DOORS," he hissed.

"Tell me more," I said.

"You kidding? I'm on to a goddamned gold mine and I'm not giving it away to some jerk in a bar . . . You come up with some heavy dough and I'll make you a partner. I'm gonna make me a fortune, so if you want in . . . scratch around and come up with some rich pals. Here's my card —I'm at the Hotel Astor."

I called Hertz early the next morning and invited him to meet me at 21 for lunch

"You outta your skull," he said, "eating in joints like that! Boy, have you gotta lot to learn."

He suggested I meet him in the lobby of the Astor and he would then show me the way to eat less expensively. I found him and we started walking. I told him about Lefty Flynn, and Hertz immediately sparked to the idea that Lefty, with his connections, was the ideal man to enlist in the project. Then he initiated me into his cheap eating plan. It was beautiful in its simplicity. He chose a big busy restaurant around Forty-eighth Street. I entered alone and sat at a table for two. Then I ordered a cup of coffee and a doughnut and opened my daily paper. After a suitable interval, Hertz came in and joined me. Not a flicker of recognition passed between us. Hertz then commanded a huge meal of soup, steak, potatoes, pie and coffee. I continued reading my paper, drank a second cup of coffee and nibbled at my doughnut.

When Hertz had finished eating, he summoned the waitress and called for his check. This was my cue.

"Would you give me mine too, please?"

The waitress slapped the two checks on the table. When she had moved away and was busy elsewhere, Hertz picked up my check for the doughnut and two cups of coffee, marched briskly over to the cashier, paid and went out into the street.

I took my time, finished my reading, then picked up Hertz' very sizable account.

"Oh, waitress . . . look, there's a mistake here! I haven't had all this steak and pie and stuff—I've just had a doughnut and a couple of cups of coffee."

Consternation and consultations followed, but there was nothing for them to do but write out a second bill for two cups of coffee and a doughnut. I paid and joined Hertz at a prearranged street corner far away. A second busy restaurant was selected, and there, following the same routine, Hertz got the doughnuts and coffee and I tucked in to a sizable repast.

Lefty Flynn was always becoming involved in schemes to make his fortune overnight, so it was only natural that when I told him about Doug Hertz, he insisted on meeting him the very next day.

They made an extraordinary couple walking side by side down Fifth Avenue. Lefty towered over Doug by a good twelve inches in spite of Doug's high-heeled boots and high-crowned hat. Doug was obviously impressed by Lefty, and I could see that he agreed with me that this great ex-athlete, with his mass of friends, could be more than useful in finding backing for his dream. Horse races lasting fifteen minutes! Over coffee he explained it to us in detail.

"Simple," said Doug, "you have four jockeys in each race and each jockey rides fifteen horses for one minute."

Lefty's arithmetic was no stronger than mine, and his fingers were working like a Turkish bazaar dealer's on an abacus.

"Why, that's sixty horses for each race," he said finally.

"You said it . . . so we'll need about one hundred and fifty horses all told for a card of six races—each horse running several times. Mind you, this is the time to buy . . . polo ponies! That's what we want for this setup. Who needs polo ponies in the winter? Nobody wants to feed the sons of bitches. Polo ponies! That's what we have to get."

"That's right," echoed Lefty, slapping the lunch counter, "we need polo ponies!"

I looked at him out of the corner of my eye. There was no question, he was hooked.

"It's just like a relay," said Lefty, eyes gleaming.

"Just like a relay," repeated Hertz, "except the jockeys will have to ride a different way for each minute, one bareback, another facing the pony's ass, another changing saddles, another changing mounts without touching the ground and so on."

"Gee whiz," said Lefty.

"And get this," said Hertz, "we'll be having betting concessions, peanut concessions, liquor, hot dogs—kids, we're gonna clean up."

Later that day, we formed our company, the American Pony Express Racing Association, and penciled in its officers. President, Maurice B. Flynn; secretary and treasurer, D. Niven. The experienced D. Hertz prudently kept his name off the books.

"We'll open in Atlantic City," said Hertz.

"Where do we get the ponies?" I asked.

"Sales. Pick 'em up for peanuts. So long as they're sound, doesn't matter how mean they are."

"Who's going to ride them?"

"Cowboys—I'll find them—a few ads in Montana and Oklahoma and we'll have all we want . . . thirty'll be enough."

Lefty and I sat goggled-eyed as Hertz expanded.

"Atlantic City, Municipal Auditorium, then the Boston Garden, then the big one—Madison Square. We need working capital right now for offices and my living expenses, so you fellas can get going and raise the dough. Forty people putting up a thousand bucks each'll do it."

Lefty and I were mesmerized by Hertz. We became like two schoolboys who had wandered into a power station and pulled a switch. Everything suddenly started to happen.

The first person Lefty decided to approach was Damon Runyon.

Runyon loved the idea, promptly bought a thousand dollars' worth of stock, and gave us a word of warning.

"Skip Atlantic City."

"Why?"

"Unless you can make a deal with the guy who runs it."

"Who's that?"

"Pinkie, he runs the numbers, the protection and the whores. He even gets a piece of every slot machine on the Steel Pier . . . nobody gets into Atlantic City without Pinkie . . . don't try it."

When we reported this conversation to Hertz, he poohpoohed it. "Oh, Pinkie won't bother us."

Armed with our first thousand dollars and with Damon Runyon's name as an investor, we soon found that it was not all that difficult to raise some more. Jack and Charlie bought a few shares and stifled sighs of relief when I told them I was leaving. Elsa Maxwell campaigned for us, and the sudden arrival of two old friends from England, Dennis Smith-Bingham and Ian Galloway, who both became shareholders and officers of the board, helped lay a fairly solid financial foundation.

Many people, however, were skeptical of our chances and at 1 William Street, the headquarters of Lehman Brothers, we had to throw in our reserves. I went downstairs and retrieved Hertz. We had left him sitting in full regalia in a waiting room. Hertz was subjected to a barrage of technical questions about cash flow, contracts and projected earnings. He fielded them admirably, but the day was not won till I remembered the steel plate on the top of his head.

"Oh, Doug . . . tell Mr. Lehman about the Argonne."

Hertz went into his routine about the hair growing like moss, but still Lehman wavered.

"Pull a little out for Mr. Lehman," suggested Lefty.

Hertz was as brave as a lion. Without a murmur, he

seized a great hank of his forelock and pulled it out by the roots. Victory was ours. The hair never grew in again, of course. We didn't use this impressive ploy too often, but even so, by the time we had raised twenty-five thousand dollars Doug Hertz' head looked like the bottom of a diseased moorhen.

Hertz made a deal with a decaying polo club at Poughkeepsie, eighty miles away, up the Hudson River. There was a ramshackle hotel on the property and Hertz persuaded the proprietors to give us free stabling for our ponies. In return we would provide a rodeo every Sunday for which they could sell tickets. The advance guard of ponies went to Poughkeepsie followed by a busload of cowhands from Maryland. Oklahoma, and six Indians whom "colonel" Zack Miller had persuaded to leave their reservation. I went up to take care of this group while Lefty and Hertz went to Atlantic City. A week later they returned, flushed with success, having landed a contract with the Municipal Auditorium for a grand opening in May.

Smith-Bingham and Galloway, both expert horsemen, moved up and training started with a vengeance—it was needed. The cowboys, mostly old rodeo and circus hands, operated in a haze of bourbon and rye whiskey, and the ponies, bought at an average price of around a hundred and twenty dollars, though sound in wind and limb, were mostly quite mad.

"Excellent," said Hertz, "we'll have 'em running through the orchestra and jumping into the ringside seats."

Our spartan life at Poughkeepsie was enlivened by the appearance of Hertz' blond, statuesque wife who took an instant shine to Ian Galloway. One night there was an ugly scene when Hertz accused Ian of trying to seduce her in the stables. It ended with everyone getting drunk in the hotel and swearing eternal friendship, but in the middle of the celebrations, Dennis Smith-Bingham rushed in. "Come on, quick! Somebody's left the door open and about forty ponies have got out . . . they're all over the bloody country." We dashed out.

It was a pitch-black night, so it took hours to round them up. The only casualty was Hertz, who ran very fast, straight into a large cart horse which was standing perfectly still in the middle of a field. The impact knocked him cold.

Training progressed, and in a few weeks we could see

that we had a very exciting spectacle on our hands; the only problem was money. We were approaching our grand opening in Atlantic City, and the cost of moving the whole cavalcade from Poughkeepsie was going to be astronomical. Hertz called an emergency meeting.

"We're in trouble, boys. We've gotta have another ten grand to get us to the opening. From there on in, the show'll pay for itself, but I've gotta have ten big ones this week or we fold."

We were silent.

"Get on down to New York, fellas, and beat the bushes —I mean it—or we fold."

Somehow we raised the money and we set off for Atlantic City on the appointed day.

The advance man had done his job with enthusiasm. Hoardings and walls were plastered with announcements of our coming and promises of what we were going to deliver. "CHILLS, SPILLS AND THRILLS," screamed the posters. Doug Hertz organized a parade from the railway station and tied up traffic all over town as a result. He rode at its head himself, an oval pouter-pigeon figure rolling slighly in the saddle as his round thighs tried to grip. He didn't really ride; he conned horses into letting him sit on them.

The American Pony Express Racing Association was in Atlantic City for a week before the grand opening, and Lefty and I often broached the subject of Damon Runyon's warning about the mysterious Pinkie, which still nagged us.

"Nothing to worry about at all," said Hertz confidently. "I've seen the police, nobody's going to interfere with us."

"How do we get any betting? It's illegal in the state of New Jersey."

Hertz winked broadly. "Everything is just Jim Dandy."

On the night of the grand opening, it was pouring with rain but the lines were at the box office, and by the time the parade started the auditorium was packed—fifteen thousand people. We were so short of cash that we couldn't afford an orchestra for our opening night. The best we could provide was an organist. The organ blared out stirring music as the parade trotted around the arena. Dorothy Fell and McClain came down with a big party from New York to cheer us on.

A master of ceremonies, wearing full fox-hunting regalia, explained over the loudspeaker the finer points of the races. The teams of ponies were guaranteed to be evenly matched, he said, so it was a question of picking the jockey with the most prowess.

I had a feeling of cement in my stomach when the teams came out for the first race, but Hertz waddled about exuding conficence.

"Good luck, kids," he said to the riders. "You're gonna be great."

The ponies sensed the tension and acted up like thoroughbreds. One or two, which had been tubed, whistled loudly through holes in their necks. Suddenly the auditorium went dark except for the brightly floodlit track. Crack! went the opening gun and away went the first race. The entire audience rose to their feet. Terrible chances were taken on the sharp turns. The cowboys excelled themselves, the courageous Indians staged some hair-raising falls, and at the end of the evening, we listened almost unbelievingly to loud and prolonged applause.

"We're in business, kids," said Hertz, clapping Lefty and me on our backs. "Next stop Boston and then the Garden!"

The morning after, I was sitting in our little office in the auditorium smugly reading the reviews of our show in the local press when four extremely hostile characters barged in. They wore fedoras and tight double-breasted suits.

"Where's Hertz?" they demanded.

Almost before I could answer, the avocado shape of our leader appeared in the doorway behind them. When Hertz saw his visitors, he went the color of cat-sick.

"Okay, creep," said one of the hostile men to me, "we don't need you. Beat it." I left with what dignity I could summon.

For about twenty minutes, I watched the approach to our office from a discreet distance, and when I saw the men depart, I hurried back in. Hertz was sitting slumped behind the desk. He looked stricken.

"What did they want?" I asked

Hertz smiled wanly. "It was a shakedown," he said, "but nothing's gonna happen. Like I said, I'm right in there with the cops." He didn't sound too confident, and in the event, a number of things did happen. That second night, we had a house only slightly less well filled than the previous one. Everything was going according to plan and the audience was enjoying itself hugely. Suddenly, in the middle of the second race, all the lights in the auditorium went out. For a while chaos reigned, ponies were crashing into each other, cowboys were swearing, and women were screaming. The lights stayed out for fifteen minutes and the slow hand-claps started. Finally, the lights came on again and we re-started the show. During the fourth race, the same thing oc-curred only this time, when the lights went on again, the people were streaming toward the exits and many went to the box office and demanded their money back.

On the third night, it was discovered that at least half the cowboys had packed up and left during the day.

The next day, the forage for the animals never arrived, and during the night a large number of saddles mysteri-ously disappeared.

On the fifth night, the lights went out again. More cow-boys defected the next day, and on the Saturday night our show was pitiful. It didn't matter anymore; the audiences had eroded to a point where only a handful had turned up.

Hertz, who had certainly never lacked courage, was stoic in defeat, but all chance of selling the show to other audito-riums in the country had evaporated. We were living on a shoestring. Everything had depended on making a big prof-it during that first week.

It was decided to liquidate our assets immediately and salvage what we could from the wreck.

Lefty could take all the disappointments except the de-sertion of the cowboys. He had loved them dearly, and he couldn't believe that they had allowed themselves to be in-duced to sink us. Sadly, he left for Greenwich and I stayed on to help Hertz arrange a sale of the livestock and remain-ing saddlery—all the assets we had. They didn't fetch much, and by the time we had tied everything up in Atlan-tic City I am afraid our gallant band of backers did not see very much of their original investment.

When I came to think of it, I, too, was in far worse fi-nancial shape than when I had first become involved with the American Pony Express Racing Association, and in ad-dition, I had given up my job with Jack and Charlie. But please don't feel that, at the end of this chapter, you are leaving me, like Pearl White, strapped to the financial railroad tracks, because, thank God, succor was already puffing toward me aboard the American Express.

10

Back in New York, I found a letter from Grizel. My mother, it appeared, had left everything to Tommy in trust for the four of us, but she had stipulated something very important. Max had once borrowed three hundred pounds from her to bail himself out of debt, so if either Joyce or Grizel or I were in desperate need, the small estate must try to provide the same amount for us.

Within a week, I had collected my share. It came to a little over eight hundred dollars—I was rich.

Lefty and Norah had gone to Bermuda where they had rented a small cottage at Devonshire Bay.

Lefty met me in Hamilton and I spent several blissful weeks on that spectacular island at a time that must have been its golden era. No cars, no motorcycles—just bicycles or horsedrawn carriages—no muttering groups at street corners, no sullen looks from under pork-pie hats, no cut-off conversations, just smiling happy faces and music everywhere.

Joe Benivides was our carriage driver, a mixture of Negro and Portuguese blood. He had bright-blue eyes and the broadest smile I had ever seen.

As we clip-clopped along the dazzling white-coral road, we passed through orchid farms and dense plantations of palm trees. Bright-hued little birds darted in and out of the oleander and giant hibiscus bushes, and when we arrived at the cottage, the bay in front of it was aquamarine and the sea gulls flying lazily in the blue above had long graceful forked tails.

"Norah's got a big surprise for you, Davey," said Lefty. "Somebody very special is coming to supper tonight."

In a day spent swimming on a pink-sand beach, reminiscing about our ill-fated venture and laughing—oh! how much we laughed—I forgot about my big surprise until

Anthony Pleydell-Bouverie walked into the cottage, accompanied by a diminutive Finnish wife called Peanut.

Anthony had been made flag lieutenant to Admiral Sir Ernle Erle Drax, commander in chief of a large fleet based on Bermuda. It was a classic reunion.

A week later, Tommy Phipps arrived. He had lately come back from California, and was full of stories of Hollywood. He had also sold his first piece of writing, a short story to *Harper's Bazaar*. The days flew by. We bicycled off in the mornings to various beaches or explored the islands. We were never out of the water and became burned the color of mahogany. I fell slightly in love with a dark-haired beauty of eighteen from Richmond, Virginia. She wore a camellia in her hair on the night I took her for a romantic drive in the full moon. Joe Benivides, though himself the soul of tact on these occasions, sitting bolt upright on his box and staring straight ahead oblivious to what was going on behind him, had unknowingly sabotaged my very delicate preliminary moves by giving his horse some wet grass. It is quite impossible to impress a beautiful girl with your sincerity if your carefully worded murmurings into a shell-pink ear have to compete with a barrage of farts.

A lot of time we spent planning our lives. Lefty and Norah were quite decided to sell up and leave the suburbia of Greenwich for the real country. They had masses of places to choose from, and plans and prospectuses went with us everywhere. Their hearts were more or less set on the little village of Tryon, North Carolina, nestling at the foot of the Smoky Mountains. There they had their eyes on a delicious low white-frame farmhouse called Little Orchard.

Tommy had more or less decided to follow a literary career and looked like installing himself in New York.

I was the problem, and much of the planning time was allotted to my future moves. A letter from Dennis Smith-Bingham decided them.

Lefty's stories of his time in Hollywood had fired my imagination. Now Tommy had stoked the fires. Dennis' letter clinched it.

Immediately after Atlantic City, he had left for California and was presently in Pasadena. He felt sure, he said, that the pony racing would go well in that part of the world.

"Come out and see for yourself," he wrote. "I'll find you a place to live."

I didn't for one minute believe that we would revive the pony racing, nor did I want to try, but I did feel deep down that I might be able to make a go of it in the movies. Norah and Lefty urged me on, but Tommy was more forthright. "Your legs are too big," he said.

Big legs or not, at the end of July, I packed my worldly belongings in my suitcase and the Flynns, Tommy, Anthony and the Peanut came to see me off. I sailed on a dirty old freighter for Cuba.

I had a week to wait in Cuba before the *President Pierce* sailed for the Panama Canal and California.

Havana enthralled me and I loved the gay jostling mobs, but there was a strange undercurrent of uneasiness and much that I did not understand. A lot of heavily armed soldiers were about, and almost as soon as I arrived, I witnessed a very brutal arrest.

One night in Sloppy Joe's Bar, I met an Irishman. He explained what was going on. The power behind President Mendieta was his chief of staff, Batista—"a ruthless bastard," according to my informant. "He won't even let them have an election." The man was fascinating and, I think, a little mad. I met him every evening. He tried to sell me the idea of becoming a soldier of fortune with him and joining some strange group who were forming "to fight for the rights of the people."

One night, on my way to Sloppy Joe's, an English voice spoke to me from a doorway near the entrance to my cheap hotel.

"May I have a word with you?" The man was about thirty-five and wore a white linen suit.

"Of course."

"You hold a British passport, do you not?"

"Yes."

"I'm from the British Embassy. How long are you planning to stay here?"

"I'm sailing on the *President Pierce* the day after tomorrow."

"Good. I hope you'll do just that. You've been seen with a man whom the local authorities don't view too highly. We got the word from them this morning. I expect you

have been followed because they told me where to find you
... Take my tip ... don't miss that ship."

He refused to join me for a drink and hurried away. I
avoided Sloppy Joe's that night and was the first in line
when the gangway of the *President Pierce* was lowered.

When traveling, I have always lived in the hope that I
will find myself seated on planes next to the most beautiful
girl. It never happens. It is usually a mid-European busi-
nessman who spreads himself over my seat and smokes a
foul cigar.

I knew I would be sharing my cabin on the *President
Pierce* with someone, and I prayed that the agents might
have slipped up and that I would find myself with one of
the several attractive ladies I noticed going through the Immigration. My roommate turned out to be an Indian
male—a red Indian male—but this was no lean copper-col-
ored warrior; mine was about two hundred and fifty
pounds of pure blubber and he smelled like a badger.

According to the purser, he had just become a millionaire because oil had been found on a small plot of land he
owned in Oklahoma.

The *President Pierce* had started its cruise in New York,
so by the time I joined it everyone was more or less ac-
quainted and I was the new boy in the school. Most of the
passengers were elderly, but there were a few families
headed for Panama and California. It came as something
of a shock when I realized the ship was dry. I was fascinated by the passage through the Canal, and at Panama,
where we spent a day, I went ashore and played golf in a
thunderstorm.

The smell of hot Indian was so overpowering in my
cabin that I regularly slept in a deck chair behind a funnel.

I spent a great deal of time and energy avoiding the
cruise director, a man who looked and behaved like a
games mistress.

"Come, come," he would say, clapping his hands, "who's
for shuffleboard ... we don't want to get pepless, do we?"
"You look like a perfect ping-pong type," he said to me,
just as I was settling down to a good book. "This is Miss
Weyhauser from Toledo, Ohio. She'll give you a good
game ... come ... come ..."

Miss Weyhauser had a small brother of nine, and he became the bane of my existence—a really horrid little boy

who wore white plus fours, a white shirt with a red bow tie and a white peaked cap with a pom-pom on the top.

His name was Cyrus—Cy for short—and he never left my side. He was intrigued by my "English accent" and followed me around all day, saying "Pip-pip, old chappie, jolly good show—what! any teabags anyone . . .?"

His father was a Hollywood scriptwriter.

Finally, after several warnings, I hit him. I was playing ping-pong with his sister, and when Cyrus was not picking up the ball and throwing it overboard, he was pinching my bottom and crying out, "The Redcoats are coming," so I let him have one really hard with the flat of my hand. It made a noise like a pistol shot. Everyone looked up from his chair to find Cyrus lying on the deck holding the side of his face, pointing and howling, "The limey hit me! The limey hit me!"

Miss Weyhauser took a backhander at me with her ping-pong paddle and said, "Oh! How dare you strike a child!" The cruise director materialized as if by magic.

"Well, we all thought you were a gentleman!" He swished off, picked up the blubbering little brute and cradled him in his arms.

That night the cruise director said he thought it might be a nice gesture if I apologized publicly to Cyrus and his mother after dinner. I had nothing to lose; no one was speaking to me anyway, so in the lounge, I stood up and asked for attention. I said that I was really sorry that it had happened and begged them all not to think it was typical of my race. "I am an orphan," I said. "I was abandoned in a cemetery by my mother when I was a few weeks old. I never knew who my father was. I was brought up by the parson, but he drank the Communion wine and beat me every Sunday night." I went on along those lines. I was good—there was no question—and as I warmed to my work, I saw several good ladies sniffling and taking out their handkerchiefs. I began to wonder if my trip to Hollywood might perhaps not be in vain.

I sat down to rapturous applause. My apology was accepted with smug bad grace by Cyrus and his mother, and for the remaining days of the voyage, he redoubled his efforts to annoy me. I got even with the little son of a bitch on the day we docked at San Pedro.

"I'm really sorry, Cy, about what happened," I said.

"Oh, that's okay, limey, forget it."

"No, really, Cy, to show there's no hard feelings, come and have an ice-cream soda with me."

"Okay."

We sat on two stools at the only bar in the ship.

"Bannana split with cream?"

"Okay."

Then a little later, "How about a chocolate sundae with pistachio nuts?"

"Okay."

"A nice prune whip and caramel sauce?"

"Okay."

I must say it was an expensive revenge. He was a veritable human disposal, but, finally, after about seven mountainous concoctions his color began to change.

His mother's last-minute packing must have been very interesting.

Dennis had cabled that he would meet the ship, and there he was with a beautiful golden-haired girl. I recognized her at once as Sally Blane. Sally was a fast-rising young star of the movies.

The usual shipboard reporters were sniffing around for stories. They spotted Sally and I found myself improvising about the pony racing and my plans. The next day, there was a picture of me in the Los Angeles *Examiner* with the caption:

BRITISH SPORTSMAN ARRIVES,
PLANS TO BRING OVER A HUNDRED
HEAD OF POLO PONIES

Sally was marvelous, with a lovely open face. "It's all arranged," she said. "Mom's got a room for you. You are going to come and visit with us till you find someplace to live."

Mrs. Belzer was Sally's mother, and with her three other daughters she lived in a charming Colonial-style house on Sunset Boulevard between Holmby Hills and Westwood.

On the drive up from San Pedro, we passed first through oil fields and citrus groves, then we stayed on the Coastal Highway with the endless sandy beaches and pounding Pacific surf on the left. In the distance were the high hills behind Los Angeles and far away to our right, the snowy top of Mount Baldy.

Mrs. Belzer was a beautiful woman, wonderfully sweet and seemingly vague, with an impeccable taste in antique furniture. The girls all worshiped her.

When I met the others, I gaped. They all were spectacular beauties. Blond Georgiana was the youngest, only about eleven. Polly Ann Young, an excellent and successful actress, was the oldest, probably twenty-two, a glowing brunette. Then there was Gretchen. Gretchen was already a big movie star, and her working name, Loretta Young, was known all over the world.

There has never been, in my experience, such a beautiful family to look at, and the beauty came from within because each and every one of them was filled with concern for others and kindness and generosity. They have never changed.

It was impossible to lie to people like these, so when Dennis, a few days later, left suddenly for England, I confessed one night to Mrs. Belzer and the girls that I was hoping to break into movies. I felt an idiot doing it in front of three already-established professionals, but they took it in their stride and took great care not to put me off by telling me too many facts that I was soon to discover for myself.

The next day I got my first taste of a major studio.

Loretta was making a picture at Fox, something about hospital nurses, and it was arranged that when the family car came to fetch her in the evening, I would be smuggled past the eagle-eyed police at the gate lying on the floor under a rug.

Once inside the gate it was a dream world. The car slipped through Indian villages, jungles, sections of Venice, complete Western streets, New York streets and passed a medieval castle and a lake with a large schooner and native canoes on it.

The studio buildings, the executive offices, cutting rooms, fire department, casting office and the huge towering sound stages seemed like a miniature city, and everywhere the streets teemed with cowboys, Indians, Southern gentlemen, soldiers, policemen, troupes of dancers and tall willowy show girls. I just gaped and gaped and wondered if I could ever be part of it.

Loretta's driver took me inside Stage 19 and I watched fascinated from a dark corner while she was powdered and primped and prepared for a close-up. What a strange, wonderful secret world! It pulled me like a magnet.

I really cannot remember what I was using for money at that time. I know I didn't borrow any and I don't remember stealing it, but I do know that within a very few days of arrival, I realized the vastness of the distances and the urgent necessity for some wheels and for an augmentation of my funds.

The girls took me to a used-car lot in Culver City and I bought a very old Auburn for ninety dollars. It went quite well on the flat but hated hills, and the small incline of the Belzer driveway could be negotiated only in reverse.

They also helped me in my search for a place to live. They never gave any sign of it, but they must have prayed that I would soon be successful. It is with great embarrassment that I have to record that nothing suitable was found for a considerable time.

The central casting office was down on Western Avenue. It handled only the extras. Anybody who spoke lines was a bit player or a small-part actor; these the studios employed through agents. In the Auburn I drove to central casting thinking that all I had to do was enroll myself and go to work. It was a forbidding moment. Outside the building was a large sign:

DON'T TRY TO BECOME AN ACTOR.
FOR EVERY ONE WE EMPLOY,
WE TURN AWAY A THOUSAND.

I stood in a long line and finally was interviewed by a brisk elderly woman with protruding teeth and glasses so dark that I could not see her eyes.

"Yes?"

"I'd like to be a movie actor."

"So would millions of others. What professional experience have you?"

"None, I'm afraid."

"Nationality?"

"British."

"Do you realize how many Americans there are looking

for work these days?" Before I could answer, she went on, "Well, the studios are making a lot of British stories right now, so we might find something for you. Fill in this form and mail it to us . . . you got a work permit okay?"

"Work permit?"

"You can't work without one—it's against the law. You got one?"

"No."

"Give me back that form . . . the way out's over there."

There is an antidote to everything, even, we are told, hopefully, to the Intercontinental Ballistic Missile, and usually, when those old Chinese weeds we wrote about earlier start clogging up the garden and things look pretty hopeless, out of the blue comes a weed killer.

The weed killer at this point was Alvin Weingand, now a highly respected Congressman from California, but then a junior reception clerk at the Roosevelt Hotel on Hollywood Boulevard. My search for cheap accommodation had not been going well, and Al gave me a room between a service elevator and a huge machine that shrieked and thumped all night as it inhaled cool air and belched it downstairs for the benefit of the guests. When I say "gave" me the room, he charged me so little that it almost amounted to a gift. I had a bed, a shower and a telephone. I needed no more.

Unpacking, I came across a telephone number—a girl I had met in New York, Lydia Macy, who lived in Montecito. I called her and was invited for the weekend.

Not feeling I could trust the Auburn to undertake the eighty-mile trip, I packed my bag, including my frayed and frightful dinner jacket, and thumbed a ride up U.S. Highway 101, arriving in Montecito, in a fruit truck, in plenty of time for dinner.

Montecito has more resident millionaires per acre than any other community in the United States. The houses are beautiful; the mountains behind them are purple in the evening light; and between them and the white sandy beaches lies a palm-covered plateau, inhabited by charming lotus-eaters.

On the Saturday morning, I looked out of my bedroom window, and I beheld an old friend, HMS *Norfolk* a county-class cruiser, riding at anchor in the bay, off Santa Barbara. She had been in Malta when I was there, and more lately, I had found her again in Bermuda. Now, she was on a goodwill tour of the West Coast of Mexico, the United States and Canada.

I told Lydia that I would love to go and visit her, as I knew several people on board. "Well, you're going to-night," said Lydia. "The officers are giving a party and all of Montecito is going."

That night, in a dinner jacket that had been rejuvenated by Lydia's maid, I escorted her on board *Norfolk*.

A huge awning covered the afterdeck, and the ship was dressed with garlands of lights and bunting. The Royal Marine Band was grinding out a fox-trot. I looked around for a familiar face and nearly fell over the side—there stood Anthony Pleydell-Bouverie. Apparently, Admiral Sir Ernle Erle Drax had decided to join the cruise and his flag lieutenant had come too.

Poor Lydia! I didn't behave very well. The reunions were continuous and strenuous, and I spent far too long in the wardroom. She left without me. All guests were asked to be off the ship by 3 A.M. At about that time, I mumbled to Anthony that it was time I left.

"Nonsense," he said, "don't go ashore . . . we'll look after you . . . there's a bunk you can have . . . go to bed and have a nice rest."

It sounded fine and I was past being analytical anyway, so I removed my clothes and fell immediately into a deep black sleep.

Next morning, about ten thirty, I woke with a mouth like the inside of a chauffeur's glove. Nobody was around. It was Sunday and the ship's company was at Divine Service. I looked out the porthole and couldn't see much except sea, and the sea was passing the window at a great rate.

I lay there wondering what to do next. Whatever Anthony had said, it made no sense to be at sea, in the middle of the Pacific, in one of His Majesty's county-class cruisers . . . in broad daylight . . . in a dinner jacket.

I continued to lie there. About noon a sailor poked his head around the door. "Compliments of the wardroom, sir, the officers would like to see you."

I doused my head with cold water, donned my crumpled suit, and followed him through the humming interior maze of the ship. Sailors gave me surprised glances as I passed.

Several of last night's drinking companions were already at the bar.

"Morning, Niven. Pink gin?"

"Yes, thanks."

"Enjoy yourself last night? Pretty girl you had with you." Small talk, chatter, more pink gin, no sign of Anthony and nobody bringing up the question of why I was still with them.

I thought to myself, "Well, I'd better just play this by ear. . . . If they're not going to mention it, I'm not." So I relaxed, joined in the small talk, accepted the pink gins and closed my mind to the future.

At last, Anthony appeared. "Sorry," he said, "I've been with the admiral. He wants to see you!"

"Like this?" I said, looking down.

"You look fine," said Anthony. "Let's go—he's waiting for you."

By now I was sure I was going to be made to walk the plank.

In the captain's dining room, the admiral was waiting, a spare, ruddy, typical sailor.

"Morning, Niven."

"Morning, sir."

"Enjoy yourself last night?"

"Very much, thank you, sir."

"Care for a pink gin?"

"Thank you, sir."

There I stood in my dinner jacket, wondering, and there half an hour later, I sat having luncheon, still wondering. Small talk, shoptalk, Malta talk, Bermuda talk, but the subject of my presence never broached.

Toward the end of the meal, a signalman knocked and entered. He handed the admiral a message using the flat white top of his headgear as a tray.

"H'm," said the admiral, "HMS *Bounty* off the starboard bow. . . . Niven, look out of that scupper and see if you can see her, will you?"

I moved to the indicated porthole, wondering if delirium tremens was always so fascinating. I had just finished reading Charles Nordhoff and James Hall's brilliant historical novel which Lefty had taken to Bermuda.

Sure enough, I beheld the *Bounty* with all sails set, moving gently on the Pacific swells. Suddenly, little white puffs of smoke like cotton wool erupted from her side, followed by the champagne cork pops of its cannon. HMS *Norfolk* slowed to a dead stop. The *Bounty* came close and I could see her crew wearing pigtails and striped stockings, then victory cheers floated across the water. I turned toward the admiral and Anthony, and they both burst out laughing.

"This is where you get off, young man," said the admiral.

As he led me on deck, Anthony explained that the great Metro-Goldwyn-Mayer producer Irving Thalberg was about to make a film of *Mutiny on the Bounty*. A complete replica of the original eighteenth-century warship had been built, and now, as a publicity stunt for the promotion of the picture, a meeting with her modern counterpart had been arranged in the Catalina Channel.

A rope ladder was dropped over the side, and an incongruous figure in my dinner jacket and cheered on by Anthony and a large number of the ship's company, I clambered nervously down onto the deck of the press tender which had materialized alongside.

Several of today's Hollywood Press Corps, including Jimmy Starr of the Los Angeles *Herald Express* and Bill Mooring of *Tidings*, witnessed my arrival, and I got the reputation of being the first man to crash Hollywood in a battleship.

Also on the tender were Frank Lloyd, the director of the picture, and Robert Montgomery, one of the reigning Hollywood stars. Clark Gable and Charles Laughton, who were to make the film as Fletcher Christian and Captain Bligh, were not present. Bob Montgomery had come along for the ride. The camera crews, the press, Frank Lloyd and Montgomery were most hospitable to their unexpected charge, and as *Norfolk* gathered speed and resumed her course south, I was carried unprotesting, for the second time in about three weeks, to the port of San Pedro.

Montgomery had a new sports Bentley—very impressive for me to see this beautiful machine so far from home and very helpful to me when he offered me a lift to M-G-M Studios, which lay some hundred miles north.

We arrived at about seven o'clock just as the day's work was coming to an end. The departing crowds of extras stood, respectfully, aside as Montgomery's Bentley was saluted through the main gate by the studio's police.

Horrible little boy, age two.

Above: Nessie's friend, eighteen and a half years old.

Left: Normandy, June, 1944.

Primmie with David, Jr., 1942.

*Bogie and Betty arriving for charity show in London;
author dressed as doorman to surprise them.*

Frank Lloyd offered me a drink in his own office and there I met another great director of the day, Edmund Goulding.

Goulding had lately completed the epic *Grand Hotel* with Garbo, John Barrymore, Joan Crawford, Wallace Beery, Jean Harlow, and a host of other great names as his stars. He was about to start a film with Ruth Chatterton.

Goulding was about five feet ten, of square stocky build, had sandy hair and a broken nose spread halfway across his face. About forty, a man of enduring charm, I owe more to him than to anyone else in the business.

Goulding was wearing the Goulding uniform: sweat shirt, silk handkerchief around his neck, a blue blazer and white slacks turned up at the bottoms displaying highly polished loafers. He laughed with a deep rumble when he heard from Frank Lloyd about my arrival on *Norfolk*.

"Ever done any acting?" he asked.

"None to speak of."

"Good. I'm looking for a new face to play the drunken, dissolute, younger brother of Chatterton. Will you make a test for me tomorrow?"

I thought it better with this wonderful opportunity being dangled before me to leave nothing unsaid that ought to be said, so I told him about my abortive trip to central casting a few days before.

"No problem," said Goulding, "you don't need any permit to make a test. If it works out, the studio will arrange things."

"What do I have to do?"

"Just be yourself . . . Harry Bouquet, the test director, will make it. He'll give you something easy to do." Goulding then invited me to his home for dinner. He was married to the famous dancer Marjorie Moss.

After dinner when I made a move to go home, Goulding and Marjorie would have none of it.

"Why?" they asked.

"To sleep, shave and change."

"You can sleep and shave here," said Goulding, "but I want that test made exactly as you are now—in the dinner jacket."

The next morning at 8:30 A.M. I presented myself to Harry Bouquet on Stage 29. I had been painted a strange yellow ochre by Bill Tuttle in the makeup department, and my eyes and lips had been made up like a Piccadilly tart—I felt ridiculous.

Harry Bouquet, a frustrated man, was in a hurry. "Christ," he said, "I've got six of these goddamned things to get through by lunchtime; waddaya gonna do?"

"Mr. Goulding said you'd give me something easy," I said.

"Jesus! Nothing's easy in this business! Okay, stand over there by that table while they light you."

The set was decorated as a New York apartment. Under the bright lights I could vaguely make out the outlines of the camera and about forty people. A man with evil-smelling fingers stuck a light meter immediately beneath my nose.

"Light 'em all," came a voice from the camera. "Okay, Harry, let's go."

Bouquet loomed out of the shadows.

"Okay, now start off facing the camera, then turn slowly when I tell you—wait a beat at each profile. Then wind up facing the camera again, got it?"

"Yes, sir."

"Turn 'em over."

I stood blinded by the lights and stared in the direction of the camera like a dog watching a snake.

"Turn slowly," said Bouquet, "hold the profile, goddammit. . . . Okay, now hold the full face . . . try to come alive, for Chrissake . . . tell us a funny story."

Out of my panic and my subconscious came a very old schoolboy limerick. I recited it:

> There once was an old man of Leeds
> Who swallowed a packet of seeds,
> Great tufts of grass
> Shot out of his arse
> And his cock was covered in weeds.

"Cut!!!"

Bouquet loomed up again. "Whattayou trying to do, for Chrissake? Get me fired? Everyone sees these things . . . L. B. Mayer . . . Mannix, the whole bunch."

He softened and smiled. "Okay, kid, now relax, we'll pick it up from there . . . think of some little story. When you're ready, tell me and we'll shoot it . . . clean it up though, will ya?"

Finally, I recounted a story that had happened to Tommy Phipps when he first went into an automat. Not knowing how it worked, he put five cents in the slot machine for a cup of coffee and collected a jet of hot fluid in the fly buttons. Later somebody ate his sandwich and somebody else dunked his doughnut in the coffee he had finally managed to collect in a cup.

I had laughed when Tommy told it, and there was, I thought, quite a gratifying reaction when I had finished this homely little tale.

The next day, Goulding called me and told me to meet him at his office.

"That test was really pretty bad—except for the natural bit when you told the limerick. Except for that, you were all frozen up. You won't get the part this time. . . . L. B. wants Louis Hayward anyway . . . but I think you can make it and I'm going to help you. I'll be through with my picture in about twelve weeks. Till that's over, I can do nothing. Call me in three months and we'll see what can be done."

Al Hall was Mae West's director, and she was about to start a picture, *Going to Town,* at Paramount. Goulding told Hall about me. Hall got hold of my test and a week later I got a call from the Paramount casting office. Mae West would like to interview me as her possible leading man.

I was welcomed at Paramount almost with eagerness. Anybody Mae West might want, they might want too, so before I was even seen by Miss West, I found myself being asked if I would be interested in a seven-year contract with options. Did I have a work permit?

"No."

"Never mind, we can fix that."

I was ushered into a huge office, and seated behind a Mussolini-type desk was a small round platinum-blond woman flanked on one side by a large American-Irish manager and on the other by Al Hall.

She never spoke. The men asked various questions. Then, after a whispered conversation Al Hall said, "Would you mind taking off your coat?"

"Now turn around please."

More whispers, then the manager spoke. "Who is your agent?"

"I don't have one."

Incredulous looks were passed. "We'd like to see you again. Please be sure that casting knows where you are."

The men rose and shook hands cordially, Mae West said nothing. She was munching something.

The next day, I had an urgent call from the Paramount casting office. I also had a visitor. A pale-faced man in a dark suit was waiting for me in the hotel lobby.

"I'm from United States Immigration Service, Mr. Niven. Now let me see. . . ." He had some documents. "You arrived in San Pedro four weeks ago. You asked for and were granted a ten days' visitor's visa. You are, therefore, now in this country illegally. We also understand you are contemplating signing an employment contract with a U.S. firm, so you are about to break the law on a second count."

"What do I do?" I asked.

He was a kind man but a tired one. He must have been through this a thousand times. His voice was weary.

"You have twenty-four hours to be off United States territory. You understand that, don't you?"

"Yes."

"Then sign this."

I glanced at a mimeographed slip. It was a statement admitting that I had been told to leave and that I understood the dire penalties involved if I did not comply.

"Where the hell do I go?"

"That's your problem, son. If you want to work in this country, you must get a resident alien visa. So long now."

Al Weingand advised me, and that afternoon I boarded a train that clanked and bumped for hours through a sandstorm to the border post of Calexico. There I left the United States and walked on foot into Mexico.

Mexicali may be a thriving metropolis by now. I hope it is, for its own sake. In late 1934, it was the most awful dump I had ever seen. A single dirt road ran through the center of the small township and petered out at each end into dry brown hills. In the center of the town there was one hotel, a few broken-down lodging houses, a grocery store that must have been the official breeding ground for all the flies in northern Mexico and one small clean-looking house, the American Consulate.

The American consul was a busy man, mostly because he had to cope with the problems and grievances of the sad daily flow of underpaid Mexicans who crossed the border to be driven in stinking buses to work crippling hours picking fruit, cotton and vegetables in the Imperial Valley.

He advised me kindly that he would be able to arrange a visa for me as a resident alien in the United States but first I must produce my birth certificate and a copy of my police record from Scotland Yard.

I took a room for a dollar a night in a loathsome lodging house and sent my sister, Grizel, a cable: "SEND BIRTH CERTIFICATE IMMEDIATELY."

She got the cable two weeks later when she returned from a trip to Spain. She did not distinguish herself by her reply: "WHOSE BIRTH CERTIFICATE?" I really had to sweat it out—there was little transatlantic air mail in those days and most of that went by ship. The mail service to Mexicali via Mexico City must have gone by donkey. My little pile of money was dwindling alarmingly, but many Americans came to Mexicali to hunt quail and other game in the surrounding brown hills. I became the "gun man" in the only moderately clean bar in the town and in exchange for chile or tortillas, I cleaned and polished the guns while their owners drank and boasted. Sometimes I was given a tip. I never refused.

It was just after New Year's Day, 1935, when I triumphantly presented myself at the U.S. border at Calexico. In my hand was my resident alien visa—my permit to work.

I jumped trucks back to Los Angeles. Al Weingand let me have my old room back and manfully swallowed the difficulties of payment.

I telephoned Goulding, but he had finished his picture and gone to New York. Mae West, I learned, was halfway through her picture with an English actor called Paul Cavanaugh playing opposite her.

I visited central casting and, after an agonizing wait of several days, was finally accepted and enrolled as "Anglo-Saxon Type No. 2008."

Such was the efficiency of central casting that the first call I got to work as a professional actor was as a Mexican.

Los Angeles is one of the largest cities in area in the world. The film studios are mostly strategically placed in faraway suburbs miles from its center.

Universal Studios is in the San Fernando Valley. I was told to be there at 5 A.M. The Auburn broke down the night before, so I started a zigzag journey across the city by streetcar at 3 A.M.

Once at the studios, I was handed a chit through a small window and instructed to report to wardrobe. There I waited in line, showed my chit which was stamped, and was issued with a baggy white suit, a large sombrero, some sandals and a blanket.

I changed in a huge barnlike dressing room. Other "Mexicans" were putting on their outfits. "Indians" were also preparing themselves and honest townsfolk were getting into tailcoats, top hats and bowlers. The women extras were dressing in an adjacent barn.

I followed my fellow "Mexicans" to the makeup department and once more stood in line. While those, including myself, who had fair skins had our faces and hands and feet sprayed with a brown mixture from a spray gun, on some of us they glued mustaches. The "Indians" lined up opposite were being similarly treated all over their bodies with a reddish color. Somewhere the Chinese were getting it in yellow.

There was not much happy chatter, I noticed.

At six thirty, we were all marshaled by an assistant director and loaded into buses for a one-hour drive to a remote movie ranch where the permanent Western town had been erected. There we were positioned by other assistants and told when to move slowly, when to scatter in alarm, etc., etc. The cowboy star, whoever he was, appeared, and at eight o'clock sharp shooting started. The director's name was Aubrey Scotto. He did not bother with us; we were pushed around all day by a harassed assistant.

At one o'clock we were given a cardboard box and told we had half an hour to eat. The contents consisted of a piece of chicken fried in batter, some cookies, an orange and a small carton of milk. After lunch we resumed shooting till the sun became too low and its light too feeble to continue.

There had been a lot of pushing and pulling by the extras during the filming of the last scene, it being essential to be "established" so that you would automatically be called back the following day.

Back at the studios, I waited my turn to wash the make-up off in a basin. When I handed in my mustache and clothing, my chit was stamped again; then a last long wait at the cashier's office to present my chit and be paid.

I was lucky enough to get a lift back to Hollywood from a group who lived there, but even so, it was ten o'clock before I sat down on a stool in the drugstore for the "50-cent Blue-Plate Special." My salary for my first day as a professional actor amounted to $2.50.

My fellow extras, I discovered during the new few weeks, fell into two distinct categories. There were the professional "crowd artists" and the actors who were "would-be stars."

The professionals were content to remain extras. They had no acting ambitions. They worked all the angles and were not above slipping a percentage of their daily salaries to unscrupulous assistant directors to guarantee being called the next day. Among these "professionals" could be counted the specialists such as the mounted extras who worked almost exclusively in Westerns and the dress extras. The latter group were much more highly paid, getting as much as twenty dollars a day because they provided their own modern wardrobe for every occasion, including evening dress for the women, white tie and tails for the men, beach outfits, city outfits, and the correct clothes for race meetings, football games, fox hunting and graduation days.

The acknowledged leaders of the professional dress extras were two elderly English people, Mrs. Wicks and a white-mustached ex-Indian Army man known as Major.

This couple were in great demand, lending dignity and refinement to the drabbest pictures. They had their own little coterie of friends, and sitting in full evening dress, they all played bridge together from morning to night.

There were a few younger professional dress extras also totally devoid of acting ambition and perfectly content to put on their smart clothes and work two or three days a week. Stuart Hall was one of these. Born in Cyprus, he had been brought to California as a child and had drifted into the movies. Stuart was a striking-looking man of my age. He was constantly being offered small speaking parts; he always refused them.

I did not have the finances to set myself up as a dress extra, but Stuart became a good friend and if we were called to the same studio, he always gave me a lift.

The would-be stars were almost exclusively in the dress-extra category because it was there that one got placed in the foreground with a chance of being noticed, and people in this group were occasionally singled out to say a line or play a small bit. At night they went to acting schools or formed small theater groups. The studios sent talent scouts to cover these showcases. Unless you were a big star brought out specially from Broadway, the only door into Hollywood was within Hollywood itself.

These were the golden days. The movie business was booming. Hundreds of films were being made each year and there was little competition in the entertainment world. Television had not been heard of. Night football and night baseball were in the future. Nobody played bingo or went bowling.

This was the era of the great stars. The studios had not yet been emasculated by the Supreme Court in antitrust suits and the newspapers still had several pages each day devoted to nothing but Hollywood news and gossip.

The studios looked ahead and carefully built up their stables of favorites.

When I worked in crowds at Metro-Goldwyn-Mayer, I used to stare in awe at the names on the dressing-room doors: Garbo, Cable, Norma Shearer, Jean Harlow, Joan Crawford, W. C. Fields, Wallace Beery, Spencer Tracy, Hedy Lamarr, William Powell, Myrna Loy, Luise Rainer, Robert Montgomery, Lionel Barrymore, John Barrymore, Charles Laughton.

The supporting actors were a powerful lot too. Frank Morgan, Louis Calhern, Robert Young, Franchot Tone, Reginald Owen, Lewis Stone, H. B. Warner. And the "ba-bies," some of them doing their school work in little canvas cubicles on the sound stages so many hours each day by California law: Elizabeth Taylor, Mickey Rooney, Lana Turner, Judy Garland and Ava Gardner. All those under contract to one studio at the same time!

Other studios had their stables too. James Cagney, Pat O'Brien, Edward G. Robinson and Bette Davis were at Warners. Gary Cooper, Charles Boyer, Claudette Colbert and Marlene Dietrich at Paramount, while Fred Astaire,

Ginger Rogers and Cary Grant reigned at RKO.

Small wonder that young people with stars in their eyes flocked to Hollywood from all parts of the world. There was hardly a beauty contest winner anywhere who didn't hopefully book a one-way ticket.

Small wonder . . . outside central casting:

> DON'T TRY TO BECOME AN ACTOR
> FOR EVERY ONE WE EMPLOY,
> WE TURN AWAY A THOUSAND.

And small wonder that behind cosmetic counters, serving as carhops and waitresses, selling theater tickets, swimsuits, ice creams, or their bodies, were the most beautiful girls in the world.

I soon got the feel of it and was able to take shortcuts. Friends among the extras tipped me off about jobs that might be coming up, and riding very much with the Sandhurst "forward seat," I worked in a number of Westerns.

I got to know a few assistant directors and they put me on their personal lists. I also made the rounds of all the studio casting offices when the Auburn was in the mood.

Once or twice a week, I worked as deckhand on a swordfish boat operating out of Balboa.

Chet Liebert had a 45-foot charter boat rigged up for marlin fishing with rod and line from the stern and a 10-foot spear platform forward for tackling the giant broadbill. He was a dour, rather unpleasant man but a wonderful fisherman. He found it hard to keep deckhands.

During the week he went for the broadbill—monsters running to 1,400 pounds—and weekends he took sports fishermen hunting the marlin.

The broadbill, though selling well in the market, were a bore to catch. The method was to spot the sickle-shaped fin when the fish were lying on the surface. Chet said they came up for a couple of hours a day to sleep. Then switching off the engines to glide up from behind and from the spear platform, they planted the "lily head" harpoon just behind the head. The harpoon pole was detachable, but the "lily head" was spliced to several hundred fathoms of thick line. At the end of this was an empty oil drum. When the broadbill was hit, it would immediately "sound," finally taking the oil drum down with it.

After that, it was a question of waiting for the poor brute to exhaust itself fighting against the upward pull of the air in the drum, then gaffing it, tying a rope around its tail, and heaving it aboard—a backbreaking job.

Spearing from the end of a narrow platform that could be rising and falling in the big Pacific swells was a highly skilled job, and the risk of getting a foot caught in the hissing uncoiling line as the fish dived was ever present. If anything went wrong Liebert made life hell for the spearman. For the rest of the day, he would either pour out abuse or go into a black, muttering sulk, which was even more unnerving.

I enjoyed the marlin fishing much more. The charterers were usually nice businessmen, from Long Beach mostly. My job was to look after them, settle them in their swivel chairs and body harness, then bait their hooks by attaching a gutted flying fish. Trolling astern, the flying fish weaved and wriggled like a live thing.

Then I climbed the mast and looked for fins. Very suspicious feeders are marlin. Sometimes one would follow the bait for a mile or so, coloring up bright blue in the water with excitement, then come in for the strike when it would grab the bait and pinch it between its sword and lower jaw to kill it, then throw it out again. Liebert was expert. He knew just when to cut his motor and yell to the sportsman to pay off line so the flying fish would sink down deep followed by the marlin. This was when most fish were lost. We had to beg the man on the rod not to strike till the big fish had time to make up its mind to swallow. "COUNT TO HUNDRED!" Liebert would yell. "NOW HIT HIM HARD."

The singing line and the bending rod always thrilled me. Sometimes the sportsmen had to fight a big one for two or three hours. Once both rods had strikes at the same time and we lost both fish. Another time a fat oil executive became so exhausted and frustrated that when he had brought a beauty almost to gaff (my job) for the tenth time only to see it make another leaping, slashing run standing on its tail on top of the water, he stood up, unhooked rod and reel from his harness, and shouted after the disappearing fish, "If you want it that bad . . . take the goddamned thing!" He then threw two thousand dollars' worth of equipment into the sea.

Liebert was a poor companion but he was generous. He gave me ten dollars a day, more if we had fish to sell, and allowed me to keep my tips. I enjoyed the fishing more than the filming.

I don't believe this is one of the thoughts of Chairman Mao, but breaks, good or bad, do come when you least expect them.

I had been doing a fruitless round of the studio casting offices and my last port of call was the United Artists Studio on Santa Monica Boulevard. "Nothing just now, call next week. . . ." So that the sanctity of the studio could be preserved, the entrance to the casting office was separated from the main gate by a twelve-foot high wall of wire netting. I was walking out again when I was hailed from a large limousine on the other side of the cage. "Hi! How's the golf?" It was the great Douglas Fairbanks himself. He never forgot a face, but he had the greatest difficulty in coming up with a name to match it.

Soon I was on his side of the barricade and setting him right that I was not Bobby Sweeny. He asked what I was doing in Hollywood and I told him. He thought for a moment and said kindly, "Gee, I hope you make it. . . . I'm here with Sylvia at the beach house and we'd love to see you anytime. I'd like to take you to play at Bel Air—it's a great course. Come around, I mean it, any time, but please don't ask me to help you with your career."

This was the completely honest expression of a completely honest man and a breath of fresh air in a place where the empty promise was the easy way out.

"Now," he said, "I'm going to take a steam. Come on in and join me."

Actually, I would have preferred the offer of a good hot meal, but I gratefully tagged along. He greeted everyone he passed with a wide smile and "Hi! How are you?" It was obvious that he was greatly loved but he was never quite sure who was loving him.

Inside the steam room, I was introduced to various mist-shrouded figures and I found myself sitting stark-naked on a marble slab between Darryl Zanuck, the head of Twentieth Century, a new thrusting company which he was just forming, and Joe Schenck, his partner. Opposite sat Charlie Chaplin and Sid Grauman, a famous theater owner. Present too were Bill Goetz, another associate of Zanuck's,

Lew Schreiber, his casting director, Bill Dover, Sam the Barber and Aidan Roark.

The sight and proximity of these great men, combined with the intense heat, was almost too much for me, but I decided to sit there if it took all night. It might lead to something. They were used to these steam baths. I wasn't. After ten minutes, my lungs felt scalded and my head was spinning.

Fairbanks, above all, loved jokes of any sort—funny jokes, practical jokes, any jokes. He had, of course, caught on that I was practically broke, so he couldn't resist saying, "Oh, Niven, what are you planning this winter? Playing polo or bringing the yacht around?"

"Polo . . . polo," I croaked and made for the exit. Sam the Barber grabbed me before I fell to the marble floor and put me forcibly into the ice-cold plunge. I was reviving when the others came out of the steam room.

"Doug says you played for the British Army," said Zanuck.

"Well, I played a bit in Malta," I said.

"Come and play a few chukkas on Sunday. We'll have a good game."

"Er . . . my clothes haven't arrived yet, I'm afraid."

"Aidan here will fix you up."

Aidan Roark was a ten-goal international. He and his brother, Pat, both played for Great Britain. Now he was employed by Zanuck in some capacity and organized Zanuck's polo team. A quiet, dark-haired, olive-skinned Irishman, he looked more like a South American. I decided to tell him the truth, and in a corner, I explained my limitations.

"Don't worry about it—I'll lend you all the stuff you need. Just play a couple of chukkas—you'll have fun."

So it was arranged. I was to play polo at the Uplifters Club the following Sunday afternoon with Darryl Zanuck! How many two-dollar-and-fifty-cent extras were getting that break?

On the fateful day, Aidan Roark lent me some jodhpurs that were much too tight and drove me to the ground. The first thing that worried me was when I noticed that the stands were full of people. Douglas Fairbanks and the gorgeous Sylvia Ashley were in a box. The second thing which unnerved me more was the sight of the other players.

Among them were "Big Boy" Williams, a formidable performer, Elmer Boeseke and Cecil Smith, both ten-goal internationals. The final thing—and this nearly completed my disintegration—was the sight of Saint George.

Saint George was a white Arab stallion. He bit savagely at everything in sight, and at that moment a groom was struggling to put him into a muzzle.

"You can play Saint George," said Aidan. "Play him in the first and fourth chukkas. It's only a pickup game. You play at number one and I'll hit the ball up to you ... Mark Darryl, he's playing back on the other team ... wear the red vest."

The bell went. It was a nightmare. I didn't know who was playing in which position on what team. Those great experts were hitting the ball like a rocket from every direction, but during that first chukka, I was far too busy stopping Saint George from leaving the ground altogether to care. When Aidan passed the ball up to me, I made vague flourishes at it with my stick but quickly needed both hands again to control the brute. It was during one of these mad dashes that Saint George kicked a goal.

Zanuck, I tried to cover but generally passed him at high speed without making contact.

At the end of the first chukka, Aidan was laughing so much he could hardly change ponies.

"Come back in for the fourth one ... you'll find him easier now he's worked some of it off."

I toyed with the idea of slinking from the ground, but I still hoped that I might impress Zanuck and further my movie career, so I waited apprehensively for my next appearance. My riding muscles being suddenly forced into violent action were now reacting and causing me to shake like a leaf. This did not go unnoticed by Saint George when I mounted him once more for the fourth chukka.

I was determined to make my mark on Zanuck, and I stayed as close to him as Saint George would let me. I even hit the ball a couple of times, which encouraged me enormously. The experts continued to charge about, playing a spectacular game, shouting oaths and instructions at each other, but Aidan, I suspected, had deliberately stopped sending the ball up to me. It all seemed more peaceful.

Suddenly, "Big Boy" Williams, renowned as one of the longest hitters in the game, connected from the far end of the ground and the ball sailed over Zanuck's head toward the goal. Zanuck turned fast and galloped off to backhand it away. I chased after him to try and ride him off the line, and if miracles could happen, to score. The two of us were now the focal point of all eyes. People were shouting and clods of earth were flying up into my face from Zanuck's pony's hooves.

Saint George was the faster and we gained inexorably.

As we drew almost level and I was getting into position to bump Zanuck off the line of the ball, Saint George leaned forward and through his muzzle sank his teeth into the seat of Zanuck's breeches. Zanuck roared with alarm and pain, and in the ensuing shambles his pony trod on the ball. It became embedded in the turf. I caught a momentary glimpse of the white mushroom top passing below us, and trying to ignore the embarrassing action at the front end of my steed, I made a vague swipe at it as it fell astern. I missed and my stick passed beneath Zanuck's pony's tail. His mount being extremely sensitive in that area, with a maidenly reaction, clamped its tail to its behind. The head of my stick was thus imprisoned. I was attached by a leather thong around my wrist to the other end of the stick. Saint George had a firm grip on Zanuck's buttocks and our horrible triangle galloped past the stands.

Zanuck was good about it. I was not invited to play polo with him again, but he mentions it to this day when I see him.

With the help of Saint George, I must, after all, have made my mark.

Goulding came back from New York and kept his word . . . he really tried to help me.

"You must stop being an extra and have a good agent," he said.

He talked to Bill Hawks, an important man in that line, and I found myself with a representative. It was vitally important to "have something on film" so I was delighted when I was given tests for various roles. I did tests with Mady Christians, with Elizabeth Allan and Claudette Colbert, but I never landed the parts I was being tested for.

Three men did the same tests on the same day with Claudette Colbert for *The Gilded Lily*—a scene on a park bench complete with popcorn and pigeons. The other two both got contracts at Paramount, but nothing happened to me . . . their names were Fred MacMurray and Ray Milland. I was a new face and the lifeblood of movies is new faces. I also had a good agent and a powerful director pushing me; furthermore, I was meeting the people who mattered. I was interviewed and tested for dozens of roles at all the major studios. I had the contacts and the chances, no one could have had more, but I was a hopeless amateur and in front of the camera, I congealed with nerves.

As the weeks went by, I changed from being "a new face" to being "a face that's been around and hasn't made it." Invitations to the houses of the great became fewer. Tests no longer came my way and it began to dawn on me that after all, it might all be beyond my reach.

Irving Thalberg had been the boy genius of Hollywood. Now just in his mid-thirties, he was the undisputed master producer of Metro-Goldwyn-Mayer. Married to the beautiful Norma Shearer, they were the golden couple of Hollywood.

Production on his epic *Mutiny on the Bounty* was getting under way, and having been told by Goulding of my bizarre connection with his ship, Thalberg decided that, as an additional drop in the publicity bucket, it might be worthwhile to sign me up as one of the nonspeaking mutineers.

He happened to phrase it more glamorously at some Friday night gathering: "I'm thinking of signing David Niven to a contract on Monday."

That did it. The word went around. If the great Irving Thalberg was going to put me under contract, then I must be worth having. Three studios sent people looking for me, but I was out chasing marlin. When I got back on Sunday night, Al Weingand gave me a sheaf of messages. I called Goulding and told him of the sudden activity. He and Bill Hawks came over to the hotel and held a council of war. Then Goulding fetched my original and only relaxed test from the M-G-M studios vault, put it in his car, and went directly to the house of Samuel Goldwyn, Hollywood's legendary and most successful independent producer.

Goldwyn ran the test there and then while Frances, his wife, listened sympathetically to Goulding's sales talk.

On Monday morning, Goldwyn sent for me. He sat behind a huge desk in a tastefully furnished office. He was almost entirely bald, very well dressed, with small intense eyes set in a brown face. He was about fifty and looked extremely fit. He spoke without smiling in a strangely high-pitched voice.

"I'm giving you a seven-year contract," he said. "I'll pay you very little, and I won't put you in a Goldwyn picture till you've learned your job. Now you have a base. Go out and tell the studios you're under contract to Goldwyn, do anything they offer you, get experience, work hard, and in a year or so, if you're any good, I'll give you a role."

I was ushered out in a daze and taken to see the head of publicity—Jock Lawrence, a dynamo.

"Jesus," said Jock, "you realize what a break you've got? Mr. Goldwyn never signs unknowns. He only has three people under contract—Eddie Cantor, Anna Sten and Ronald Colman. Colman's leaving next month and he's taking on Gary Cooper and Joel McCrea."

He looked at me quizzically. "What do you think of Mr. Goldwyn?"

"He didn't give me time," I said. "I was in and out of there in about two minutes."

"He's the greatest," said Lawrence. "All his pictures are hits and he is the only producer in Hollywood who uses his own money—Mr. Goldwyn never goes to the banks—he's the greatest, all right, but, boy, can he be rough sometimes. Now, he's told me to build you up, so let's hear all about you."

I gave Jock Lawrence a brief résumé of my life so far while he made notes.

"Mother?"

"French."

"Good, we can use that."

"Father?"

"Killed in the war."

"GREAT! What rank?"

"Lieutenant."

"Jesus, that's terrible! We'd better make him a general."

I was taken to see Reeves Espy, Goldwyn's assistant, a gentle, intelligent man who explained that my contract started at a hundred dollars a week for the first two years, with twelve weeks' layoff each year. During the first two years, Goldwyn had an option every three months to terminate the contract. In the third year, a little more money and fewer options, and so on for seven years. I hardly listened . . . it was all too unbelievable. I was taken to see Bob

McIntyre, the production manager, and Lola Unger, his assistant. Lola said, "We have a nice dressing room for you," and gave me a key. "We'll put your name on the door tomorrow."

I found my little cubbyhole and sat there in a wicker chair for a long time. Then I wandered about the studio, the same United Artists Studio where Fairbanks had invited me to take a steam.

I wandered over by the main gate. Near it was a familiar high wire fence. On the other side was a shuffling line of extras inquiring for work at the casting office.

The Auburn had finally collapsed altogether, so I walked to the hotel and told Al Weingand the good news. He was genuinely overjoyed, but he also said, "Thank Christ, now you can pay your goddamned bill!"

Together we crossed Hollywood Boulevard to the showroom of the Ford Motor Company. The new models were in the window and priced at just under five hundred dollars. I told the snooty salesman I had just signed a seven-year contract with Samuel Goldwyn, and at the magic name, he became, immediately, deferential.

"I'll take that one." I said, pointing. He gave me some forms to sign to do with monthly payments. Then he pulled a chain, the whole window moved aside, and I drove out into my Brave New World and took Goulding and Al Weingand to lunch.

11

Goldwyn signs unknown! That was the headline of super-powerful columnist Louella Parsons the next morning. The Hollywood *Reporter* and *Daily Variety, the twin bibles of the industry,* similarly alerted their readers to this earth-shaking occurrence.

In my new Ford, I drove out to bask in the congratulations of the Belzer-Young family.

Within a week I had evacuated from Al Weingand's haven and found myself a tiny, brown cuckoo clock of a chalet at the top of North Vista Street, with a view looking over the whole of the Los Angeles Basin. I shared the chalet with several scorpions and black-widow spiders and a garage with the madam of a well-known whorehouse situated immediately below me.

I joined the Hollywood Cricket Club.

There were twenty-two cricket clubs in California at that time. The Hollywood Cricket Club was deservedly the most famous, and crashes were frequent on Sunset Boulevard on Sunday afternoons when amazed local drivers became distracted by the sight of white flannel trousers and blazers on the football ground of UCLA.

Hollywood was going through a "British period," and the studios were indulging themselves with such epics as *Mutiny on the Bounty, David Copperfield, National Velvet, Bengal Lancers, Edwin Drood, Disraeli, Lloyds of London* and *Sherlock Holmes . . .* It was a bonanza for the British character actors. The captain of the Hollywood Cricket Club was the redoubtable, craggy C. Aubrey Smith. A famous county cricketer, he had a penchant for suddenly nipping out from behind the umpire and firing down his fast ball . . . He had been nicknamed 'Round-the-Corner Smith. His house on Mulholland Drive was called

The Round Corner; on his roof were three cricket stumps and a bat and ball serving as a weather vane.

Ernest Torrance and his wife, Elsie, were other leaders of the "British Colony." Henry Stephenson. E. E. Clive, Eric Blore and H. B. Warner were members. Later arrivals, Basil Rathbone and Nigel Bruce, were fiercely independent of the label "British Colony." Herbert Marshall spent all his time with Gloria Swanson and Reggie Gardiner with Hedy Lamarr, while aloof from it all, living the life of a hermit in his house at the end of Mound Street, was Ronnie Colman. There he entertained only his intimate circle: William Powell, Richard Barthelmess and Noll Gurney. Colman had just overcome an unhappy marriage and was trying not to fall in love with Benita Hume.

The hard-core "British Colony" took tea on Sundays at the Torrances' or the Aubrey Smiths'; the atmosphere was very like the Marsa Polo Club in Malta.

Nigel and Bunnie Bruce became, for me, the Norah and Lefty of Hollywood.

"Willie" Bruce, immortal as Doctor Watson in *Sherlock Holmes*, was fat and jovial and generous. Bunnie was thin and gay and generous. They both adored their two little girls, Pauline and Jennifer. They kept open house in an old Spanish-style mansion on Alpine Drive and happily spent every penny that Willie earned.

It was Willie who made me join the Hollywood Cricket Club. He was keen and had played first-class cricket before he collected eleven machine-gun bullets in his left leg at Cambrai. After the war he went on the stage and appeared often with Gerald du Maurier and Gladys Cooper. Once he was invited for the weekend to play country-house cricket at some ducal monstrosity.

He arrived the night before the match and was shown his room by the butler with that subtle mixture of alarm and condescension reserved exclusively for actors.

Out of his window, Willie saw the house party gathered around the duke, sitting under a giant yew tree; teacups and cucumber sandwiches were in evidence; and Willie shuddered.

Finally, he plucked up courage to go down and meet his host and fellow guests; but to put off the evil moment as long as possible, he made a long detour through the orchards and greenhouses. There he came across a small peach tree bearing a solitary peach. He ate it and continued on his way to the giant yew. Nobody, including the duke, took the slightest notice of him, so he huddled miserably at the back of the group and toyed with a piece of fruitcake. The butler appeared and announced, "The gentlemen of the press are here, Your Grace." This caused considerable excitement and an anticipatory buzz rose. Willie tapped his nearest neighbor. "What's going on?"

"Oh, haven't you heard? The duke is the first man in the world to succeed in growing a full-sized peach on a miniature tree."

Willie tiptoed away, packed, and left before dinner.

Having a highly publicized contract with Goldwyn made it obvious that I was not about to parlay an invitation to dinner or tennis into an embarrassing hint for work. New doors were ajar. I played tennis with Constance Bennett and Gilbert Roland, with Dolores del Rio and Cedric Gibbons, golf with Jean Harlow and William Powell. When Garbo was not nursing him, I spent sad afternoons with John Gilbert, who was fighting a losing battle with the bottle in his hilltop hideaway. The Thalbergs, Douglas Fairbanks and Sylvia became close friends; so did Merle Oberon of unbeatable beauty. Ronald Colman slowly made me persona grata at Mound Street, and when Fifi Fell called from New York insisting that I contact Phyllis Astaire, a lasting bond was formed with Phyllis and Fred.

John McClain suddenly arrived from the East with a contract to write scripts for RKO, and my cup overflowed.

My social life was picking up nicely, but my professional career was not in top gear. My first speaking part was at Paramount in *Without Regret*. Elissa Landi was the star and I said, "Good-bye, my dear," to her on a station platform.

Howard Hawks produced *The Barbary Coast* with Miriam Hopkins; I got the part of a Cockney sailor, with drooping mustache.

"Orl rite, I'll go," I said, and was thrown out of the window of a brothel in San Francisco and into the mud. Miriam Hopkins, Joel McCrea, Walter Brennan, thirty vigilantes and some donkeys walked over the top of me.

I was employed by Woody Van Dyke to play a whole

scene with Jeanette MacDonald in *Rose Marie* at M-G-M. She and Nelson Eddy were the stars, and a lanky young actor from New York was making his debut in the same picture. James Stewart was his name.

This looked better—a whole scene in a big important musical!

It was a short piece, so I was not given a complete script, just a couple of sides with my stuff on it. It took place in a theater in Toronto. Jeanette MacDonald had just come off the stage from singing some aria to a packed house and was rushing to the arms of Nelson Eddy, her lover in the Mounties, who was supposed to be waiting in the dressing room.

She flung open the door expectantly and all she found was a top hat protruding above a screen. Underneath the hat was a drunken stage-door Johnny (me) who, after a short altercation, was forcibly removed.

Van Dyke seemed happy enough with my efforts and by eleven o'clock I was out of the studio.

He was a very fast worker. M-G-M sent me two tickets to the preview and I took a girlfriend along.

"What's the story?" she asked.

"I've no idea, but when they get to Toronto, that's me after the song—a top hat behind a screen. I'll tell you when it's coming." We settled back expectantly.

The picture trailed on, and finally it was clear that the song in Toronto was over and Jeanette MacDonald was heading for her dressing room.

"Here I come," I whispered. The girl held my hand.

"There! There's the hat—this is me!!"

The hat moved and a perfectly strange man stepped out from behind the screen and played my scene.

Apparently, I had been so bad that they had got rid of me early and sent for another actor to come and do it correctly. Van Dyke was a very fast worker.

My next try was at Columbia where I was hired to act the part of Leo, a poet, in *A Feather in Her Hat* starring Ruth Chatterton. Al Santell was the director and I have blessed him forever. I had only one scene, but it was a long and difficult one taking place during a big party sequence.

The party had been in full swing for some time with much buildup toward the arrival of Leo, the poet.

"I *wish* Leo would come, he'll liven it up," etc., etc.

Finally, all gaiety and light, I had to burst in through a door, and for at least three minutes I was single-handedly supposed to raise the whole tempo of the party, with a wisecrack here and a kiss there. The scene was in a continuous shot with the camera on a rail moving with me group to group.

The extras on the set, some hundred or so, were dress extras. Stuart Hall was there full of encouragement, but most of the others were of the highly critical "would-be star" category. It was an appallingly difficult scene and I hadn't slept all night from anxiety.

I didn't own the tailcoat I needed for the occasion, so Herbert Marshall lent me his. "Bart" Marshall had lost a leg on the Somme, so for some technical reason his fly buttons did up the wrong way, like a woman's coat.

I was shaking so badly in the wardrobe department that a seamstress had to do my flies up for me with a button hook.

I waited around in an agony of apprehension till, finally, I was sent for to do the scene. Santell was kindness and patience itself and walked me gently through many rehearsals, but I still couldn't relax.

This was my big chance but I was rigid with terror.

"Okay, Dave, let's take a crack at it. Do it just like that last rehearsal—that was just fine."

Miserable and sweating, I stood outside the door and listened to the happy sounds of the party inside. After an eternity, a red light glowed—my signal to burst in.

I did. My toe caught in the track and I nearly fell over. I bumped a dowager in a chair; I spilled somebody else's drink and said all the wrong lines to the wrong people, but, somehow, I staggered through to the end.

Everyone on the set applauded.

I couldn't believe my ears. Santell rushed up.

"Hey, that's great, Dave! Just what I wanted . . . perfect! Now we have that one in the can, we'll just take another for safety. . . . Oh, this time don't hit the track, and watch out for the old dame's chair . . . one or two little changes . . . just clean it up a little . . . but it's great and we have it already—this one's a luxury."

I stood outside the door looking at that red light . . . I

couldn't wait for it to go on. "This is easy," I thought, "this is fun!"

I sailed through the second take, loving every minute of it, completely relaxed.

At the end of the day, Stuart Hall and I were celebrating in a bar; he told me the secret. Santell had addressed the whole set while I had been shivering and shaking in my dressing room.

"The boy who's playing Leo—this is his first big scene in a picture and we've all got to help him loosen up. After the first take, however bad he is, I want you all to applaud, then I'll put some film in the camera."

Santell is in my private Hall of Fame.

"Go get yourself experience," Goldwyn had said, so I went to the Pasadena Playhouse. This was by far the most highly regarded of all the showcases and almost impossible to break into. The magic name of Goldwyn opened the door.

I was welcomed by Gilmore Brown, the playhouse director, and given a minute part in *Wedding*.

It was all very arty. The curtain was up when the audience arrived. It never came down between acts and it remained up when they left.

I was one of the guests. There were sixty others and most of them were queer. One with whom I shared a cubicle dressing room was different. He was an ex-footballer from Notre Dame with a forgettable Polish name. When last heard of, he was a dentist in Lansing, Michigan. He was a devotee of scotch whisky and had a large stock of a brand called Mist o' the Moors.

It tasted like rubbing alcohol. I think it was made in Japan.

My part was as follows: Early in Act I, I sauntered on, carrying a large bowl of punch. This was a very important prop as there was an urgent message for someone underneath it. I arranged the bowl carefully on the table and sauntered off again.

Act II. I had to enter left, looking distracted, suddenly see offstage someone I was looking for, smile with relief, and exit hurriedly, right.

Act III. My big moment. I had a snatch of conversation with my footballer friend:

NIVEN: I tell you the King of Siam *does*.

F. F.: Well, I *know* the King of Siam . . . and I tell you he *doesn't*.

NIVEN: I see. (Exit.)

During the two weeks' rehearsal, I went to many parties in Hollywood, and without actually lying, I propagated the idea that I was starring in a play at the Pasadena Playhouse —good propaganda. . . . "Yes, I am opening with a very interesting girl at the playhouse next week. . . . I think she'll go a long way. . . ." That sort of thing, not lies really.

On opening night, thanks to the ever-present Mist o' the Moors, I was completely relaxed. When my moment came, I picked up my bowl of punch and wandered onstage.

I received a thunderous ovation.

In alarm I shielded my eyes from the footlights, an unforgivable thing to do, and saw that "Bart Marshall had brought a surprise party of about thirty people to witness my great star debut. I caught a glimpse of Gloria Swanson and Charles Laughton among other famous people filling the first three rows and tottered off the stage with the bowl of punch, thereby ripping irreparable holes in the plot.

Downstairs in our cubicle, the F.F. tried to calm me.

"Have a little Mist, Dave. Don't worry about 'em . . . screw 'em. . . ." He gave me a great umbrella stand full of the stuff.

Act II. I thought, "They mustn't see me," so I shot across the stage from left to right like a meteor.

Act III. And after several more calming draughts of Mist, I had changed considerably. "Many of these people," I said to the F. F., "have come from as far as Malibu to see me . . . let's go." He blinked and shook his head in a dazed way, then followed me meekly onstage for our snatch of conversation.

We swayed on and I led him by the arm right down to the footlights.

"Now look," I said, giving him an intimidating stare, "I don't want to impose my rather strong personality on your very dull brain . . . but I have it . . . on the very finest authority . . . straight from the horse's mouth . . . that the KING OF SIAM *DOES*."

The F. F. looked utterly stunned, then in an awed voice he said, "Jesus Christ!"

Gilmore Brown was waiting for us in the wings. "Get out of my theater, both of you."

Reactions to my performance were mixed.

"Bart" Marshall said he wouldn't have missed it for the world.

Charles Laughton gave me an angry lecture about "bastardizing my profession."

Goldwyn treated me to a mild dressing down. He had been pacified in advance by the news that the great Ernst Lubitsch had just seen my "relaxed" performance as Leo, the poet, and wanted me to start immediately at Paramount in a very good part in *Bluebeard's Eighth Wife* with Gary Cooper and Claudette Colbert.

Working with Lubitsch in the company of such professional experts and such privately wonderful human beings as Gary Cooper and Claudette Colbert was a joy that lasted for about three months. The screenplay was by another expert, Billy Wilder.

Lubitsch sat, like a little gnome, beside the camera, perched on a small stepladder, giggling and hugging himself at all his own wonderful inventiveness. A huge cigar was always in his mouth. He was patient, understanding and encouraging; what more could any actor ask?

I learned major lessons about playing comedy during that time and will forever remember a statement of his: "Nobody should try to play comedy unless they have a circus going on inside."

Thank You, Jeeves was the next. I was borrowed from Goldwyn by RKO to play Bertie Wooster, and the indelible Arthur Treacher played Jeeves. But it was a B picture . . . on the program a curtain raiser for the main feature. It was my first leading role, however. Virginia Field was the leading lady.

Sent for by Warner Brothers, where Michael Curtiz was testing actors for *The Charge of the Light Brigade*. Errol Flynn was the star—his second picture. His first had been a smash hit, *Captain Blood*. Now he was the big white hope of the studio.

Curtiz had a reputation for eating actors for breakfast. An ex-cavalry officer and very Prussian in his approach to subordinates, he was a daunting sight when I reported for work, outfitted in riding boots and breeches and carrying a whip.

I was testing for the part of Flynn's friend, destined for a sticky end in the Charge. The whole scenario was a loose adaption of the true story and the Charge itself took place on the North-West Frontier of India; but, no matter, those were the days when Hollywood was reshaping British history to conform to budgets and available locations. I was to play the test scene with Olivia de Havilland; so, I realized with dismay, were a dozen other hopeful young actors all dressed in exactly the same uniform as myself, all standing around and, a refinement of sadism, allowed to watch each other perform.

By the time the scene had been played half a dozen times and six actors curtly dismissed by Curtiz everything I had hoped to do had already been done. My mind was a blank when Curtiz, with heavy accent, called out, "Next man."

I was led out of the shadows by an assistant and introduced to Miss de Havilland and Curtiz. She smiled a tired resigned smile and shook hands. Curtiz said, "Where's your script?"

I said, "You mean the four pages I was given for the scene, Mr. Curtiz?"

"Yes, where is it?"

"Well," I said, hoping it was true, "I've learned it, Mr. Curtiz. I don't have it with me."

"I asked you *where* it is!"

"Well, it's in my dressing room at the other end of the studio."

"Run and get it," he shouted.

My uniform was thick and tight. It was 100° in the shade and the sound stage was not air-conditioned; also, after witnessing the efforts of the others, I reckoned I had no chance of getting the part anyway.

"You fucking well run and get it," I said.

His reaction was instantaneous: "Dismiss the others—this man gets the part."

We got along famously all through the picture. "That goddamned Sandhurst man," Mike called me and built up my part.

My friendship with Flynn dated from that picture. I had met him once or twice at Lili Damita's bungalow in the Garden of Allah and we had reacted to each other with wary distaste. Now he was married to Lili and we made a new appraisal of each other.

Flynn was a magnificent specimen of the rampant male. Outrageously good looking, he was also a great natural athlete who played tennis with Donald Budge and boxed with "Mushy" Callahan. The extras, among whom I had many old friends, disliked him intensely.

They were a rough lot, too, the toughest of the riders from Westerns, plus the stunt men who specialized in galloping falls. Flynn, they decided, had a swollen head, having made too big a success too soon. They were the 27th Lancers. Flynn was their commander. I was the second-in-command.

One day they were lined up on the parade ground of our fort, somewhere in the San Fernando Valley. Flynn and I were slightly in front of the others when one of the stunt men leaned forward with his lance, rubber-tipped to cut down accidents, and wriggled it in Flynn's charger's dock. The animal reared up and Flynn completed the perfect parabola and landed on his back.

Six hundred very muscular gentlemen roared with laughter.

Flynn picked himself up. "Which of you sons of bitches did that?"

"I did, sonny," said a huge gorilla of a man. "Want to make anything of it?"

"Yes, I do," said Flynn. "Get off your horse."

Nobody could stop it and the fight lasted a long time. At the end of it the gorilla lay flat on his back. After that everyone liked Errol much more.

Goldwyn decided that I was ripe to appear in one of his own superpictures and cast me as Captain Lockert in *Dodsworth* with Walter Huston and Ruth Chatterton. Walter had created the role on Broadway and had now moved to California. His son, John, then a scriptwriter, also worked on the picture. He and his father were wonderful to me; so was Ruth Chatterton. William Wyler, the director, was not.

Willie Wyler, as his record all too plainly shows, is one of the world's all-time great directors. Practically without exception, his films have been hugely successful, both critically and financially. He may have mellowed by now, but in 1936 he was a Jekyll-and-Hyde character.

Kind, fun and cozy at all other times, he became a fiend

the moment his bottom touched down in his director's chair.

Some directors, especially those touched by the Max Reinhardt school. believed in breaking actors down completely so that they became putty in their hands. As practiced by Willie. he even managed to reduce the experienced Ruth Chatterton to such a state that she slapped his face and locked herself in her dressing room.

I became a gibbering wreck.

Whenever I was working, it was perfectly normal for Willie to sit beneath the camera reading the Hollywood *Reporter* and not even look up till I had plowed through the scene a couple of dozen times. "Just do it again," he'd say, turning a page.

The picture was a big hit in spite of my wooden performance. I have only kept one review during my life. It is of *Dodsworth* and appeared in the Detroit *Free Press*:

> In this picture we were privileged to see the great Samuel Goldwyn's latest discovery—all we can say about this actor? is that he is tall, dark and not the slightest bit handsome.

It has the place of honor in my lavatory.

Irving and Norma. like all the top movie people, had a private projection room in their home.

One night Lubitsch brought down a print of *Bluebeard's Eighth Wife*, and they ran it after dinner for their friends.

I sat squirming with embarrassment throughout the showing, but after it was over. everyone, with one exception, was overly flattering and enthusiastic. Fairbanks and Sylvia, Merle, the Astaires. Paulette Goddard and Frederick Lonsdale all puffed me up most pleasantly. One guest sat silent in his chair. Finally, I could stand it no longer. "What did *you* think, Mr. Chaplin?"

His answer constituted the greatest advice to any beginner in my profession. "Don't be like the great majority of actors . . . don't just stand around waiting your turn to speak. LEARN TO LISTEN."

By the autumn of 1936 I was very much involved with a GBS (Great Big Star).

The GBS was doing a week of publicity in New York for her latest vehicle, and we had a rendezvous to meet there.

I made a side trip to see Lefty and Norah, by now bliss-fully happy in Little Orchard in Tyron, North Carolina.

Tommy Phipps was there and his highly talented sister, Joyce Grenfell, was over from England.

Lefty took me to see the local high school football games, and among the glorious colors of the fall, we rode along the foothill trails of the Smoky Mountains.

It was a wonderful few days and a most salutary contrast to the life I had been leading in Tinsel City, but I fear the lesson passed almost unnoticed and I hurried off to keep my tryst with the GBS in the St. Regis Hotel.

The GBS was gorgeous and quite adventurous. "Let's not fly back to California. Let's take the sleeper to Detroit, buy a Ford, and drive it out."

She bought the car. I drove, and the first night we spent together in Chicago.

She disguised her well-known face with a black wig and dark glasses and called herself Mrs. Thompson. In the lobby nobody recognized her. Although it was highly un-likely that anyone would recognize me, I went along with the game and called myself Mr. Thompson.

The desk clerk handed GBS a telegram. "For you, Mrs. Thompson."

I was mystified. "How could that happen?" I said.

"I promised Jock Lawrence I'd tell him exactly where we'll be all the way across in case the studio needs me ur-gently, then I can hop a plane."

She opened the envelope.

TELL NIVEN CALL GOLDWYN IMMEDIATELY
                    JOCK

"Forget it," said the GBS. "Call him tomorrow—it's too late now." We went to bed.

The next night we spent in Cedar Rapids, Iowa.

"Telegram for you, Mrs. Thompson," said the desk clerk.

TELL NIVEN CALL ME TONIGHT WITHOUT FAIL
                    GOLDWYN

We didn't want the idyll spoiled, even though the new signature gave me an eerie feeling of impending doom.

In North Platte, Nebraska, the wording was crisper:

> ASK NIVEN WHAT HE THINK'S HE'S DOING HAVE HIM
> CALL TONIGHT OR ELSE
> GOLDWYN

Still we pressed happily on across the country, and the telegrams became more alarming at each stop. The one at the Grand Canyon was very unattractive indeed:

> TELL NIVEN HE'S FIRED
> GOLDWYN

The GBS was made of stern stuff. "He can't do that," she said, "and anyway he wants me for two more pictures. We'll call him when we get to California—not before."

I was so besotted by the GBS that I even managed to enjoy the rest of the trip, except when we turned off the main road in the middle of New Mexico and got stuck in the desert at sunset.

Finally, the ten-day trip ended and we crossed the state line into California. From a motel in Needles, with great apprehension, I called Goldwyn.

"Do you know what you're doing, you stupid son of a bitch?" he yelled. "You're doing about a hundred and thirty-five years in jail. Ever heard of the Mann Act and taking women across state lines for immoral purposes? Think what Winchell would do to that girl, too, if he got the story—you're through I tell you . . . you're . . ."

His voice was pitched even higher than usual. The GBS leaned across the bedside table and grabbed the phone out of my hand.

"Sam, darling," she purred, "I've had a simply gorgeous time, so don't be angry with David . . . I'll explain it all to you when we get back tomorrow . . ." She motioned me to go out of the room and finished her conversation alone. When she found me later, she said, "Sam's sweet really. Everything's OK again, you've been reinstated."

The "actor's nightmare" is the role of Edgar in *Wuthering Heights*. Soon after I came back from my trip with the GBS, Goldwyn called me in and told me he had cast me to play it. "Laurence Olivier will play Heathcliff and Merle Oberon, Cathy," he said.

"But it's the most awful part ever written," I said, "and one of the most difficult; please don't make me do it."

"You'll have the best director in the business," said Goldwyn. "He'll make it easy for you."

"Who?"

"Willie Wyler."

I could not afford it, but I immediately opted to be put on suspension, but the combination of Edgar and Wyler was too daunting.

On paper, if a contract actor refused to work, he could not, of course, complain if his weekly salary was suspended, but what happened in practice was that not only was the actor suspended for the duration of the picture—four months for a big one—but the producer had the right to suspend him for half that amount of time again as a punishment; then a whole six months was added onto the end of the original contract In studios with unscrupulous managements that purposely gave actors assignments which they knew would be refused players were sometimes trapped for twelve or fifteen years working off a seven-year contract. Years later Olivia de Havilland fought this and took it all the way to the Supreme Court. She won, and thereafter, if someone refused to work, he didn't get paid, but it became illegal for the length of his contract to be altered without his consent.

Olivia struck a great blow for freedom and everyone in the industry should bless her, but she hardly ever worked in Hollywood again.

Goldwyn did not offer people roles in order to prolong their contracts, and he found it hard to understand my intransigence.

By now Flynn had separated from Lili Damita and I was looking for new quarters so together we rented Rosalind Russell's house, 601 North Linden Drive, and settled into a fairly ostentatious bachelor existence.

601 became a hotbed of fun and bad behavior, the booze flowed freely, the girls formed an ever-changing pattern, and after Flynn came back from a trip to North Africa, we went through a long period when we smoked or chewed kef.

Kef had strange effects on me: Sometimes everything seemed hilariously funny, sometimes I became quiet and introspective, sometimes I experienced pleasant imaginings or hallucinations. I got bored with it one day and just stopped taking it. Nowadays it is better known as marijuana.

Flynn had a more lucrative contract at Warners than I had with Goldwyn, so he paid the most rent and, consequently, had the big double bedroom. I was allowed to borrow it for special occasions.

One day after I had been on suspension for two or three weeks, Willie Wyler called me.

"Come and have dinner at Dave Chasen's," he said.

Over drinks he asked, "Tell me truly, why you don't want to play Edgar?"

"Because it is such an awful part," I said.

"It's not, you know," said Willie, "and you are one of the few people in the business who can make it better than it is."

Now that was pretty heady stuff coming from one of the great directors to someone with my minimal experience.

"There's something else, isn't there?" Willie said.

"Honestly, Willie, I love you. I love being here with you, but I was so bloody miserable working for you on *Dodsworth*—I just couldn't go through it again. You're a son of a bitch to work with."

Willie laughed. "I've changed," he said. "Come and play the part. It's a wonderful cast . . . it'll be a great picture and I'll make you great in it."

I weakened at once, of course.

"Okay, under one condition: that the night before I start work, you come and have dinner with me here, and I'll remind you that you've changed—that you're no longer a son of a bitch."

It was arranged.

I reported to the studio next day and did all the costume fittings and renewed my acquaintanceship with Laurence Olivier, who had arrived that morning from England.

Larry appeared with a fantastically beautiful kittenlike creature on his arm, Vivien Leigh.

Viv had come out to be with Larry during the shooting of our picture, and within a week of that day, she met David O. Selznick, was tested, and over the furious heads of all the big established female stars was handed the role of Scarlett O'Hara in *Gone with the Wind*.

The night before I was to start filming, Willie Wyler kept

his word. We had a good dinner at Chasen's and played ping-pong on the back patio.

As we bade each other good night, Willie laughed. "Don't worry, you'll have fun. . . . I'm no a son of a bitch anymore."

The shooting next day was on location in the San Fernando Valley. Goldwyn had reconstructed Wuthering Heights in rolling hills, and except for the fact that the heather of the moors was about four feet high, it looked wonderfully like Yorkshire. In the first scene, I had to drive up in a two-horse buggy with Merle looking very demure as Cathy at my side. Once I had stopped at exactly the right mark, the dialogue commenced. Wyler was up on a rostrum about fifty feet in the air, with the camera.

A few rehearsals to practice that tricky stop and we made the first take.

The horses halted just right.

Cathy: "Come in, Edgar, and have some tea."

Edgar: "As soon as I've put the horses away."

Wyler: "CUT! Just play it perfectly straight, David. This is not a comedy, you know."

After a long drive, breasting through the heather, we arrived back for the second take.

"Come in Edgar, and have some tea."

"As soon as I've put the horses away."

"CUT! What's so funny, David? This is not a Marx Brothers picture. Do it again!!" Off we drove.

Forty-something times I drove those damn horses around the San Fernando Valley. Finally, Wyler said, "Well, if that's the best you can do, we'd better print the first one, I suppose."

"Willie," I said, "remember last night at Chasen's?"

"Yeah, I remember. What about it?"

"You really are a son of bitch, aren't you?"

"Yes—and I'm going to be one for fourteen weeks!"

No one was spared by Willie. The girls were reduced to tears on several occasions and even Olivier was brought up all standing.

The most talented and most reasonable of performers, after being told twenty or thirty times to play some long scene once again, without any specific instructions as to how to alter it, he finally confronted Wyler.

"Willie, look. I've done it thirty times. I've done it differently thirty times. Just *tell* me, that's all, *what do you want me to do?*"

Wyler considered this for a long moment. "Just—just be *better.*"

When Cathy was lying dead in her big bed with her family all around her, and a lot of great performers they were too—Flora Robson, Geraldine Fitzgerald, Hugh Williams, all weeping silently and Larry circling purposefully around the fireplace, carrying a vast log—I glanced nervously at the instructions in my script: Edgar breaks down at foot of bed and sobs.

"Willie," I whispered, "I can't do that."

"Do what?"

"Sob. I don't know how to."

"Speak up."

"I don't know how to sob, Willie."

"Speak up . . . louder."

"I DON'T KNOW HOW TO SOB," I yelled.

Wyler addressed the whole set: "Well, you've all heard it. Here's an actor who says he doesn't know how to act . . . now . . . SOB."

I tried and it was pretty grisly. "Tam" Williams got hiccups bottling his laughter and Larry looked up the chimney.

I tried again.

"Jesus," said Wyler, "can you make a crying face?"

I made some sort of squashed-up grimace.

"Oh, God," he groaned, "IRVING!"

Irving Sindler, the prop man, was instantly at his side.

"Give him the blower," said Wyler.

Greg Toland, the cameraman, gave his signals, and the film started passing through the sprockets.

"The blower, Irving!" said Wyler.

Through a handkerchief, Sindler puffed menthol into my open eyes.

"Bend over the corpse . . . Heave your shoulders." crying face . . . Blink your eyes . . . Squeeze a little . . . "Bend over the corpse . . . Heave your shoulders."

A terrible thing happened. Instead of tears coming out of my eyes, green slime came out of my nose.

"Ooh!!! How *HORRID!*" shrieked the corpse, who shot out of bed and disappeared at high speed into her dressing room.

Thanks to Wyler. the picture was a big hit and has remained one of the all-time classics, and, incidentally, any time Wyler wants me in one of his pictures I'll be there.

There was an excitement and generosity of spirit in Hollywood, a minimum of jealousy and pettiness; everyone felt they were still pioneering in a wonderful entertainment medium.

The premieres of the big pictures were black-tie events and all the big names turned out to cheer on their friends. Outside bleachers were erected to enable the screaming fans to catch a glimpse of their favorites and searchlights weaved to and fro across the sky. After the show. a loudspeaker alerted the fans to the departing of the great: "Mr. Clark Gable's car! Miss Marlene Dietrich's car! Miss Constance Bennett's car! Miss Shirley Temple's mother's car!" And on one glorious occasion: "Mr. Alfred Hitchcar's cock!"

Some of the conveyances were a trifle exotic. Connie Bennett sat inside the wicker-box body of a Rolls Phaeton with a spotlight on her . . . outside in all weathers sat her chauffeur.

Tom Mix drove himself in a white open Packard wearing a white ten-gallon hat.

Marlene Dietrich had a black Cadillac driven by a chauffeur named Briggs who carried two revolvers and in winter wore a uniform with a mink collar.

Marlene, the most glamorous of all, was also one of the kindest Once I was ill with flu in my chalet shack on North Vista Street. She hardly knew me, but Briggs was a friend and he told her I was sick. Marlene arrived with soup and medicine. She then went to work and cleaned the whole place from top to bottom changed my bedclothes and departed. She came back every day till I was well.

Goldwyn continued my buildup and gave me a good part in *The Real Glory* with Gary Cooper. Then I was loaned to Darryl Zanuck to play two important roles at Twentieth Century-Fox, both with Loretta Young, still as sweet and as generous as ever. The whole Young family turned up for the first day's shooting. John Ford directed one of these, an experience actors prayed for. So incredibly sure was his touch that he cut the film with his camera as he went along. All the editor could do was join the pieces together in the correct order and there was the picture.

Ford, like many movie greats, had a soft spot for the practical joke. I had a birthday during the picture, and Loretta presented me with a huge cake, which the whole crew devoured.

"David," said Ford, "tomorrow you have very little to do—you'll just be background—so tonight go on out and enjoy yourself—really tie one on."

I hate getting drunk, but I felt that I had more or less been ordered to do so and I did my best to oblige. I started slowly, after work, in Tyrone Power's dressing room, then home, where Flynn joined me enthusiastically, continued at the Trocadero with Mike Romanoff, then I visited two German lesbians in Encino and after making the rounds of Chasen's, the Brown Derby and various bars in Hollywood. I finished up in Doc Law's All-Night Café in Santa Monica. From there, I went directly to the studio at eight o'clock in the morning, very drunk indeed and thinking how pleased John Ford would be.

We were rehearsing the first scene. All I had to do was bind up the arm of George Sanders, who had been shot. Suddenly, I heard Ford say, "Hold it. What's the matter with you, Niven? Why don't you stand still?"

"Sorry, Mr. Ford."

"Just a minute. Are you drunk or something?"

"Well, I did have a few, Mr. Ford . . . I thought you said. . . ."

"Cut the lights," said Ford.

"Send for Mr. Zanuck. Tell him I have a drunken actor on my set—ask him to come down right away."

I was sobering up rapidly but still not registering too clearly. All I knew was that people were backing away from me, not wanting to be part of the impending showdown.

Zanuck marched onto the set, looking ferocious, followed by his henchmen.

"What's the problem, Jack?"

"Goddamned limeys," said Ford, "they're all alike . . . give 'em an inch . . . this actor reported for work drunk."

"Let me see a take," said Zanuck.

"Put a white coat on him," said Ford, "and give him the first-aid box . . . all right, now try to pull yourself together, for Christ's sake . . . on your cue pull the stethoscope out of your pocket, then open the box and take out a dressing. Okay, let's go."

White coat? Stethoscope? Dressing? These were last-minute instructions.

The camera turned and George Sanders and Richard Greene played a lengthy scene. Out of the corner of my eye, I could see Zanuck watching intently. I tried to concentrate on my cue, and when it came, I put my hand in the pocket for the stethoscope and pulled out a large snake. Trying manfully to continue the scene, I dropped it on the floor and opened the first-aid box. When I saw it was full of little green turtles, I let out a yell and flung it in the air.

"Print it," yelled Ford, admidst the ensuing guffaws. The scene which Zanuck had been a party to was run constantly in private projection rooms thereafter.

Fairbanks had a small ranch down near San Diego, where he used to take the Astaires and me duck shooting and coyote hunting. A rather bigger spread lay north, near San Luis Obispo, where the super-publisher and newspaper tycoon William Randolph Hearst had built himself a hilltop castle dominating some 200,000 acres.

His sons, George, Bill, Jack, Randy and David, constantly invited me up there. They were all about the same age as myself and all were either just married, about to become engaged, or sliding down the other side into divorce. The girls were beautiful, the boys were great fun, and I spent some of the happiest times of my life at San Simeon.

W. R. Hearst lived there openly for years with the blue-eyed beauty Marion Davies. The sons loved their mother, who lived on Long Island. They also loved their father and they liked Marion enormously. It was impossible not to . . . a warm-hearted scatterbrain who worshiped W. R.

Mr. Hearst fascinated me. He was an avid collector of antiques on a massive scale. An entire Greek temple had been dismantled, shipped over, and reassembled by the swimming pool. Glorious frescoes, paintings and tapestries were everywhere. Often I slept in Richelieu's bed. Hearst had repositories of treasure still not unpacked and a large private zoo. He enjoyed going for rambles with the young and discoursing on every subject under the sun. One heard rumbles that he was utterly ruthless in business, but, rather naturally, I saw no sign of that.

In the huge paneled dining hall, flanked by monks' stalls, and decorated up high by sixty or seventy ducal banners from Venice, Siena and Florence, it always intrigued me that down the center of the largest refectory table in the world stood clusters of H. P. sauce, Heinz Tomato Ketchup and paper napkins.

At the end of 1936, Irving Thalberg died. He was thirty-seven years old. He had caught a chill playing cards out of doors, pneumonia followed, and very quickly he was gone. Hollywood was stunned. It was a staggering loss.

Fairbanks organized the ushers at the funeral service at the synagogue, B'nai B'rith. He told me to help at the entrance and said that he would personally seat the family in the front, as he knew them all by sight. Knowing his penchant for putting the wrong name to the wrong face, this made me rather nervous, a condition that increased when I walked down the aisle to ask his advice about something and he showed me into a pew.

By Hollywood standards, the funeral was conducted with great decorum. The fans were kept at bay, so nobody had a chance to repeat an earlier disaster when the widow had her veils ripped off—"Let's see your face, dearie."

The only sour note was when some moron in the M-G-M publicity department saw to it that the child actor, Freddie Bartholomew, who had just completed the name part in the film showed up in his black velvet *Little Lord Fauntleroy* suit.

It was probably the same source of good taste which, when Jean Harlow died, took out full page ads in the trade papers showing the Metro lion dressed in white tie and tails with tears pouring down its face, placing a wreath on a tombstone: JEAN HARLOW IN MEMORIAM. And below on a scroll, the full list of her screen credits.

Norma was inconsolable and disappeared from view for months.

David O. Selznick was as big an independent producer as Goldwyn, so when he borrowed me to play Fritz von Tarlenheim in *The Prisoner of Zenda*, I was very excited. Not only was it to be one of the biggest pictures of the year, but also it had a spectacular cast: Ronald Colman, Madeleine Carroll, Raymond Massey, Douglas Fairbanks, Jr., Mary Astor and C. Aubrey Smith.

Colman was now very close to me, and I did not doubt that on my behalf he had put in his two cents' worth with Selznick. Doug, Jr., I was meeting for the first time and we immediately struck up a friendship which is just as warm today. An added bonus was that Madeleine's husband, Philip Astley, was coming out to spend three months with her in Malibu.

My part was excellent, seemingly the only comedy relief, so all in all, I had never had it so good.

John Cromwell, the director, was rather solemn and steadfastly refused to let me play my part for comedy. I plowed on, playing it straight as ordered, but was pretty sure the result was dim. Colman found it hard to be encouraging.

After about a week, I decided to make a stand and upon completion of a scene, I said, "Mr. Cromwell, would you let me do it again—my way?"

This was unheard-of insubordination and the entire crew shuffled about, looking embarrassed.

"All right," said Cromwell. "Do it once more—your way."

By now whatever it was I had dreamed up felt profoundly unfunny, but I did it anyway.

"Next scene," said Cromwell with no change of expression.

That night David Selznick called me.

"I'm sorry, David, but somehow you're not giving the part what I thought you would. . . . I'm afraid I have to replace you."

My legs turned to water. I went up to my room and sat on my bed in the dark. "So I really couldn't do it after all. Lubitsch and Wyler might have pulled me through, but the first big chance had found me out. . . . What was I going to tell everyone?"

My next option with Goldwyn was just coming up . . . he would surely drop me. I felt panic rising. I heard Flynn come back about two o'clock and still I sat there.

At nine in the morning, Selznick called me.

"I want to see you at once . . . come on down."

I was taken straight to his office. With him was John Cromwell.

"Look, David," said Selznick, "we have just seen yesterday's stuff . . . the last thing you did was exactly what I want from you and John here agrees."

"I certainly do," said Cromwell. "It's my fault entirely and David and I are going to build up the part so that we can get much more fun out of it. . . . You'll be great . . . go and get dressed."

How many big directors are really that big? I wonder. Cromwell is another for my private Hall of Fame.

It was a long picture—more than four months—and every day was fascinating. We all felt we were making a success and the enthusiasm ran high.

I was given my own stand-in for the first time. I asked Stuart Hall if he would like the job, and for years after, he stood patiently being lighted by cameramen so that I would be fresh when the moment came to play a scene.

I had problems with my old chums among the extras. At six thirty at night, they automatically went on a quarter-extra salary. If I was playing a scene around that magic hour, they would make it clear they expected me to blow my lines and put them safely into overtime. My loyalty to David Selznick, who would have to pay them, also came into question. . . . It was very tricky.

In the coronation procession, Colman and Madeleine were in the royal coach, C. Aubrey Smith and I rode alongside, and the two heavies, Doug, Jr., and Ray Massey, rode behind us.

Knowing the fixation that studios have that leading actors should be seen riding highly strung prancing steeds, I had a little chat with the head wrangler and exchanged mine for a quiet old mare. Unfortunately, she was in heat and the stallion that Ray Massey was riding decided to mount her, and me, in the middle of a take. I heard snapping teeth behind my head and just caught a glimpse of Ray's appalled expression far above me as I flung myself to the ground.

Toward the end of the picture, King George VI and Queen Elizabeth visited President Roosevelt.

Someone had the bright idea that the "British Colony" should do a special radio show on the Sunday that would coincide with a hot dog picnic the President was giving for his royal guests at Hyde Park, up the Hudson River.

We rehearsed for days and bashed our brains out, being loyal and talented.

Olivier gave the "Into the breach . . ." speech from *Henry V.*

Brian Aherne recited Rupert Brooke's "The Soldier."

Aubrey Smith, Nigel Bruce and Roland Young sang "Three Little Fishes."

Reggie Gardiner imitated a train.

Ray Noble's band played and the rest of us—Vivien Leigh, Flynn, Colman, Madeleine, Cary Grant and myself —all did something.

I had an unexpected moment alone with Her Majesty a few years later and asked her how they all had enjoyed our efforts.

"Oh, wasn't it awful?" she said. "The President's battery ran down just before it came on."

At the end of *Zenda,* Goulding called in a high state of excitement from his house in Palm Springs.

"Come at once, I have good news, I think."

I drove down to the desert to find Goulding hopping up and down in the driveway.

He led me down to his pool. There was a naked figure in it.

"Oh, I forgot," said Goulding, "Garbo was coming over for a swim . . . we'd better go back up to the house."

Up there he told me the news.

"You've got it!" he said. "They just called from Warners and confirmed it."

"Got what?"

"Scotty in *Dawn Patrol*—it's the best part ever written for an actor."

Warners borrowed me from Goldwyn and Goulding was right. It was a marvelous part . . . a World War I story of the Royal Flying Corps. Flynn and I were pilots. At one point I was hungover and late and went up in my Sopwith Camel in red-and-white spotted pajamas. I was shot down and fell in a lake. The officers' mess was plunged in gloom at the loss when I suddenly walked in, still in pajamas, with an armful of champagne bottles. This was a true incident that had happened near Arras to a certain flying officer, Pope.

Basil Rathbone played the CO and Donald Crisp was the adjutant.

Goulding was a most sensitive and inventive director.

The picture really hit the jackpot, and he achieved what he had always promised: He launched me in a great part in a great picture.

After that, things moved rapidly. I was given star billing and borrowed by Twentieth Century-Fox to do a picture in England with the beautiful French actress Annabella.

Trubshawe came to Southampton to meet the ship. He was now the squire of Barton Hall in Norfolk and Margie had presented him with two daughters. For old times' sake, he carried the Dipsomaniac's Delight. He also displayed a placard:

BARTON HALL VILLAGE FETE

CRICKET MATCH
SIDESHOWS
RAFFLE
BOWLING FOR THE PIG
CAWSTON SILVER BAND
TO BE OPENED BY FAMOUS HOLLYWOOD STAR
DAVID NIVEN

"Better come, old man," he said. "It's tomorrow and I've stuck these bloody things up all over the county."

It was marvelous to be home again.

The picture was shot at Denham. Angie and Ken Thornton let me be a paying guest in their lovely old house at Ascot, near the Weigalls, and a hundred old threads were picked up.

I was given a stand-in named Reynolds who was an ex-Royal Navy master-at-arms. He had never been inside a studio before and disapproved heavily of a makeup man who had dyed-blond hair and rather tight trousers. "One of those others," sniffed Reynolds.

I had time to go to Bembridge. Everyone made a great fuss of me and I wallowed in it.

On the return journey on *Île-de-France*, I met an Austrian named Felix Schaffcotsh. He was on his way to Sun Valley, Idaho, where, at the request of Averell Harriman, he had designed and built a new ski resort.

A handsome and affable *Graf*, he was also a dyed-in-the-wool Nazi. He spent hours extolling the virtues of Hitler, sympathizing with his problems and enthusing over his plans. I listened politely but took none of it seriously. I was far more interested in the script of my next film.

Shortly before sailing, I had been advised that Goldwyn had loaned me to Walter Wanger to co-star with Loretta in *Eternally Yours*.

Felix said that he was bringing over a dozen good ski instructors from near his home in Austria—"all Nazis too." I promised to go to Sun Valley after I finished the picture.

I arrived back in Hollywood to find that Flynn and Lili Damita had signed a truce and I had to find somewhere else to live.

John McClain was at the Garden of Allah, so I rented a bungalow there, and although I missed F. Scott Fitzgerald, who had moved to Malibu with Sheilah Graham, I had the great joy of meeting Robert Benchley and Dorothy Parker.

Benchley was one of the wittiest men alive, but unlike most people full of funny things to say, he was rather retiring. Long the theater critic for the *New Yorker*, he was now bravely putting on the other hat and embarking on a highly successful career as an actor. He loved to drink . . . "I must step out of these wet things and into a dry martini. . . ."

There had lately been a big influx of Easterners, and with McClain and Benchley, I spent fascinating evenings at Cole Porter's house, where it was quite usual to listen to Cole or Irving Berlin or George Gershwin playing numbers from the half-written scores of their future smash-hit musicals.

Benchley disappeared to Europe. I made him promise to go to Venice, which he had never before visited.

One day he cabled me, and in view of the address he used, the fact that it was delivered was flattering enough:

VENICE
NIVENTRAVEL
HOLLYWOOD
STREETS FULL OF WATER. ADVISE
BENCHLEY

When McClain moved back to New York, I moved down to Santa Monica and rented a small guest beach house from Marion Davies. I shared this with Robert Coote, an excellent English actor, and a mysterious Australian named Walter Kerry Davis.

Bob was quickly making a big name for himself as a character actor, and Walter was hovering hopefully on the fringe of Los Angeles and Pasadena society where, rumor had it, he was trying to snag a rich wife. He so often failed to pay his share of the rent that he must have been finding the going very uphill.

It was a very happy combination, however, and we entertained twenty-four hours a day . . . so much so that Carole Lombard, Alice Faye, Ida Lupino and Cary Grant christened the house Cirrhosis by the Sea. We had this painted on a board outside the front door, where it remained for more than a year, till we received instructions from W. R. Hearst to take it down.

Fred Astaire and Ginger Rogers decided to make no more musicals together and the whole world mourned. Fred went on from strength to strength with a series of different dancing partners; and Ginger decided to return to straight acting. They were the king and queen of RKO, so it was immensely flattering for me when Goldwyn told me that he had loaned me out to co-star with Ginger in her first solo for a long time, *Bachelor Mother*, to be directed by the immensely talented writer-director Garson Kanin.

"Everyone's going to expect you to dance," said Goldwyn. "Show them that you can act instead."

The script, by Norman Krasna, was a dream, and Goldwyn decided that this picture was so important that he would not put me into anything else before it. It was then February, 1938.

"You don't have to report to RKO till May, so you can have yourself a good vacation," said Goldwyn.

Later the same day, Reeves Espy called me. "You've a long layoff—for twelve weeks," he said.

I kept my promise and went skiing at Sun Valley. The resort was only just open, new and small. Only two hotels were built, the Lodge, very good and very expensive, and the Challenger Inn, where I went, more fun and much cheaper.

Averell Harriman had his own charming chalet and others were building. The skiing was perfect and I had a wonderful six weeks. Felix had made a huge success of the place. Given half a chance, he was still liable to lay down the law about *Lebensraum*, but he was a most agreeable companion. Toward the end of my stay, I was surprised to get a phone call from Norma Shearer, who had been virtually incommunicado since Irving's death.

She sounded desperately lonely, so I persuaded her to come on up and booked her a suite in the Lodge. When she arrived, Averell Harriman went out of his way to make life pleasant for her. She fell in love with the place, with skiing, and a few years later with a great skier and happily remarried.

Bachelor Mother took most of the summer to shoot and was a most happy assignment. Thanks to Garson's sure hand and novel ideas the result surprised the highest hopes and it was widely acclaimed as the best comedy of the year. It went straight to my head of course and I bought a Leica and went all over Los Angeles taking pictures of my name and likeness on the billboards.

During the filming, Garson said something that gave me pause for thought. "Do you realize," he said, "that I am the director of this picture and you are the co-star, but between us we are being paid less than half what the cameraman is getting?"

Garson, obviously, had his own studio problems, and in my case there was no doubt that every time Goldwyn loaned me out, he demanded huge sums for my services; but I was still basically amazed that I was being paid at all and Goldwyn after all, had given me a chance when nobody else would touch me. Nevertheless, the flea was in my ear, so I had a talk with Bill Hawks, my agent. He was unenthusiastic about tackling Goldwyn, so I went to see Leland Hayward, the top agent in Hollywood.

"Leave Goldwyn to me," he said. "You're making a fortune for him. I'm going in there and ask for a lot of money and a contract for five years straight with no layoff and no options, a limited number of pictures and six weeks' guaranteed vacation."

On the day of Leland's meeting with Goldwyn, he went into the office brimming with confidence. I waited in the anteroom. Two minutes later he was back.

"Did you get it?" I asked.

"Not exactly," said Leland, "Goldwyn has barred me from the lot. Now I can't even talk to him."

A really ridiculous war of nerves then started with Goldwyn. He didn't speak to me when I met him, and when I
turned down what I thought was a really awful script, I was
promptly put on suspension.

One day I saw a headline in Louella Parsons' daily gossip
column read avidly by the whole industry: NIVEN
IMPOSSIBLE, SAY FELLOW WORKERS. It went on to charge
that because of recent successes I had got such a swollen
head I refused to speak to old friends in the studio.

I was appalled, and when I discovered through a secretary in the publicity department that the story had emanat-
ed from there, I confronted Jock Lawrence.

As usual he was urbane.

"Remember that first day you came in here? I told you
then Mr. Goldwyn is the greatest, but he's rough sometimes."

Being suspended, I started earning a nice amount by
working on radio in the *Lux Radio Theatre* and other programs; very serious they were, too, with a week's rehearsal
and the performance given before a live audience of several
hundred to an unseen one of 50,000,000.

Reeves Espy spoke to me—poor man, he hated to deliver bad news. "Dave, Mr. Goldwyn says that you have
been working on radio without his permission. Under the
terms of the contract he has the right to everything you
earn. However, he'll let you keep half."

The next radio show I did was with Bing Crosby; the
sponsor was Kraft. At the end of the show, as was often
the custom, I was presented with a large hamper filled with
all the Kraft products—cheeses, spreads and sardines.

When I got home, Coote helped me, and I meticulously
removed half the spread from the jars, cut every cheese in
half, every sardine in half; then with an envelope containing a check for half my salary from the show, I sent the lot
to Goldwin inside half the basket.

It was ridiculous and childish, and I was behaving like a
small boy attacking a heavy tank with a water pistol but
rather enjoying it.

Fred and Phyllis Astaire arranged a cease-fire and Goldwyn sent for me. All smiles, he received me in his office—he
had immense charm. He told me that he wanted to give me
a new seven-year contract, mentioned the figures, which

seemed colossal to me, and added that the first picture I would do would be *Raffles*.

I had always wanted to tackle the part of the famous gentleman crook: now it was being dangled before me like a carrot. It all seemed perfect.

"I'll call Leland and have him come over and we'll make a deal," said Goldwyn. I left in a high state of excitement.

I remember that September evening very vividly because in the car park. outside Leland's office, I listened to the hysterical voice of Hitler addressing the Nuremberg Rally. The doom-filled tones of the commentator, Gabriel Heatter, left one in no doubt as to the intentions of the man and the rolling *Sieg heils* of his massed Storm Troopers underlined them in an ominous and frightening way.

I thought about Felix and his dire prognostications.

Leland blithely turned down Goldwyn's offer.

"You've got to have some guts," he said. when I remonstrated. "Sit him out. play it disinterested. Your contract is running out. He doesn't want to lose you—he's just playing games. I know Sam. We'll get the deal we want."

I just hoped that Leland knew what he was doing, and went sailing with Flynn on one of our weekend jaunts to Catalina Island in *Sirocco*. Normally, the arrangement was that we provided the booze, and the girls, whoever they were, brought the food. There was one lady who had made a habit of showing up only with a loaf of bread and a douche bag.

We were on our way back to the mainland on Sunday evening, and the sea had kicked up quite considerably.

About fifteen miles out of Balboa, we sighted a large cabin cruiser. It was stopped and wallowing about and signaling to us frantically.

When we came near enough, we could see its name, *Jobella*, and sitting in the stern with a cigar clamped between his teeth was the owner, Harry Cohn, the head of Columbia Studios.

"Give us a tow, for Christ's sake," yelled Cohn. "Goddamned engines broke down."

Jobella was a heavy boat and we didn't bring her into Balboa till well after midnight.

Cohn in his rough, tough, East Side way was only moderately grateful, so the next day I thought I'd have a little fun with him. I persuaded a lawyer friend to send him an official letter quoting maritime law on the question of asking for help at sea, and mentioning the Salvage Act of 1912, I claimed one half of the *Jobella*.

No answer came and I forgot all about it. One day Leland called me. "What the hell have you done at Columbia? You've been barred from the lot for life!!"

"I haven't set foot in the place for three years," I said.

"Well, you must have done *something*," said Leland.

Then I remembered and told him about the lawyer's letter. "But it couldn't be that," I said.

"Knowing Cohn, that's exactly what it is," said Leland. "You'd better call him up and explain."

I called Cohn and couldn't get him on the phone. I left messages—he never called back.

I became nervous. There were only six major studios. Goldwyn was highly displeased with me at the moment and he had an option coming up in a few days. Suppose Goldwyn dropped me? Out for life at Columbia!! And the black list really did exist. Too many actors who had quarreled with their studios had sunk without trace. I might never work again anywhere. I panicked.

Leland tried to calm me down, but it was obvious that he, too, was concerned.

Finally, Cohn consented to see me and I was granted an interview at 9 A.M.

He kept me waiting in the outer office all morning. At lunchtime, he walked out, right past me, and never said a word. But I was frightened. I was chicken. I didn't have the guts to leave too.

After lunch, Cohn came back. He never looked at me. All afternoon I sat under the pitying eye of a secretary. Finally, at 6:30, "Mr. Cohn will see you now."

In his big office he growled at me, "Waddaya want?"

I said, "About that night Errol and I towed you home. . . ."

"Yeah . . . well, whattabout it?"

". . . Did you get a lawyer's letter about the salvage?"

"Yeah, I got it. D'you want apologize?"

"Look, the idea was to make you laugh—if it made you unhappy, of course, I apologize."

"Okay, I accept the apology—now get your ass outta here."

I didn't work at Columbia till after Cohn died twenty years later.

The ridiculous war of nerves with Goldwyn continued, although I suspect that the nerves were strictly on my side.

I was called to the studio to make some costume tests for a picture with Gary Cooper. I began to notice a man hovering about in white tie and tails. He was posing for stills with Bob Coburn, the Goldwyn photographer—posing, I noticed, half-way up a ladder with a revolver in one hand and a pearl necklace in the other . . . obviously he was meant to look like Raffles, the gentleman crook.

During the afternoon, I approached him and asked him what he was doing. He was a little mystified himself. "Well, I've been told to put on these clothes and follow you around having these pictures taken."

The ploy was pretty juvenile: to get me to rush off and sign the Goldwyn offer for fear of losing Raffles. After work, I went to the May Company and sent Goldwyn a boy scout's outfit.

The name of the man was Dana Andrews.

Finally, in the spring, Goldwyn and Leland made a deal. Goldwyn, who had a great capacity for letting bygones be bygones, welcomed me to his office with open arms and Jock Lawrence had pictures taken of the two of us signing the contract.

Goldwyn, himself, escorted me to one of the huge star suites and ordered it to be redecorated to my taste. Olivia de Haviland was signed to play opposite me and Sam Wood to direct.

I was pampered and spoiled and my every whim was catered to. When I asked for some of my old "extra" chums to be employed in the English country house sequences, they were immediately, and when I walked on the set, I thought it was the Crystal Palace. To a man they were sporting monocles. When Sam Wood fell ill, the picture was completed by a gentle and helpful Willie Wyler.

We finished shooting on September 1. The picture looked good and Goldwyn was delighted. My contract was munificent. Goldwyn's plans for me were most exciting, and all this had happened in less than four years. But at that very moment when I was preening myself, something bigger than a weed was blowing into many people's gardens.

Hitler, without a declaration of war, was invading Poland.

Doug, Jr., with attractive new Virginia-born wife, Mary Lee, had chartered a yacht for a weekend trip to Catalina. On board were Larry Olivier and Vivien Leigh. Ronnie Colman and Benita Hume were anchored nearby in Colman's ketch, *Dragoon*. Coote and I were supposedly sailing across to join them in a small sloop, the *Huralu*. Coote and I drank an immense amount of rum at a party in the Balboa Yacht Club and did not quite make the tide.

We were woken up at 4 A.M. by a man in a dinghy banging on the side of our boat.

"You guys English?"

We peered blearily over the side. "Yes."

"Well, lotsa luck. You've just declared war on Germany."

We never spoke a word . . . just went below and filled two teacups with warm gin. I can't believe it was a toast to anything in particular.

When we finally arrived at Catalina and joined the others, we found a somber group. Nobody knew quite what to do; like millions all over the world, it was beginning to dawn on us that we were pawns in a game that had got out of control.

After a gloomy couple of days, Coote and I sailed back. I got a call from Felix Schaffcotsh from New York. "Hello, enemy," he said gaily, "what are you going to do?"

"I'll go back, I suppose," I said, very gloomily.

Felix sounded very bright. "I'm leaving the day after tomorrow. Let's go together."

The next day, I told Goldwyn that I had been called up and had to leave immediately. Goldwyn, as usual, was far smarter than I gave him credit for. Within half an hour he had checked with the British Embassy in Washington and had been told that nobody outside the British Isles had yet been called up. Luckily, nobody told Goldwyn that, having resigned my commission, I was no longer on the Reserve and in all probability would never be called up at all.

I cabled my brother, Max, with certain instructions and was able to show Goldwyn a cable which read:

REPORT REGIMENTAL DEPOT IMMEDIATELY
                                    ADJUTANT

Doug gave me a splendid sendoff—a bachelor party complete with pipers. The guests included Colman, Nigel Bruce, Olivier, Brian Aherne, George Sanders, Cary Grant, Roland Young, Basil Rathbone, Kerry Davis and Coote, and the next day I took off from the Burbank airport for New York.

As the plane circled over the San Fernando Valley, gaining sufficient height to cross the mountains, the whole of Los Angeles stretched out below me in the early morning light. Warner Brothers and Universal studios were easy to pick out. I had a nasty feeling that I might be seeing them for the last time. I also wondered what the hell I was doing up there.

Felix had gone on ahead and made a rendezvous with me in Rome.

Dreading the idea of being back again in the British Army, I had a vague idea that I might save time and money by offering myself to the Canadian Army instead, so from New York I went to Washington to ask the advice of the military attaché at the embassy.

The military attaché was sympathetic but explained that the few divisions at present being raised in Canada were already oversubscribed nine times down to cooks. "Anyway," he added, "the ambassador would like to see you."

Lord Lothian was flattering, but gave me a very peculiar directive: "It is, of course, admirable that you want to join up, but if you really would like my advice, the best thing you can possibly do is to go back to Hollywood and represent your country on the screen."

I thanked him and sailed in the Italian liner *Rex* for Naples.

The ship was fairly empty except for a group of extremely hostile young Germans who made it obvious that the war had already started. I was delighted when a British destroyer stopped *Rex* outside Gibraltar. Officers boarded her, interrogated all the passengers, and over the vehement protestations of the Italian captain, removed the young Germans.

Felix met me at Naples and we embarked on a week of liquid farewells in Rome.

He seemed very well connected, and twice I found myself at the Golf Club di Roma, playing with Count Ciano, the foreign minister and son-in-law of Mussolini.

Ciano was a highly attractive man, and both times we played, beautiful Roman ladies walked around with us twittering like birds. When he heard that I was on my way to England to join up, he wished me luck very solemnly and said that he was sure it all would be settled very soon.

Felix and I decided that we would both leave Rome on the same day. The night before, he arranged a glorious finale.

It started with drinks in somebody's palazzo and continued through a series of visits to the houses, apartments and rooms of Felix's smart Roman friends.

In the early hours, we took two carefully selected girls to a nightclub—a Spanish one for Felix, a Norwegian for me—and all the time we drank and drank without getting drunkard's drunk or noisy drunk—an evident danger on this occasion. Toward dawn Felix said, "Let's go to the Vatican and all kiss a Swiss guard."

When we arrived, the sky above St. Peter's was changing from black to palest blue and the viridescent beauty of the place was almost unearthly. The Spanish girl surreptitiously crossed herself; the Norwegian whispered irreverently in my ear, "Every time I've been in that place, I've been groped."

Soon they were both asking to be taken home. Ungallantly, we did not accompany them, but this was our night and they sensed it.

Alone in a little bistro in Trastevere, we drank Vino di Frascati as though they were never going to make anymore; still we didn't get drunk. Felix talked about the new ski lifts he was planning for Sun Valley, and I talked of the pictures I was going to make. A long silence enveloped us. We watched the newly awakened swifts wheeling and darting and miraculously missing each other in the darker-blue sky. Suddenly, Felix slammed his glass down on the table and jumped to his feet.

"Let's say good-bye now," he said almost angrily.

I stood up. I think we both wept anyway.

We embraced and parted quickly. A few hours later, Felix headed northeast for the Brenner Pass to join the S.S. and I headed northwest for the French border at Modane to join God knew what.

Felix was killed in Russia.

12

Duce! Duce! on every station in letters ten feet high, and the train services in Italy were running perfectly. By way of Genoa and Torino, I was quickly transported to the French border and crossed into Savoie at Modane.

Not a bomb had yet fallen on the French railway system, but chaos was reigning supreme. I had the greatest difficulty convincing a pompous little official that I was not a spy.

"Why does an Englishman come from Italy, monsieur?"

At last I persuaded him I was trying to be on his side if only he would let me, and with a shrug of resignation, he stamped my passport and wrote a special pass.

"Se rendre en Angleterre pour faire la guerre."

The distance between Modane and Paris is a little less than five hundred miles. The train took three full days. It was packed with drunken reservists, and if I ever found a seat, I vacated it only *in extremis*. The corridor was jammed with eagle-eyed opportunists. At night, train and stations were blacked out and we stumbled about bitterly cold platforms looking for bread and cheese and wine being sold by ill-tempered ladies with flashlights and no change.

Most of the time, the train stood in sidings. Nothing seemed to go past, and rumors of bombings farther up the line ran up and down the coaches.

I was constantly told by thick garlic-laden voices that the whole thing was the fault of England, and now, having forced France to join them against the Germans, the English would never show up to fight—"just like the last time."

I thought of the 3,000,000 British Empire casualties, including my own father, and finally, through pure exhaustion, I placated the accusing red faces by explaining that I was half French anyway.

On arrival in Paris, I managed to find a room in a hotel

on the Left Bank and slept for twenty-four hours.

Refreshed, I decided to give myself a week in Paris and then join the RAF. I wondered if, perhaps, I could do this in France, so I called at the British Embassy, but it was a seething mass of expatriate British looking for permits, visas and transportation, so I gave up and contacted Claude.

Claude had appeared in Hollywood for a very short period and had twice made the hazardous crossing to Catalina aboard *Sirocco*.

She had been a model in a famous Paris fashion house and had graduated to become the mistress of a rich industrialist. He had, rather sneakily, sabotaged her movie ambitions by sending her to Hollywood with a return ticket and just enough money for three months. She was now once more under his roof . . . actually, if not technically. He had built an apartment building in Neuilly and lived on the top floor with his plump wife and two children. Directly beneath, he had installed the beautiful Claude. She was given a certain amount of freedom, but he was adamant that she must never receive gentlemen friends alone in her flat.

Although monsieur paid the concierge on the ground floor, he paid her so poorly that instead of being a built-in spy system for him, she had become the *gardienne* of Claude's freedom.

Once monsieur was home for the evening, *en famille*, he never made surprise visits below, explaining to Claude, with Gallic logic, that he would never insult his wife. Claude's only enemy then was the extreme cheapness of the materials which monsieur had used in the construction of his building; he could hear everything, even the squeaking of bed springs, and once had questioned her closely as to why she had got out of bed and used her bidet at four in the morning.

Bumping about for long periods in motorcars, trains or planes always had a strangely exuberant effect on my sexual ambitions; the problem now was how to gratify them without making a sound.

If monsieur had had the foresight to install a pane of glass in his floor, he could have gazed down on the ridiculous spectacle of two people thrashing around below with handkerchiefs stuffed in their mouths. As it was, it was a miracle he didn't come down to investigate because Claude, toward the end of the evening, decided to freshen me up with an alcohol rub. She intimated this in sign language and fetched a huge bottle of Eau de Cologne. Unfortunately, as I turned over to have my back done, I knocked the bottle out of her hand with my elbow and most of its contents went straight up my behind. Shrieking agony in whispers is a difficult thing to accomplish.

Noël Coward had come to visit my beach neighbor, Cary Grant, about six months previously, and like hundreds before and since, I had fallen under his spell within a few minutes of meeting him.

Quite apart from the searing talent and biting wit, there is a largely unknown gentleness and a kindliness backed by lots and lots of guts. He also has a tremendous sense of loyalty and is a tiger in defense of friends or causes.

When I had last seen him, we had lunched together at the Cock 'n Bull on Sunset Boulevard and he had been quite definite in his prognostications that Neville Chamberlain and his government were unerringly leading us all into war.

Now he was appointed to a job in Naval Intelligence in Paris, although he later had a misunderstanding with Winston Churchill, who was never on his wavelength; he was for the moment installed in a beautiful apartment in Place Vendôme.

I went to see him one evening. The apartment was filled with a mixture of French and British diplomats and a sprinkling of officers in uniform. One of them, a very tall RAF group captain, cornered me and introduced himself by the name of Pope. "It might amuse you," he said, "but that character you played in *Dawn Patrol* was me! And I still have the pajamas."

Pope told me that I was probably too old to be taken on and trained as a fighter pilot but thought I might get fitted in elsewhere in the service. I was only twenty-nine, so this came as a rude shock. However, he recommended that I go to see John Acheson, the air attaché, at the embassy, and I presented myself once more, the next morning.

"No way to join up here in France," said Acheson. "You'll have to get to England. Keep your mouth shut and I'll get you on the mail plane—it goes every evening."

He signaled me later in the day, and I found myself clasping my suitcase, sitting on a pile of mailbags, and gazing down on, of all things, the white cliffs of Dover topped by those ghastly Citadel Barracks.

It was a gloomy, drizzly gray evening in late October, and as the pilot circled over Hendon airfield, I caught my first glimpse of the barrage balloons flying like monstrous gray toys over the city. I had not let anybody know I was coming, and by the time I found Grizel's studio flat in Chelsea it was blackout time.

We sat for hours and she brought me up to date. Max had joined my father's old regiment, the Berkshire Yeomanry, and was billeted underneath the grandstand of Newbury Race-course.

Joyce was making camouflage nets and driving for the Women's Volunteer Service and pointing down at her own coarse blue trousers said, "I've joined the Chelsea Fire Service."

After contacting a few friends and being given a great deal of conflicting advice, I set about the business of getting into uniform myself. There seemed to be a certain amount of difficulty over this because it was the time of the "Phony War." The Navy, indeed, was fully involved, but the RAF was confined to dropping leaflets on the Germans suggesting politely that it would be much wiser for them to quit before they got hurt, and the Army was stagnant on the Belgian border. All reservists had been called up, plus sufficient classes of conscripts.

An added snag was that my face was all over London. *Dawn Patrol* and *Bachelor Mother* were enormously successful and the publicity department was excelling itself. Everywhere, I was grinning out of newspapers or leering down from billboards. It was impossible to go unnoticed, and the press quickly caught up with me.

To save myself from endless harrying, it seemed wiser to get the whole thing done at once, so I telephoned Goldwyn's representative, and still being Hollywood-minded, I allowed him to arrange a press conference with one or two newspapers.

He set it up in the Odeon Cinema, in Leicester Square, and more than a hundred reporters and photographers showed up. I explained that I had come to join up and added that I hoped to get into the RAF.

The next morning Grizel called in a state of shock.

When I read the front pages, I wanted to cut my throat. HOLLYWOOD'S FIRST RECRUIT! RELAX! THE *Dawn Patrol* IS HERE! NIVEN SPURNS ARMY! "IT'S THE RAF FOR ME!"

I stayed hidden with friends in the country for a week to give things time to settle down and then visited the Air Ministry to make inquiries . . . On the way, I noticed with rising panic that the ads for *Bachelor Mother* had been altered; above my name, red stickers had been added: THE STAR WHO CAME HOME TO JOIN THE RAF.

I was directed to the office of a certain Group Captain Fletcher. Unfortunately, I was swept into it on the crest of a giggling wave of secretaries, clutching pieces of paper and pencils.

Fletcher restored order and eyed me with distaste. He knew who I was; poor man, unless he had been blind, he couldn't have avoided it. Nevertheless, he went through the motions of asking my name and occupation and what I wanted to do.

When I told him, he pursed his lips, sucked in some breath with a whistling noise, and shook his head.

"Ever heard of Wilfrid Lawson?"

"Yes . . . he's a wonderful actor."

"Maybe . . . we took him on and we've had trouble, nothing but trouble ever since. . . . Drink."

I said, "Look, all sorts of people drink, but I've come seven thousand miles at my own expense and I'd like to join the RAF."

"So I've read," he said nastily, "but we don't encourage actors to join this service.

For a moment I sat there stunned, then I felt anger rising from the soles of my feet.

"Then fuck you!" I said.

"Get out of my office," he shouted. "Get out!"

We were standing toe to toe when an inner door opened and an air commodore appeared. "What the devil's going on in here?"

"And FUCK YOU TOO!" I shouted unreasonably and made for the door and the giggling crowd outside it.

A week passed. I heard that Henry Clowes, whom I had nearly killed five years before when the Guinness-label Bentley overturned on Salisbury Plain, was now adjutant of the Scots Guards.

Philip Astley was separated from Madeleine Carroll, and he offered me a room as a paying guest in his flat at the top of Hay Hill.

"It won't work," he said. "They have blinkers on about the theatrical profession in 'The Brigade.' Look at me: I was adjutant of the Life Guards when I got engaged to Madeleine, but I was out of the regiment before I married her. Don't try it—it's a waste of time."

I did try it and I asked Henry Clowes if he could get me into the Scots Guards.

"No problem at all," said Henry when I warned him about the footlight barrier. "That was in peacetime. I'll talk to the colonel tomorrow and phone you at once."

Another week passed, so I called Henry at Wellington Barracks. "It didn't work, did it?" I asked.

"I'm terribly embarrassed," said Henry. "No, it didn't."

Goldwyn's representative called me daily. "Look, Dave, I've got about thirty offers for you on my desk. Shall I forward them to Mr. Goldwyn?"

I was in no mood to be tampered with by the end of November when David Kelburn, now a full lieutenant just back from a North Atlantic convoy, told me the naval facts of life.

"Of course you can get into the Navy tomorrow if you want to—as a stoker—but you want to be an officer, don't you? . . . Well, that means standing in line with thousands of people who know about the sea . . . little things like navigation. Go back to your old regiment."

"No," I said firmly, "I'm going to change my butcher. I don't want a lot of childish black marks hanging over me today."

We were having a late supper on the balcony of the Café de Paris . . . I stared gloomily down on the dancers. Most of the young men were in uniform, the Regular Army men, very smart and self-assured in blue patrols, the cavalrymen with colorful stripes on their pants and chain mail on their shoulders and the exotic Rifle Brigade and 60th, who wore green patrols with black patent-leather crossbelts and silver buckles, the newly commissioned, proud but self-conscious in drab khaki. Many RAF and naval officers were also present.

Suddenly, the orchestra leader stopped the music, and Poulsen, the owner, stepped forward. "Ladies and gentlemen, in case anyone is interested, the air raid warning just sounded." Such was the effect of the "Phony War" that this announcement was greeted with cheers, hunting cries and catcalls . . . in ten seconds it was forgotten.

Less than a year later, at the height of the blitz, a bomb shrieked through the roof and exploded on the dance floor, killing Poulsen, nearly all the orchestra and a huge percentage of the dancers.

David got up to speak to some friends, and I was left looking jealously at a table of RAF pilots and their girls immediately below me. Although I was sitting unobtrusively in the balcony, they noticed me and raised their glasses, perhaps mockingly, perhaps not, but I was so self-conscious about the blaring publicity of my arrival in the country that I preferred not to speculate. One girl had her back to me. She, too, was in the sky-blue uniform of the RAF. She turned and looked up. Long blond hair fell away and I found myself gazing into a face of such beauty and such sweetness that I just stared blankly back.

Her complexion was so perfect that the inevitable description "English rose" would have been an insult. Her eyes were the merriest and the bluest I had ever seen. She looked at me for a long moment, and when she got up to dance, I saw that she was tall with a divinely willowy figure. I had a funny feeling that I would never forget her, and in my mind she became marked down as "The WAAF."

I was shaken out of my musings by a rude voice behind my chair. I turned to see a beefy young man in Army uniform. He was swaying slightly. "When are you going to win the war single-handed?" he asked. A girl was plucking ineffectually at his sleeve. To avoid him, I looked again down on the scene below. A hefty shove in the back nearly embedded my front teeth in the tabletop.

"I'm talking to *you*, Niven," said the young man.

"Please, Sidney," said the girl, "you promised not to."

"Piss off, Janet," said Sidney, loudly.

Heads were turning and I could see even more unpleasant publicity looming ahead. Luckily, David arrived with some naval reinforcements and Janet led a glowering Sidney back to his table.

"I don't know why you rush it," said David. "The bloody war will probably last a hundred years anyway. . . . Everybody's waiting to get into uniform—you're not the only one."

"My name's Jimmy Bosvile." I looked up and saw, in the darkness of the nightclub, what I took to be a small wiry, elderly subaltern, wearing khaki with black buttons.

"I was with an air commodore this morning who was talking about your visit to his office the other day . . . how splendid! I wish I'd been there.

Bosvile sat down and I filled his glass.

"Having trouble finding a home, are you?" he said. "Why don't you come to the Rifle Brigade?"

"You couldn't get me into the ladies' lavatory in Leicester Square," I said.

He laughed. "I happen to command the Second Battalion."

Only then did I notice that one of the pips on his shoulder was a crown—a lieutenant colonel.

So it was arranged. I told him very briefly of my previous military history and he said, "You'll be commissioned as a second lieutenant, but put your two pips on anyway. Mark Kerr is my adjutant. He'll write and tell you what you'll need in the way of kit. When you've got it together, come down to Tidworth. I'll expect you in about three weeks." He smiled and we shook hands.

The Rifle Brigade! Probably the most famous of all the elite Light Infantry Regiments in the British Army . . . Army again . . . oh! well, the die was now cast. I had achieved what I had set out to do several weeks before in California . . . I had a strange feeling of anticlimax.

Philip Astley himself was waiting to be called up in some capacity. Some ten years older than I, he was doubtful what jobs could be found for him. "Ever been to a war cemetery?" he asked. "It doesn't matter what war or which army . . . the average age of those crosses is about twenty —it'll be the same this time."

When instructions arrived, I visited a recommended tailor. While he was measuring me for my uniform, I asked him, "How's business in these days of drastic clothing rationing?"

"Very slow, sir, very slow indeed . . . Of course, it'll pick up nicely once we start having heavy casualties."

I decided to visit my club. My brother and Brian Franks and others had insisted that I join during my last visit to

England. My name had been put down, and some months later, I had been duly elected to Boodle's.

Mr. White, Mr. Boodle and Mr. Brook all kept coffee-houses in St. James's Street in the days of the Prince Regent. The horse racing, gambling "bloods" had frequented White's, the politicians Brook's, and Boodle's had been the haunt of the landed gentry. Upon the demise of the owners, these coffee shops became clubs.

It is arguable which, today, has the most attractive interior, but Boodle's, with its cream-colored columns and bow windows, certainly has the most beautiful face.

Davy, the hall porter, showed me around the premises at eleven o'clock one morning. The perfect club servant, he had spent his whole life in Boodle's since he had started there as a page.

"Of course, some of my older members are a little awkward nowadays, sir. They don't take to the rationing at all, sir . . . luckily chef can still put on a good table because so many of my members bring game from home. . . ."

He prattled on as he showed me the beautifully proportioned rooms. "Of course, the Scarlet Pimpernel, he was a member, sir, and all his gang too . . . very exciting times those must have been, sir."

He showed me a secluded corner of the main room. Large leather chairs discreetly separated one from the other were placed beneath portraits of former members, prime ministers, dukes and masters of foxhounds. "In this corner, sir, Beau Brummell used to sit looking out into the street . . . this is the silence corner, sir. . . . In here my members speak only to the waiters, never to each other.

"Welcome to the club, sir, we've never had a movie star in Boodle's before." He withdrew.

No other members were about at that hour, so I settled myself in the silence corner with a weekly magazine and rang the bell. The waiter brought me my glass and tidied up an ashtray; without looking up he whispered, "I took my wife to see *Bachelor Mother* last night, sir . . . you're her favorite fan. Lovely pictures of you and Miss Rogers in all the papers today, sir."

I had seen them. The film had just gone on general release, and once more, I was staring out of the movie pages from enormous advertisements.

From Beau Brummell's corner, I had an interesting view

of the passersby on St. James's Street. Always fascinated by
the expressions of people who do not know they are being
observed, I was too occupied to realize that I was myself
being examined, with some distaste by an elderly gentleman with a white walrus mustache. He stood right over me
and flapped at me with a newspaper . . . a sort of fly-remov-
ing underhand flick.

"Hhhrrump!" he said. I looked up at him. "Hhhrr-
rump!" he went again and flicked once more. I wondered if
he wanted me to throw him a fish. He "hhhrrrumped" and
flicked at me for quite a while and finally subsided angrily
into a leather chair directly facing mine. There he breathed
heavily and furious, intolerant, upper-class eyes stared out
at me malevolently from beneath cotton-wool eyebrows.

I tried to concentrate on my magazine, but the tension
between us was oppressive. At last, he appeared to relax
somewhat. He sat back and opened his newspaper.

Suddenly, he sat bolt upright as though he had sat on a
nail. He stared at the paper in front of him as though he
had seen a ghost; then very slowly, like eighteen-inch guns
on a warship, his horrified eyes zeroed on me. They never
left my face as he rang the bell beside his chair.

"Bring me a list of members," he commanded with the
voice of doom.

"Very good, m'lord."

Those terrible orbs bored into me till the members' list
was brought to him on a silver tray. Before he opened it, he
took one last look at his paper, then his finger traveled up
and down the pages. The waiter hovered nervously. Finally, the old man closed the list with a snap, looked at me for
fully a minute, then let out a long moaning sound of deep
despair. "Treachery! Treachery!" it said.

He turned to the waiter and trying to keep his voice
steady, said bravely, "Double brandy—quick!"

"I enjoyed that very much," said a naval lieutenant commander, with a pleasant ruddy face and a broad smile.
"That's our oldest member. He hates people sitting in his
chair."

I had moved out of silence corner in a hurry and a few
members were now filtering in. Over drinks and luncheon
he told me he was in Naval Intelligence "probably stuck in
the Admiralty for the duration." Ian Fleming was his name

and we laughed together at the same things for years to come.

While I was gathering my necessaries together for a second military career, I found Trubshawe.

He was still living at Barton, waiting, like so many others, to be called up, but his marriage to Margie was foundering and he was being increasingly comforted by the beautiful Mrs. Tower.

Ditchley Park in Oxfordshire was the beautiful home of Nancy and Ronnie Tree.

Nancy was a cousin of Norah Flynn, and Ronnie had lately distinguished himself by being one of the small band of rebel Conservative M.P.'s who had voted with Winston Churchill against Chamberlain at the time of Munich. They invited me for the weekend, and in the lovely house, decorated with sublime taste by Nancy, I have since spent some of my happiest times.

For some reason I returned on Sunday afternoon instead of Monday morning. Philip had also gone away, so I was surprised when I let myself into the flat to find myself greeted by a minute Yorkshire terrier. Further shocks greeted me when I heard strange cries coming from my bedroom. I tiptoed down the passage and peered around the open door.

There, stark-naked and strapped to the foot of my bed was a well-known social figure and a senior member of the royal household. Thrashing him with great concentration with a birch was a large red-haired lady wearing a black bra, black gauntlets and black thigh boots. . . .

"Mercy, mistress!" he squealed as the birch rose and fell. The little dog sniffed at his heels. Nobody saw me, so I left quietly and went to a movie. When I came back later, there was no trace of the activity except for a small puddle in the room. Philip promised to reduce my rent if he lent my room to anyone in the future.

Being the owner of a well-known movie face has opened all sorts of doors. It has also closed a few, but I have, thanks to my years in a profession which fascinates almost everyone, had the chance to meet people whom I would only have read about if I had been a successful bank clerk or a well-to-do butcher.

The last weekend before I went to Tidworth, I was invited to the home in Kent of Sir Adrian and Lady Baillie, Leeds Castle. Here, I was to see some of the big wheels of government at play. David Margesson was chief whip of the Conservative Party and, later, Secretary of State for War. Geoffrey Lloyd was Minister of Transport and "Crinks" Johnston was head of the Liberal Party. Individually charming and, for all I knew, performing their tasks with the greatest ability. As a group, they depressed me.

I had a feeling that they had no right to eat and drink and dress for dinner, to make small talk and gossip like ordinary people. I was quite unreasonably shocked that they were not locked in their offices for the weekend, working tirelessly to find ways to finish the war before it got properly started.

For £190 I bought a Hillman Minx. With the gasoline ration of a few gallons a month, its tiny consumption would at least allow me some freedom.

I spent my last night in London at the Café de Paris, hoping to see the WAAF again, but she did not show up. The next afternoon, I put on my new uniform, threw my baggage onto the back seat of the Hillman and headed out on the Great West Road.

It was a cold, wet, windy and altogether miserable winter's evening when I stopped the car on a hilltop on Salisbury Plain. Wood pigeons were homing into the dark isolated clumps of firs, the sodden turf on either side of the road had been chewed up by tanks. Below me lay Tidworth . . . acres and acres of Victorian barrack squares in all their red-brick horror. Gray-slate roofs glistened in the drizzle. A band of blue smoke hung above the place and the sound of bugles rose.

With every mile that Tidworth had come nearer, my depression had increased. "What have you done?" I asked myself. "Nobody asked you to come—they even told you not to . . . you hate the Army . . . you certainly are not very brave and you don't want to get hurt . . . you've thrown away a wonderful life and career in Hollywood . . . you're going to miss all that, you know. . . . Why did you do it? . . . Are you sure it was not just to show off?"

I put my head on the steering wheel and warm tears of self pity pricked my eyeballs. After a while, I drove downhill.

The Second Battalion was a motor training battalion. I

was, by at least eight years, the oldest of the subalterns
under training and being an ex-regular but knowing less
than the others, a bit of a freak. It didn't take long to catch
up. All too soon, I realized that in the intervening years,
there had been pitifully few innovations. We now formed
threes instead of fours; the Lewis light automatic had been
replaced by the Bren; a few small Bren carriers with tracks
had been added; and instead of marching into battle, we
were now driven there in trucks. Once there, we performed
in the same way as before.

In the battalion, all the senior officers down to second-in-
command of companies and all senior NCO's were regu-
lars. Everyone else had either volunteered or been con-
scripted.

Jimmy Bosvile was an excellent commanding officer;
Dick Southby, my company commander, was first class as
was Mark Kerr, the adjutant.

The officers came from all corners of the British Isles,
the men recruited almost exclusively from London with a
preponderance from the East End.

Conscripts, particularly Cockney ones, were, I soon discovered, very different from the professional peacetime
Jocks of the Highland Light Infantry, and it took me a
while to get used to the grumbling of bored soldiers who
resented being pulled out of good jobs and warm homes to
train in acute discomfort for a war they didn't believe
would ever come to anything.

Jimmy Bosvile made it clear that I was earmarked for
the First Battalion, which was already on the Belgian
border, and in the meanwhile, I settled down to a deadening routine of teaching men to drive trucks and to march
and march and march. . . .

A tall flaxen-haired Danish model, a nyphomaniac of
heroic proportions, came down from London most weekends, and I installed her in a cottage in a nearby village.
The great Dane did not pack a prodigious intellectual
punch, but her bed, though every bit as tiring, was a welcome change from spending cold frustrating nights chasing
nonexistent German parachutists all over Salisbury Plain. I
introduced her to a rather dubious Jimmy Bosvile . . . he
was convinced she was a spy.

A few days' leave came my way in February and I spent
them at Ditchley. Winston Churchill was there with Mrs.

Churchill. Also, Brendan Bracken, his trusted lieutenant, and Anthony Eden.

I arrived in uniform just in time for dinner—the meal had, in fact, already been announced and a move was being made in the direction of the dining room. Nancy Tree took me by the hand. "Come and sit next to me," she said. "It's too late for introductions."

We were twenty in number, and just as we were about to sit down, Churchill spotted me from the far end of the table. I had heard before that he was an ardent moviegoer, but I was unprepared for what was to come. He marched the whole length of the dining room and shook me by the hand.

"Young man," he growled, "you did a very fine thing to give up a most promising career to fight for your country."

I was conscious that the great and the near-great in the room had remained standing and were listening with interest.

I stammered some inane reply and Churchill continued with a twinkle, "Mark you, had you not done so, it would have been despicable!" He marched back to his seat.

After dinner Churchill talked and expounded on every subject under the sun. Eden took issue with him on several occasions, but Bracken, always so opinionated on his own, was very subdued in the presence of the champion.

After church on Sunday, Churchill requisitioned me for a walk around the walled garden.

He talked at great length about vegetables and the joy of growing one's own. He made it clear that before long, rationing would become so severe that "every square inch of our island will be pressed into service." He questioned me about the problems of a junior officer in the Army and listened most attentively to answers. It saddens me greatly that I had the enormous good fortune to have several of these garden tours with this unique human being and that I remember so little of what he actually said.

That first weekend he extolled the virtues of Deanna Durbin, "a formidable talent," and whenever he spoke of Hitler, he referred to him either as "Corporal Hitler" or as "Herr Schicklgruber."

Ronnie Tree asked me if I could arrange an occasional private showing of a movie for Churchill. "He loves films, but he doesn't want to go out in public to see them for obvious reasons."

The next morning I got busy, and on the last evening of my leave I booked a projection room in Soho and obtained a copy of the latest Deanna Durbin musical. I installed a bar in the projection room and gave a small dinner in the private room of a nearby restaurant before the showing.

The Trees and Eden came to dinner. Churchill was detained at the Admiralty, but he joined us for the show. When he arrived, he accepted a large liqueur brandy, lit a cigar and settled happily down in his seat.

Halfway through the film, whispering started at the back and I saw that Churchill was leaving. I followed him out, and he thanked me kindly for my efforts but said that "something important" had come up and he must return to the Admiralty.

The next day the headlines were ecstatic. Churchill had given the order for HMS *Cossack* to enter the Josing Fjord "to board with cutlasses" the German naval auxiliary *Altmark* and free three hundred British prisoners—seamen of merchant ships sunk by the *Graf Spee*.

The "Phony War" continued, and the deadening boredom of the training battalion melted into that which I had found so intolerable in the Citadel Barracks, Dover. I felt I had never been away.

New battalions were being formed, but I still waited for my posting to the First Battalion in France.

Suddenly, at the beginning of May, all hell broke loose. Norway fell. Holland and Belgium were invaded, and Churchill became Prime Minister.

By the end of the month our First Battalion were fighting desperately in Calais, with their backs to the Channel, as rear guard, protecting the evacuation from Dunkirk. I was ordered to stand by to move there with two hundred replacements. Events moved too quickly. By June 4 the last troops had left Dunkirk and our entire gallant First Battalion was wiped out—either killed or taken prisoner.

My brother decided that this was the moment to get married to a beautiful South African from Durban, Doreen Platt. After their three-day honeymoon ended, he was sent out to the Eighth Army in the desert and did not see his wife again till he came back in one piece six years later. Miraculously, the marriage also survived.

I was shown an interesting document by Mark Kerr, calling for volunteers for a new "elite force" of a highly secret nature. There followed qualifications about age and questions about liability to air and seasickness.

"I think it must be parachuting," said Mark. "I heard rumors that they are forming something like that."

"Jesus!" I said. "I don't want any part of *that*," but the Tidworth boredom prevailed and "anything to make a change," I put my name down.

It turned out to be something equally alarming . . . the beginning of the commandos.

I was accepted and found myself being interviewed by Colonel Dudley Clarke at the War Office.

He told me the whole conception of the quick cut and thrust of raids on the enemy-held coastline. He had some special ideas, he said, which he might disclose later; in the meanwhile, I was to report to a prohibited area in Scotland, Lochailort Castle in the Western Highlands, for special training with the other volunteers.

Before leaving. I made a quick but fruitless reconnaissance of the Café de Paris in the hopes of seeing "the WAAF," whom I could not get out of my mind, and then fulfilled a noisy, bruising late-night rendezvous with the great Dane.

Volunteers usually fall into two groups. There are the genuinely courageous who are itching to get at the throat of the enemy, and the restless who will volunteer for anything in order to escape from the boredom of what they are currently doing. There were a few in my category, but most of the people I was thrown together with were made of sterner stuff.

Bill Sterling, Brian Mayfield, and the Everest climber, Jim Gavin, were the founder members of the group. They were lately recovered from being depth-charged almost to death while returning in a submarine from some secret operation on the coast of Norway. Other instructors were David Sterling, who later collected a record three DSO's for desert raids deep behind the enemy lines; "Mad Mike" Calvert, who was the demolition expert; Lord Lovat who became the great commando leader of the Dieppe Raid and the Normandy landings, where he also lost half his stomach; Colonel Newman who collected a Victoria Cross when he raided Saint-Nazaire and blew up the dock gates;

the highly decorated Freddie Chapman who spent three and a half years behind the Japanese lines in the Malayan jungle; and two very formidable Shanghai police, Mr. Sykes and Mr. Fairbairn, who concentrated on teaching us a dozen different ways of killing people without making any noise.

Volunteers of all ranks came from every conceivable outfit and were a tough adventurous group prepared for any hardship. Mixed with us, for a while, were the semimutinous remains of the independent companies, defeated in Norway and now awaiting either absorption into the commandos or disbandment. The regimental sergeant major of this ragged conglomeration was a huge man, brought by Brian Mayfield and Bill Sterling from their parent regiment, the Scots Guards. The first morning I was at Lochailort, this splendid creature passed me, ramrod-straight and mustache bristling. He let fly a tremendous salute which I acknowledged. He replied to this with an unmistakable and very loud Bronx cheer or common raspberry.

I spun round as if shot and shouted after him, "Sergeant Major!"

"SAH!"

"Come back here!"

"SAH!"

He came back, halted and snapped off another salute.

"Did you make that rude noise?"

"YESSAR."

"Why, may I ask?"

"Because you look such a cunt in a Rifle Brigade hat, SAR."

Only then did I catch on; it was John Royal of Green Beer fame!

While I gaped at him, he said. "I heard you were coming . . . I have a room in a crofter's cottage, name of Lachlan, just behind the kirk in the village. See you there this evening . . . SAR!"

Another Scots Guards' salute and he was gone.

John's cottage was a godsend. Every evening, I repaired there and tried to forget my aching, bruised body and my flea-bag bed on the hard wooden floor of a loft shared with forty or fifty others.

John, after his problems in India, had found it impossible to obtain a commission, so he had joined the Scots

Guards as a Guardsman and within a few months had risen to his present dizzy height. Later he became a parachutist and at last got his commission as a glider pilot. He was killed at Arnhem.

After two months running up and down the mountains of the Western Highlands, crawling up streams at night, and swimming in the loch with full equipment, I was unbearably fit. I spoke to Bill Sterling about my problem, and he, most understandingly, allowed me forty-eight hours' leave in London to rectify the situation.

I visited the little village sweetshop which doubled as post office and sent a telegram to the great Dane:

ARRIVING WEDNESDAY MORNING WILL COME STRAIGHT TO FLAT WITH SECRET WEAPON.

The great Dane lived in Swan Court, and I went there as soon as the night train from Glasgow had deposited me in London.

I was about to ring the bell when I was tapped on the shoulder. A major and two sergeants of the Military Police had materialized from nowhere.

"Come with us, please," said the major.

"Why? What's the matter?"

"I couldn't say—my superior wants to see you."

I was taken in a military car to a building in St. James's Street almost opposite Boodle's and shown into an office where sat a man in a blue suit. He didn't look very friendly.

"MI-V would like to ask you one little question," he said grimly. "You are a member of the most secret outfit in the British Army; you are in training in a prohibited area; you have sent a message in code to an enemy alien. WHY?"

I said, "Sir, that's not code—that's fucking."

I explained the circumstances and finally persuaded him that all was well. He melted a little but said that he would investigate the whole matter further. The upshot of it was that although I spent my holiday as planned with his daughter, the great Dane's father was discovered to be working in the Ministry of Supply in a department closely connected with the organization of convoys at sea. He was removed.

By September I was sent back to Colonel Dudley Clarke, who told me that I had been promoted to captain and was now the liaison officer between M.O.9—the War Office department which was responsible for the commandos and their operations—and the units themselves. When at the War Office, I shared a desk with a portly amiable captain who coped tirelessly and uncomplainingly with the mountainous paper work—Quintin Hogg, Lord Chancellor of Great Britain. The rest of the time, I was on the move.

A weekend leave at Ditchley provided me with a second tour of the walled garden with Winston Churchill, now Prime Minister. He asked me what I was doing at the moment, so as we walked, I filled him in on the exciting prospects with the commandos. He stopped by a greenhouse and said, "Your security is very lax. . . . You shouldn't be telling me this." He was always a superb actor, but to this day I don't know whether or not he was joking.

The first big raid was on Guernsey. We trained in the Isle of Wight. RAF crash boats were used because landing craft had not yet been built.

It was a success and a few bemused prisoners were taken out of their beds. One party made a landing by mistake on Sark which had no Germans on it at all. They were invited to the nearest pub by the locals.

The Battle of Britain was now in full swing as Hermann Goering tried to break the back of the RAF as a prelude to invasion.

As the battles over London and the south and east coasts raged, friends suddenly disappeared. Billy Fiske, the first American killed in World War II, died flying a Spitfire with 601 Squadron. The "Phony War" was over with a vengeance.

Dudley Clarke switched the role of commandos from offense to defense, and we trained to be overrun by the invaders and then to form the nucleus of an underground movement.

London was being heavily bombed, and moves were made to take the minds of the civilians off their increasing discomforts.

The National Gallery, for instance, abolished its entrance fee, and as an added inducement to relax and forget what was happening over one's head, eminent musicians gave free lunch-time concerts.

One day I walked there from the War Office and wandered around a couple of galleries. From a third, I heard a cello being played by an expert. . . . I watched her complete concentration and bathed myself in the haunting sounds for several minutes before I realized that a few feet away and totally engrossed stood "the WAAF."

Almost guiltily, I stared at her. At close quarters and under the overhead lighting of the gallery she was even more beautiful than I had remembered and so sweet looking and gentle.

When the music ended, she did not move; she stood quite still, lost in the beauty of what she had heard. People applauded and the cellist picked up her things and left. Still "the WAAF" did not move. When there were only two of us left in the gallery, she looked up and noticed me.

"Hello," she said, "wasn't that wonderful?"

I persuaded her to have a sandwich with me at a nearby coffee shop . . . we were both on the point of being late back to work.

I discovered her name, Primula, the fact that she was the cipher clerk at the RAF Reconnaissance Squadron at Heston just outside London and that she was billeted on a family friend who lived in the middle of Regent's Park.

There was never a shadow of doubt in my mind that this was the one, but the whole world flying apart at the seams, there was no time for the niceties of a prolonged courtship. That night I called at the house in Regent's Park and passed in a note saying that I was outside the door, was considering buying the park from the king, and would like some advice on the dredging of the lake.

She appeared, giggling deliciously, and invited me in.

Two days later I was invited to luncheon to meet her mother, and by the end of the week I found myself shaking and sweating and being introduced to her father, who lived apart. My mission was to persuade him to allow his daughter to become my wife.

Bill Rollo was an angel. Nobody has ever been able to say a word against him, and this despite the fact that he was a famous divorce lawyer. When I met him, he was, though over fifty, also in the uniform of the RAF . . . on his chest an impressive row of ribbons from World War I.

He worked all day at his law office and did night duty in a special war room, where on a huge wall map the Prime Minister could see the latest dispositions of flotillas, brigades and squadrons at a glance.

"But, Primmie darling," Bill protested, "you *can't* put me in this position because I don't know how to behave!"

"Don't be nervous, Papa," she said. "Leave everything to us."

He handed me an enormous drink and helped himself liberally. "Oh, God!" he said. "This is agony, isn't it?

"I ought to ask you all sorts of questions. Do you have any prospects? . . . Well, that's bloody silly for a start because the air-raid warning has just gone." It was the night of a particularly heavy blitz and bombs were soon raining down. It had been arranged that we would go out to dinner, but there was so much shrapnel flying about that we decided against it.

"I can't think why you want to marry her," said Bill. "She can't cook and she can't sew."

"You're a big help," said his daughter.

We opened some wine, some cans of beans and some cheese, and as a particularly heavy bombardment made the high old building shudder and sway, with the three of us huddling under the kitchen table, Bill Rollo gave his consent.

War is a great accelerator of events, so ten days later we were married in the tiny Norman church of Huish village at the foot of the Wiltshire Downs. Trubshawe, in the uniform of the Royal Sussex Regiment, was best man, and friends from far and near came by train, by bicycle or by blowing their gasoline rations for a month—some came on horseback.

Primmie looked like a porcelain figure in a simple pale-blue dress. The Battle of Britain on that cloudless September day was raging in the skies above; it was no time for veil and orange blossom. She carried a bouquet of pink flowers picked from her parents' garden a hundred yards away. Halfway through the service, as we were singing her favorite psalm, "Sheep May Safely Graze," a small flock, as though divinely summoned, wandered in from the downs and stood chewing benignly around the font.

Our week of honeymoon was spent finding a place for Primmie to set up a home. We had no money apart from my Army pay, so we were lucky to find a fourteenth-century, unheated, thatched cottage between Dorney and Slough. Primmie had left the RAF in order to get married, but she was determined to contribute to the war effort so

she bicycled to Slough every morning at seven o'clock and
worked at Hawker's factory, building Hurricane fighters.
She took in an elderly refugee from the London bombing
who had just lost her husband and her home near the
docks. Mrs. Wisden was a little birdlike creature who wore
pince-nez. She kept Halfway Cottage tidy and cooked after
a fashion, but she behaved rather strangely during air-raid
alerts. Hawkers being an obvious target for the Luftwaffe,
these were frequent. Thanks to a permanent smoke screen
from smudge pots, the factory itself remained untouched,
but the whole neighborhood became pitted with bomb
craters to Mrs. Wisden's apparent satisfaction. The moment the banshee wailings of the sirens started, she would
rip down the blackout curtains, turn on all the lights and
rush out into the garden, tearing at her blouse.

"Let me 'ave it, 'itler," she would scream, "rite through
me bleedin' chest. . . . I want to join my 'Arry. . . . Roll on
death!"

The commandos were being prepared for offensive
operations, but these were held up while landing craft were
being designed and built. In the meanwhile, the danger of
our own invasion by the German Army, poised across the
Channel, was very real. A new and highly secret outfit
within the Special Services was formed to help deal with
this possibility and I was ordered to join it in Richmond
Park. Before I went, I did something for which, in my
opinion, the military has never adequately rewarded me. I
suggested to my new uncle by marriage, Robert Laycock,
that he should join the commandos.

He was then a captain in the Royal Horse Guards and
had just received a posting to India to become gas officer of
a division and was due to embark in a few days' time. He
came to the War Office and I introduced him to Dudley
Clarke, who immediately decided that this was just the
man he wanted.

Bob and I paced the stone corridors of that dreary building while Clarke dashed about, pulling strings, as a result
of which somebody else went to India and Bob formed No.
8 Commando, embarking on a career of legendary gallantry which included his famous effort to blow up Field Marshal Rommel two hundred desert miles behind the German
lines. It culminated, five years later, in his becoming chief
of Combined Operations with the rank of major general.

Richmond Park was the headquarters of Phantom, the brainchild of "Hoppy." Colonel Hopkinson had realized painfully during the retreat to Dunkirk that if a general fighting a battle is not receiving a steady flow of reliable information from the front, he cannot contribute very much toward the outcome. In the heat of contact, normal communications frequently break down, radio transmitters get destroyed, and dispatch riders get killed.

Phantom was composed of a number of highly mobile squadrons of officer patrols. These were deployed among the forward units, equipped with radios, endowed with expert dispatch riders and as a last resort, a basket of carrier pigeons. The commanding officer of Phantom stayed at the Army commander's right hand, and when the situation at a certain point on the map needed clarifying, a message went direct to the nearest Phantom Squadron to find out exactly what was going on. Usually the answer came back explaining that the situation was unclear because the place was full of Germans.

After a brief period of intensive training, I was promoted to major and for more than three years I had the great honor to command A Squadron.

"Hoppy" was a short, square officer with a fertile imagination and a great gift for extracting the maximum of loyalty and hard work from all ranks. Before he was killed in action in Italy, he built up a unit that again and again proved its worth in the reconquest of the Continent.

Hugh Kindersley, a handsome giant from the Scots Guards, was second-in-command and the officers and men came from every unit in the British Army.

During the threat of seaborne invasion, the Phantom squadrons were distributed along the southern and eastern coasts where, apart from our primary function, we also made ourselves ready to go underground, and a large stock of disguises was earmarked for distribution if the invasion was successful. I, personally, was ready to reemerge dressed as a parson.

For a start "A" Squadron was attached to 5 Corps in the danger area behind Poole Harbour. The corps commander was a dynamic little man who demanded a fearsome standard of mental alertness and physical fitness. Just inside his headquarters was a large notice board:

ARE YOU 100% FIT?

ARE YOU 100% EFFICIENT?
DO YOU HAVE 100% BINGE?

We never discovered what he meant by "BINGE" because nobody dared ask him. His name was General Bernard Montgomery.

"A" Squadron was my pride and joy. The second-in-command was a sardonic Irish newspaperman, and the patrol officers included a Cameron Highlander, a Frenchman, a Lancastrian, a weight lifter, the assistant bursar at Eton College, an amateur steeplechase jockey and an interior decorator who frequently called me "Dear" instead of "Sir."

The squadron sergeant major was a Scots Guardsman, and the seventy other ranks were made up of bank clerks, burglars, shop assistants, milkmen, garage mechanics, schoolmasters, painters, bookmakers, stockbrokers and laborers.

A huge corporal told me he was "a lion tamer in usual life," and of the two men who cooked for and catered to the officers, one came from the royal household at Buckingham Palace, while the other, a Norfolk man, said he "liked a bit of poaching better than anything." In action, of course, these two were runners at squadron headquarters. Once when General Montgomery visited us unexpectedly, I was waiting under his eagle eye for an important message to be delivered when I was appalled to see my runner approaching with the message in one hand and a pheasant in the other.

In the autumn of '41, the Trees invited Primmie and me to spend my week's leave in the comfort of Ditchley. Walter Monckton, the Minister of Information, was there, also a charming American, David Bruce. As the Germans had radio beams from Norway and France pinpointing Chequers, the Prime Minister's country retreat was considered a bad risk, so Ronnie and Nancy made a large part of Ditchley available to Winston Churchill and his staff. It was fascinating to rub shoulders with such as Sir Charles Portal, the commander in chief of the RAF, and Sholto Douglas, chief of Fighter Command.

Churchill bade me take another walk in the walled garden. Things were looking grim: The war in the desert was at its lowest ebb with Rommel snapping at the gates of Alexandria, and after their spectacular success in Crete, the possibility of an enemy airborne invasion of the U.K. had now superseded the threat of a conventional one. Food was getting more and more scarce and a glance at the map sent cold shivers down one's back.

The whole of Europe was under German domination, and in Russia, von Rundstedt had just captured 600,000 prisoners at Kiev and von Bock another 600,000 at Vyazma . . . Leningrad was besieged and the road to Moscow appeared wide open.

"Do you think, sir," I asked, "that the Americans will ever come into the war?"

He fixed me with that rather intimidating gaze and unloosed the famous jaw-jutting bulldog growl. "Mark my words, something cataclysmic will occur!"

Four weeks later the Japanese attacked Pearl Harbor.

Months after, when we were once more enjoying the delights of a short leave at Ditchley, I asked in the walled garden if the Prime Minister remembered what he had said so long ago. His reply gave me goose pimples. "Certainly I remember."

"What made you say it, sir?"

"Because, young man, I study history."

When Primmie became pregnant in the spring of 1942, she stopped building fighter planes, left Mrs. Wisden baring her bosoms in the garden at the first sign of a German bomber, and followed "A" Squadron wherever it went, living in a succession of farms, stables and vicarages. We were wonderfully in love and spent a lot of time praying that Phantom would not be sent to the African desert or the Malayan jungle.

In mid-August, the ambitious raid on Dieppe was carried out. About 8,000 men, mainly Canadians, were employed. Also involved were commandos under Lord Lovat and a specially trained force from Phantom.

Although the raid taught many invaluable lessons that saved devastating loss of life later on the Normandy beaches, the cost was appalling with almost two-thirds of the attacking force being wiped out.

Writing and rewriting the letters I had to send to the wives and girlfriends of the men lost from "A" Squadron, I kept thinking of a scene from *Dawn Patrol* when the commanding officer was going through the same agonizing ritual. The adjutant watched him for a while and then said gently, "It doesn't matter how you word it, sir. It'll break her heart just the same."

By autumn Primmie was less mobile, so she moved to London during the height of the blitz and calmly waited for the arrival of her baby.

I thought perhaps Philip Astley might let her stay in his comfortable flat and tried to call him. His phone did not answer for a very good reason: The building had been demolished by a direct hit. Fortunately, Philip had been out at the time.

By a great piece of good luck, "Hoppy" had recalled "A" Squadron to Richmond to refit with new equipment, so I was well within reach when Primmie was whisked off in the middle of a December night and admitted to the Royal Northern Hospital in Camden Town in north London.

"Hoppy" gave me permission to spend the nights in the hospital so every evening after work, I borrowed a dispatch rider's motorcyle and rode through the blackout across the whole of London to be with Primmie and her little boy. They were unattractive trips. Hitler's full fury was raining down on the city and shrapnel from the antiaircraft batteries was also falling like lethal confetti. I wore a steel helmet and, too often aided by the light of the fires, chugged my way past bomb craters and debris, peering ahead at the glowworm reflection from my dimmed-out headlight. Happily the motorcycle made so much noise that I could not hear the express-train whistle of falling bombs.

I slept on the floor beside Primmie's bed and marveled at her serenity—she was totally unafraid. Camden Town, a working-class district, for some reason had become a prime target for the German bombers; the devastation around the hospital was awful. The bombing started nightly, as soon as darkness fell, and continued till dawn. More than once, on hearing a bomb screaming down in his direction, the brave major on the floor had to steel himself against taking cover under his wife's bed.

A few days after Primmie and her baby left for Dorney, the inevitable happened: The hospital received a direct hit.

During 1943 the soldier's oldest enemy—boredom—attacked Phantom.

It was quite evident to us that we were being prepared for the final assault on the Continent of Europe, but, like footballers, we were becoming overtrained, so "Hoppy" sent his squadrons whizzing all over England.

At one moment, "A" Squadron found itself isolated outside the walls of Dartmoor Prison.

"Keep the men interested," ordered "Hoppy" by radio.

"Think of novel employment for them; turn night into day; make front-line conditions."

Obediently, I arranged three days on the moors of intensive maneuvers and, at the last minute, to simulate what might easily lie ahead of us, I canceled the ration trucks.

Naturally, at the end of seventy-two hours on a windswept escarpment, covered with nothing but heather, ferns and wild-pony shit, "A" Squadron, forced to live off the land, was in a sorry condition. All, that is, except their gallant commander who had taken certain gastronomic precautions and Squadron Sergeant Major Lonsdale of the Scots Guards.

"How is it possible?" I asked him. "I am the only one who knew that the squadron would have no food or water for three days."

"Sorr," he replied, "I happened to have about my person one large fruitcake."

The naval commander of a flotilla of motor torpedo boats in Dartmouth contacted me.

"We are made of three-ply," he said, "and we are fitted with last war two-pounders. The German E boats have twin Oerlikens operated electrically from armor-plated bridges and we are supposed to protect the convoys from the bastards. Do you have any antitank weapons? If so, please come and help us."

"A" Squadron spent many miserable seasick hours as a result of my quixotic acceptance of this dangerous invitation.

"Hoppy" finally gathered all the squadrons into Richmond Park and told me to arrange a concert. I went to beg the help of the Crazy Gang at the Victoria Palace.

But Flanagan's response was typical. "Leave it to us," he said. "Just provide the transport and we'll provide the show, but you be master of ceremonies and give us some grub after."

The concert took place at midnight, in the big movie house on Richmond Hill. It was a classic show business answer to an SOS. Flanagan and Allen showed up, also

Nervo and Knox, Naughton and Gold, Debroy Sommers and his Band, Teddy Brown and his Xylophone, Sid Field, Zoe Gail, Frances Day, Naunton Wayne, Arthur Riscoe, and Leslie Henson.

The show lasted for four hours and was wildly appreciated. Civilian morale on a small beleaguered island was also in constant need of bolstering, and during the time I spent in the Home Forces, I was used for all sorts of capers. I was given four weeks' special duty, and with a radio transmitter in my dressing room from which I controlled "A" Squadron, I played a part in a film about the Spitfire, backed by the RAF, *The First of the Few* with Leslie Howard.

Two years later, I collected a few more weeks of special duty and played in an Army-backed film, directed by Carol Reed, written by Eric Ambler and Peter Ustinov, *The Way Ahead*, which not only was a huge public success but for ten years after the war was used as a training film at Sandhurst.

These short bursts of escapism were a bonanza and I was only too happy to sample the first marvelous fruits of a happy married life.

With my major's pay, Primmie had now left the numbing damp of Halfway Cottage for the roaring drafts of a phony Tudor villa nearer the center of the village of Dorney.

It was always full of friends, bringing their own food and drink of course. Larry Olivier and Vivien Leigh lived nearby as did Johnny and Mary Mills, Rex Harrison and Lilli Palmer. Noël Coward was a frequent and greatly cherished visitor, and all of them looked after Primmie while I was away and gave her a wonderful introduction into the strange, half-mad world of show business.

Del Giudice, the Italian dynamo who produced the pictures that took Arthur Rank out of his flower bags and put him at the top of the film world, was another neighbor. A popular guest at Del Giudice's house was the then Minister of Labour and later one of the greatest foreign secretaries that Britain has ever known, Ernest Bevin.

I discussed with him the problem of my soldier's boredom.

"Make 'em use their noggins," he said. "They're all intelligent fellers . . . get a few debates going. But don't take sides yourself or you'll be in a bloody mess."

The discussion periods I organized as a result of Bevin's advice were a huge success. The liveliest one was sparked off by a leading article which had appeared in the *Daily Mirror*: ". . . the accepted tip for Army leadership would, in plain truth, be this: All who aspire to mislead others in war should be brass-buttoned boneheads, socially prejudiced, arrogant and fussy. A tendency to heart disease, apoplexy, diabetes and high blood pressure is desirable in the highest posts. . . ."

One thing stuck out a mile during these debates: The vast majority of men who had been called up to fight for their country held the Conservative Party entirely responsible for the disruption of their lives and under no circumstances would they vote for it next time there was an election—Churchill or no Churchill.

Weekends at Ditchley afforded close-ups of other members of the Cabinet. Anthony Eden was unfailingly kind and charming, but, somehow, he left me with the impression that he was floating in the air far above me; and Duff Cooper, a much tougher, much more down-to-earth character, was given to bursts of ungovernable fury during which his face would congest and turn an alarming magenta color. The smallest thing could set him off and the Trees' two sons would come rushing to find me. "Come quick . . . Duff's doing a turkey cock in the library!"

I got on famously with him once he realized we had one big thing in common: We both loved America and Americans. His wife, the legendary Lady Diana, was, of course, sublime.

My fast-becoming-forgotten movie face was occasionally pressed into service and I was sent to make impassioned speeches in factories in the Midlands during "Tanks for Russia Week."

I was also sent to Glasgow to head a drive to get more volunteers for the Women's Army—the ATS.

There, for a week, I appeared in fog-filled movie houses all over the city and harangued the paying customers, whom I could barely see in the gloom.

My constant companion during that trip was a hard-bitten newspaper reporter named Andy Martin. Andy was a much-loved figure in Glasgow, and wherever we went, he was greeted like a brother.

Glasgow's seamy side makes the tougher parts of most other cities look like Fifth Avenue, but there was not a dive in the Gorbals which we could not visit with impunity. Andy would give the signal and we would be admitted to some smoky, reeking haunt. Then he would jump on a table or a barrel and, in seconds, have the whole place rocking with laughter. Whiskey was pressed on me till it came out of my ears. Andy was an accomplished drinker, but on my last evening in Glasgow, he misjudged it.

"I canna make it hame, Davie," he said. "Put twa cushions on the floor and I'll kip awhile."

When I woke queasily in the early morning, I looked down on my friend, sleeping peacefully at the foot of my bed. Andy was a dwarf.

By the beginning of 1944 the Americans were pouring into Britain and many old Hollywood friends appeared at Dorney. Bob Coote materialized in the Royal Canadian Air Force. Clark Gable, whose adored wife, Carole Lombard, had been killed in an air disaster, appeared as a major in a bombing squadron, and Jimmy Stewart showed up, a colonel in the same line of business. John Ford and Douglas Fairbanks, Jr., were in the U.S. Navy. Willie Wyler and John Huston were with combat photographic units. Garson Kanin was doing something very mysterious in the Army, and joy of joys, John McClain arrived, a lieutenant in the U.S. Navy attached to the OSS.

Dorney features so often in this account that I feel I should explain that I was in other places, too. At the end of a war one forgets, thank God, the numbing patches of boredom and frustration and remembers only the fright and the fun. I am chiefly concerned with the fun and Dorney; with Primmie was where my fun lay.

The Free French frequently cooked their rations in our kitchen, among them Claude Dauphin and Jean-Pierre Aumont. These two gave a party for us in London and Joseph Kessel ate a champagne glass, stem and all.

Guy Gibson, the master bomber, spent a weekend with us just after he had been awarded the Victoria Cross for blowing up the Eder and Möhne dams. He was in a rare state of excitement because Winston Churchill had invited him to dinner at 10 Downing Street on the Monday. Guy

made a date with us for luncheon at one o'clock on the following day so he could report everything the great man
said.

Primmie and I were at the Berkeley sharp at one—no
Gibson. Two o'clock—no Gibson. We were just finishing
our ersatz coffee around three o'clock when he came totter-
ing in, looking ghastly.

"How was it?" we asked.

"Marvelous—fabulous!" he croaked. "God! I'm tired.
That was the best yet!"

"What did he say?"

"Who?" said Gibson.

"Churchill," I said with a touch of asperity.

Gibson looked stricken, then he clutched his head.
"Jesus Christ! I FORGOT!"

A month later on his one hundred and twentieth bombing mission, he was shot down.

By the early spring of 1944 it was obvious that the Second Front would soon be opened on the Continent. Training increased in tempo and there were so many American
troops in Britain that only the barrage balloons kept the island from sinking beneath the waves under their weight.

Out of the blue, I was ordered to report to General Sir
Frederick Morgan at a highly camouflaged headquarters in
a wood near Sunningdale.

Morgan, although I did not know it, had for months
been drawing up the invasion plans that would soon be put
into effect in Normandy. He came straight to the point.
"You've lived in America for some years?"

"Yes, sir."

"Do you like Americans?"

"Very much, sir."

"Good, because you're going to be seeing a great deal of
them. . . . I'm taking you out of Phantom and promoting
you to lieutenant colonel. From now on, you will be under
the direct orders of General Barker, an American."

He told me where to go and I found General Ray Barker
in a Nissen hut under the trees. He, it transpired, had been
working with Morgan on the overall invasion plan.

"One thing we dread is a repetition of what happened
between the British and the French in the last war," he
said. "Sir John French and General Lanrezac were commanding adjoining armies. They didn't speak each other's

language; they detested each other and tried to win private feuds to impress Field Marshal Joffre.

"Their feelings percolated down to the troops. The Germans repeatedly attacked this weak link in the chain and very nearly won the war as a result."

General Barker was the finest type of contemporary American . . . quiet, courteous and full of humor, but underneath his evident compassion and gentleness, one could detect the steel. I listened attentively as he went on: "When we land on the Continent, there will be Americans, British and Canadians to start with. Later there will be Poles and French. I am charged by General Eisenhower with seeing that this time there are no weak links in the chain. . . . Misunderstandings and rumors are bound to arise, but they will have to be dealt with promptly at all levels from friction between Army commanders right down to arguments about what programs should be beamed to the troops by the BBC and the American Forces Network. After we invade, you will be in the field doing odd jobs for me and from now on you take orders only from me."

"A" Squadron gave me a silver tankard, and I handed over to John Hannay, my second-in-command for the past two years. It was a big wrench, but my love of change soon dispelled my disappointment and under the highly efficient John the squadron prospered.

A celebration luncheon with Ian Fleming at Boodle's revealed that the place was much changed. A direct hit had demolished the back of the building, but the beautiful façade and famous ceilings were still intact. Most of the windows were boarded over. Food had become very scarce.

"My members don't take to whale steaks at all," said Davy mournfully.

We were peering at the daily menu displayed in the darkened hall when the oldest member growled in my ear, "Can't see the damn thing in this gloom. What's on the card today?"

"*Moules marinières, sir,*" I said.

"Good God!" he trumpeted. "The bloody fellers have got us eatin' moles now!"

A few taxis were still to be found, and Jack, who was always outside the club, drove me to Paddington Station.

Although the flying bombs did not start roaring into

London for another few weeks, conventional night raids were still frequent.

" 'Orrible incident down our way last night, sir," said Jack. "They dropped a bloody great land mine and poor old Acacia Grove—they got it proper, flattened it was. . . . We was diggin' 'em out all night long. Number Fourteen was nothink but a pile o' rubble. We found the old lady and started diggin' 'er out—both 'er legs was busted and one ear seemed to 'ave been tore off. 'Find my Bill!' she kept on cryin' out. . . . 'Find my Bill! . . . 'E's in the shit-ouse at the back.' Well, finally, we dug the poor old bloke out, and 'e was much worse off than she wos, but 'e was larfin' like buggery.

" 'Wot you got to larf at, Dad?' I arst him.

" 'My Gawd,' " he said, " 'I always knowed this place wos built of piss and plaster, but wot 'appens? I go to the shit'ouse, sit down, do me job, stand up, pull the chain and the 'ole fuckin' 'ouse fell down!' "

We held a belated christening party for little David, and with the exception of Bob Laycock, all the godparents came to Dorney.

Larry and Vivien produced a Jacobean drinking mug with "D. W." engraved on it. I complained about this to godmother Vivien who said, "I'm not going to change it, so from now on you'll just have to be called Wiven, that's all."

Godfather Noël Coward donated a huge silver cocktail shaker on which was inscribed:

> Because, my Godson dear, I rather
> Think you'll turn out like your father.

The day, however, was made by a retired nannie, Miss Maple, who at seventy had decided that she could still "do her bit," so she struggled with little David to enable Primmie to return to work at Hawker's. Some of my methods, however, had upset this redoubtable old lady and she suddenly appeared and announced to the assembled guests, "It's bad enough when the major takes Master David's olive oil for the salad dressing, but when he steals his concentrated California orange juice for the cocktails, it's going TOO FAR!"

I was so proud of Primmie, of her flowerlike beauty of course, but everyone loved her and the reason was obvious: She never thought an unkind thought about anyone. She was incapable of saying an unkind word. On the June night before I left for Normandy, we clung together miserably. The parting was not made easier by the news that her uncle, Michael Laycock, had just been killed on the beaches and that her brother, Andrew, had been blown up when his destroyer hit a mine. His captain reported that "blown up" was the correct description because Andrew was on the foredeck when it happened and the next moment the captain, high on the bridge, saw Andrew above his head. Miraculously, he fell in the sea and survived.

I lied to Primmie about leaving after breakfast, and at dawn when she had finally fallen asleep, I slipped out of bed, dressed, looked down at her with the little boy asleep in his cot beside her, and tiptoed out of the house.

The *Empire Battleaxe* was a Liberty ship with elements of an American Division. I boarded her at Southampton.

"That's one helluvan encouraging sendoff," observed a GI as, over the side, we watched hundreds of wounded being helped or carried ashore from a tank-landing craft— boys with shocked faces and staring eyes, in their bandages and hastily applied field dressings, grown old in a few short hours.

Once opposite the Normandy beach, we were ordered into the landing craft and, to the continuous roll of gunfire, ferried ashore. Beach masters pointed to the white-taped paths through the minefields and we went our separate ways.

There is no place in these pages for harrowing blood-soaked descriptions of man's inhumanity to man; all that has been raked over a thousand times by a thousand more competent writers since that June of 1944. So let me say at once that lying in a ditch that first night in Normandy, my most vivid recollection was the sound of the nightingales.

Before the war, eminent lady cellists were employed by the BBC to sit in remote black woods to try to coax these timid little birds into song. The nightingales of Normandy were made of sterner stuff; they all but drowned out the gunfire with their racket.

Between British Second Army and American First there was a small bridge at Carentan. It was, in fact, the one vital

link between our very meager bridgeheads and, consequently, was shelled by the Germans at close range many
times a day.

Several spare Bailey bridges were kept handy so that re-
placement was speedy and the lifeline kept open, but it was
a hazardous crossing and I had to make it frequently. Fox-
holes were dug on either side of the bridge, and once,
trapped by the shelling, I was cowering in the bottom of
one of them when, after what seemed an eternity, the bombardment, like some lethal rain, seemed to have let up. I
peeked timidly out and couldn't believe my eyes. Like a
cock pheasant in the braken, a familiar head was sticking
out of a foxhole a few yards away—John McClain.

After the barrage, my transport was no longer function-
ing, so my old friend gave me a ride in his command car
driven by a very disapproving American sergeant. McClain
also pinned on my chest the Iron Cross.

Cherbourg was still in enemy hands, and McClain, with
a psychological warfare unit, had been bombarding the defenders with a verbal barrage via a sound truck. General
von Schlieben, in an attempt to shore up the morale of the
defenders, had for some days been handing out decorations
like Lady Bountiful at the village fete. He had radioed for
more Iron Crosses to be delivered by parachute, and they
had been dropped in error on McClain and his outfit.

My work completed at First Army, McClain suggested a
light luncheon at a little inn he had heard about from Captain Bob Low, an ex-*Time* reporter now working in First
Army Intelligence.

"Low says it's in a backwater," he said. "No Krauts
there—nobody—untouched by the war. Let's go."

Quettehou, on the coast about five miles south of Bar-
fleur, was all that Bob Low had predicted, and the inn, Aux
Trois Cents Hommes, was unforgettable. The disapproving
sergeant refused to join us and sat outside morosely chewing his C rations, while McClain and I, the first Allied
combatants they had seen, were treated like royalty by the
three bosomy ladies who ran the place. We were given a
sumptuous meal of omelets, delicious little flatfish and Cam-
embert cheese, washed down by bottles of Bordeaux,
which they dug up from the cabbage patch where they had
been hidden from the Germans.

On the way back, we grew strangely silent as we approached Carentan because it became obvious from the noise that we were going to have to run the gauntlet of the bridge once again.

"Er . . . lookit, Sarge," said McClain, "isn't there some way around by the beach so we can cut out that god-damned bridge?"

The Disapproving One was unbending. "The way I see it, Lieutenant, it's either got your name on it, or it hasn't."

McClain's reply was really brave. "Well, it may have your fucking name on it, but it doesn't have mine."

The Normandy battles raged around Caen and Saint-Lô longer than had been expected, and this frustration of their plans sparked the first differences of opinions between the Allied commanders. Finally, at the end of July, with the British and Canadians containing the bulk of the German armor, the Americans were able to break out on the Western flank and the charge on Paris and Brussels began.

I found "B" Squadron of Phantom hidden in a wood behind the Orne. Dennis Russell was still in command. Hugh "Tam" Williams, that fine actor, was still in the squadron. They told me that Hugh Kindersley had been badly wounded, and "Tam" and I agreed that if we had known about the German Nebelwerfer—a six-barreled mortar—we would never have joined the Army in the first place. After the war, like many others, "Tam" found his place had been filled while he had been away and that he had been largely forgotten as an actor. He went bankrupt and then emerged triumphant as one of the most successful playwrights that London has seen.

In a tent far to the rear lived a group of war correspondents typing out pages of self-glorification . . . "as the bullets sang past my head," etc. There were some heroic and exemplary war correspondents, of course—Ernie Pyle, Bob Cappa and Chester Wilmot, to name a few—but anyone who says a bullet sings past, hums past, flies past, pings or whines past, has never heard one—they go CRACK.

Just before the breakout at Falaise, General Barker recalled me for a few hours to England.

The DC-3 lumbered off the makeshift runway on a cliff top above the landing beaches. After an alarming dip, it gained height and headed home. Below much of the damage wrought by the disastrous three-day storm at the end of June was still apparent. The "Mulberry" Harbor opposite

Saint-Laurent was completely wrecked and of the eight hundred landing craft originally smashed ashore at least half still lay there like beached whales.

An American Intelligence colonel sitting on the bucket seat beside me told me that the storm had brought the unloading of vital stores and reinforcements to a halt and for two weeks it had been touch and go whether we could hang on in Normandy.

We landed at Croydon at eight o'clock in the morning. Flying bombs were now being directed into London all day long, and driving through the city, I saw more damage than I had expected.

General Barker concluded his business with me with great dispatch; then with his customary thoughtfulness, he said, "Your plane goes back at seven this evening so go on home and give your wife a surprise."

I caught the fast train to Reading, got off at Taplow, and borrowed the station master's bicycle. I could be in Dorney by one and the five o'clock train back seemed days away.

Land-girls were cutting lettuce and pulling potatoes in the fields on either side of the road. They looked up and waved as I pedaled past.

My heart was bubbling with excitement. In my mind I rehearsed all sorts of stiff-upper-lip-returning-warrior platitudes. I wished I had a toy for the little boy.

Quietly, I leaned the bicycle against a tree and pushed the back door—it was locked. The front door was locked too. I walked around and around the house . . . nobody was home. I opened a back window by breaking a pane and crawled through. The family was gone and judging by the state of the kitchen, had been gone for some days.

Disconsolate and also alarmed, I mounted the bicycle and made inquiries in the village shops.

"Mrs. Niven picked up her ration books a week ago, but nobody knows where she went."

Back at the house, I called Bill Rollo in London at his office, but he was out. I had beer, bread and cheese and pickled onions in the village pub, then went home again and waited for Bill to call back. While I was waiting, I mowed the lawn and weeded Primmie's little vegetable garden. At three o'clock Bill called and told me she had decided to evacuate the London area and take little David up to the peace and quiet of Quenby in Leicestershire.

I put through a call to Quenby, but there was a three-hour delay. I pleaded with the operator but she was granite.

"We all 'ave our little problems these days, don't we, luv?"

I drank the remainder of a bottle of gin in the kitchen and weaved off on the station master's bicycle in time to catch the five o'clock for London and Normandy.

13

By mid-August the Canadians had entered Falaise. The Poles were above Chambois, and with British and Americans in full spate, the bulk of the German Seventh Army was wiped out in the Mortain pocket. Sixteen of the twenty German generals involved, however, managed to escape to fight another day, and this touched off more asperity between the Allied commanders with everyone accusing everyone else of being too slow, too quick or too cautious.

The Americans and Free French entered Paris on the twenty-fifth, and the British, Canadians and Poles rushed headlong for the Channel ports and Belgium.

With the Germans in full retreat, conflicting plans were put forward for bringing the war to a speedy conclusion, and ever louder squabbles now broke out between those super prima donnas, Montgomery, Bradley and Patton. Distorted versions of their differences filtered down to the fighting troops and General Barker's department had a lot of fence mending to do.

I was ordered to Paris to deliver some important documents to an American colonel. "Meet him in the bar of the Hotel Crillon," was my highly sophisticated directive, and I hastened south, most anxious to see my favorite city in the full orgiastic ecstasy of its liberation.

An American corporal was driving my jeep. We got lost in Neuilly till I realized I was only a stone's throw from Claude's apartment. I bade the corporal wait, and leaving him festooned with flowers in the center of a singing, kissing, bottle-waving throng, I pushed my way into the building.

My welcome was rapturous but the setup had changed. Monsieur, having been deported to a forced-labor camp near Essen, madame and Claude, in their misery, had buried their hatchets, pooled their resources, and Claude had moved in upstairs with the family. They nourished me from their sparse supplies of food and drink, heated water in pails so I could have a hot bath, and clucked over me like two hens.

Luckily, I had kept the documents with me because when I descended to keep my rendezvous at the Crillon, the jeep and corporal had disappeared, borne off, he assured me later, on the crest of a wave of hysterical grateful citizenry . . . Claude saved the day.

"It's nothing—you take madame's bicycle. I come with you!"

From some long-forgotten celebration, madame produced two small Union Jacks, and with Claude at my side, bells ringing, and flags fluttering bravely from the handlebars, we free-wheeled down the whole length of the Champs-Elysées to the admiring plaudits of the crowd. Mounted on a woman's bicycle, I was probably the first British soldier the French of Paris had seen for five years.

The Guards Armoured Division entered Brussels on September 3. Antwerp was freed the next day. The reaction of the French of Paris to their liberation was that of an undertakers' convention compared to the behavior of the Belgians. The tired faces of the soldiers glowed; it made everything seem worthwhile.

That autumn has been described by the war historians as a lull; the soldiers didn't notice it, particularly the British Airborne troops who had to fight for their lives at Arnhem, the Canadians struggling on the Leopold Canal, or the Americans at Aachen.

"A" Squadron Phantom, with John Hannay at the helm, was living in great discomfort in flat water-logged fields near Geldrop. I spent some days with them en route to a chore in Nijmegen near the Meuse, where I ran across Tony Bushell, Olivier's production manager in usual life, and now a company commander with the Welsh Guards. We were reminiscing in the tank park when the earth shook under an appalling explosion. Instinctively, I dived for cover. I looked out to see Bushell roaring with laughter.

"What the hell was that?" I asked.

"Oh, that's an old friend," said Bushell. "They've got a bloody great gun in a railway tunnel just across the river. About once an hour they wheel it out and let off a big one; then they pop back in again. We're used to it."

In early December in Brussels, I found Bobby Sweeny who had been distinguishing himself with the RAF. He was on leave.

"They tell me," said Bobby, "that the wild duck are really flighting into the flooded farmland on the Scheldt estuary. Let's go and knock some off."

A great organizer of comfort, Sweeney conjured up a jeep, guns and ammunition, and we set off, accompanied by a carload of Bobby's Belgian friends. The shooting at dusk was spectacular. On the other side of the river it must have been equally good because we could hear the Germans taking full advantage of it.

The Belgian group returned to Brussels after dark, but "the Comfort King" had a better idea.

"Nothing in the world like wild duck cooked absolutely fresh . . . much better than after they've been hung," he said. "One of the best restaurants in Europe is the Panier d'Or in Bruges. The Canadians have probably taken the place by now. Let's go in there and if the Panier d'Or is still standing, we'll get 'em to cook for us."

At the outskirts of the beautiful little seventh-century Flemish town, the Military Police told us that the Germans had indeed been pushed out several hours before. In the center of the town there was very little damage and we found the Panier d'Or intact.

Bobby was right about the ducks—they were sensational —but we both underestimated the hospitality of the owner and his family.

They plied us for hours with every known kind of drink, and before we staggered out, they produced their "Livre d'Or" for our signatures. A special page was prepared, and after five years of German names, the two first Allied ones were scrawled with a flourish. Outside, a full moon was riding in the cold winter sky. The town, with not a chink of light showing, was unnaturally quiet; not a cat was stirring —it was eerie.

We started up the jeep and clattered through the deserted streets and back over the bridge to the main road. A Canadian patrol stopped us and told us the facts of life. During our long drunken meal, the enemy had started a vicious counterattack and the Canadians had pulled back through the town. Half an hour after we left the Panier d'Or, the center of Bruges was once more swarming with Germans.

In the middle of December, I was at Spa, American First Army Headquarters in the Ardennes. I spent the day with Bob Low and he showed me the map room of the Intelligence Section.

"What happens here?" I asked.

"You mean here in Spa?"

"Yes."

After all these years I can quote what he said, word for word—it was impossible to forget. He pointed out of the window. "You see the trees on the top of those hills?"

"Yes."

"Well, the other side of those hills, there is a forest, and in that forest they are now forming the Sixth Panzer Army and any day now the Sixth Panzer Army is going to come right through this room and out the other side, cross the Meuse, then swing right and go north to Antwerp."

"Have you told anyone?" I laughed.

"We've been telling them for days," said Low. "Every day we have to give three appreciations of what we *think* may happen. That has been our number-one appreciation."

The next day I went down through the fog-shrouded Forest of Ardennes to Marche. Within hours the last great German offensive of the war erupted. Ahead of it, Skorzeny's Trojan Horse Brigade, American speaking and wearing American uniforms, infiltrated everywhere with captured American tanks and half-tracks. Sabotaging as they went, they rushed for the Meuse. The rumors of Skorzeny's men flew wildly. In my British uniform and jeep with 21st Army Group markings, I had some anxious moments at the hands of understandably trigger-happy GI's. Identification papers meant nothing. "Hands above your head, buddy. All right, so who won the World Series in 1940?"

"I haven't the faintest idea, but I do know I made a picture with Ginger Rogers in 1938."

"OK, beat it, Dave, but watch your step, for Chrissake."

Time and again I was stopped and, thanks entirely to Sam Goldwyn, survived.

At the end of February, the British Army was fighting bloody battles in the Reichwald, where a sudden thaw had turned the frozen forest floor into a quagmire. Great battles were in progress for the Roer and the Maas. During the first week of March, the U.S. First Army reached the Rhine at Cologne, and two days later the U.S. Third Army did likewise at the junction of the Moselle. The Ninth U.S. Armored Division that week made its miraculous discovery that the Ludendorff Railway Bridge at Remagen had not been blown and secured the first small bridgehead across the Rhine, a bridgehead that cried out for exploitation. Montgomery was all set to cross in strength farther down and surge across the Ruhr plain, but first a big buildup, he felt, was necessary. This stoked up all the old friction between Montgomery's dedication to "tidy battles" and the American genius for improvisation. The super prima donnas were at it in earnest this time, and the heights, or rather the depths, of idiocy were surely reached when, according to military historians, Patton telephoned Bradley and said, "I want the world to know Third Army made it before Monty starts across."

I crossed the Rhine at Wesel and I had never seen such destruction; the smoking town had ceased to exist. At Münster nothing was left standing except a bronze statue of a horse. In the open country between Hanover and Osnabrück, both of which were totally ruined, was a huge hastily erected prisoner-of-war cage. There must have been a hundred thousand men already inside when the American Unit I was then with passed them. The first warming rays of the sun were just touching the prisoners. It had rained heavily during the night and now a cloud of steam was rising from this dejected field-gray mass of humanity.

The *Bürgermeister* of Hanover said that at least 60,000 corpses were still under the rubble of his city. Bremen was no better.

Hitler had started the whole horrible shambles, but looking at the places where his chickens had come home to roost, I watched the miserable survivors picking around in the ruins of their towns and was unable to raise a glimmer of a gloat.

In a siding near Liebenau, I came across a freight train, its flatcars loaded with V-2 rockets destined for London. In the woods nearby was a slave labor camp where they had been made. The notices in the camp were in Italian, French, Czech, Polish, Dutch, Yugoslav, Russian and Ukrainian. The liberated workers were wandering dazedly all over the place, asking how to get home, mingling with the dead-eyed prisoners from the concentration camps, gaunt and shuffling, conspicuous in their black-and-white stripes.

By May 8 the war in Europe was officially over, but people were still being killed and Hitler's werewolves were still, hopefully, stretching piano wire at head height from trees on either side of the roads. To avoid decapitation, the wiser jeeps now carried sharpened iron stanchions welded to their radiators. The routes west out of Germany were becoming clogged with an estimated 8,000,000 homeward-bound displaced persons pushing their pathetic belongings on bicycles or dragging them in little homemade carts. One became hardened to the sight of people lying under trees or in ditches too exhausted or too hungry to take another step.

On a country road near Brunswick, I drove through an attractive red-roofed village on the outskirts of which was a large manor house. Two towheaded little boys were playing in the garden. A mile or so away, I passed a farm wagon headed for the village. I glanced casually at the two men sitting up behind the horse. Both wore typical farmer head-gear, and sacks were thrown over their shoulders protecting them from a light drizzle. We were just past them when something made me slam on the brakes and back up. I was right, the man who was not driving was wearing field boots. I slipped out from behind the wheel, pulled my revolver from its holster, and told the corporal to cover me with his tommy gun.

I gestured to the men to put their hands over their heads and told them in fumbling German to produce their papers.

"I speak English," said the one with the field boots. "This man has papers—I have none."

"Who are you?" I asked.

He told me his name and rank. "General."

"We are not armed," he added as I hesitated.

Sandhurst did it; I saluted, then motioned to them to lower their hands.

"Where are you coming from, sir?"

He looked down at me. I had never seen such utter weariness, such blank despair on a human face before. He passed a hand over the stubble of his chin. "Berlin," he said quietly.

"Where are you going, sir?"

He looked ahead down the road toward the village and closed his eyes. "Home," he said almost to himself. "It's not far now—only . . . one more kilometer."

I didn't say anything. He opened his eyes again and we stared at each other. We were quite still for a long time. Then I said, "Go ahead, sir," and added ridiculously, "Please cover up your bloody boots."

Almost as though in pain, he closed his eyes and raised his head, then with sobbing intake of breath, covered his face with both hands, and they drove on.

On May 13, Churchill spoke from London and the whole world listened—or did it?

". . . we have yet to make sure that the simple and honorable purposes for which we entered the war are not brushed aside or overlooked in the months following our success, and that the words 'freedom,' 'democracy' and 'liberation' are not distorted from their true meaning as we have understood them. There would be little use in punishing the Hitlerites for their crimes if law and justice did not rule and if totalitarian or police governments were to take the place of the German invaders. . . ."

I cannot claim to have exerted much pressure on the squabbling field marshals and generals, but way down the scale, attached to various units, I must have done what General Barker wanted. At any rate, in September he pinned the American Legion of Merit on me and the British Army gave me:

1 suit, worsted gray
1 hat, Homburg, brown
2 shirts, poplin, with collars
1 tie, striped
1 pair of shoes, walking, black—and above all my FREEDOM.

Such was the stringency of the clothing rationing that Major General Robert Laycock, DSO, the chief of combined operations, asked me if I could spare him my discarded khaki shirts.

It was an unbelievable feeling to be free again. Primmie was due to have the second baby in November, so we took little David and treated ourselves to a holiday of luxury at the Ferryboat Inn on the Helford River. Then I cabled Goldwyn to the effect that I was available.

Goldwyn generously replied that he was giving me a new five-year contract at a mouth-watering figure and that in the meanwhile, he was loaning me out to Michael Powell and Emeric Pressburger to star in *A Matter of Life* and *Death* (*Stairway to Heaven* in the United States).

This was a huge relief because although I had been disguising it from Primmie, I was extremely nervous about my future. Six months is too long for an actor to be out of business; six years is almost certain disaster.

A whole new breed of stars had taken over the movie audiences, and at thirty-five I had good reason to be worried. I was also highly apprehensive lest I had forgotten how to do it.

Powell and Pressburger wrote a brilliant screenplay. Kim Hunter played the girl, and my old friend, Raymond Massey, the heavy. Jack Cardiff's fantastic color photography enormously helped make the picture a big success on both sides of the Atlantic, and in Britain it was chosen as the First Royal Command Film.

After Primmie produced Jamie, we set about planning our new life. Although she had never seen California, I had described it all to her so carefully that she knew exactly what she wanted: "an old house, falling down, that we can do over, a big rambling garden for the children and dogs, and a view of the mountains or the ocean."

She was wildly excited at the prospect of going, but nervous about the people she would meet.

"I'm not nearly beautiful enough," she would say. "I'll be lost in all that glamor."

She started buying old furniture, Regency mostly, for the house she could visualize. Vivien Leigh, a great expert, spent hours with her foraging around in the antique shops of Windsor, Amersham and Beaconsfield.

The problem of obtaining transportation to the United States appeared insurmountable; with more than 2,000,000 American servicemen champing at the bit to get home, there was obviously no room for a family of foreigners. General Barker came to the rescue and told me that he had secured a berth for me, alone, with the 101st Airborne Division leaving in a week's time on the *Queen Mary* but Primmie and the children would have to wait at least three months. We decided that I should go on ahead to take up my contract and find, if possible, our dream house.

I gave myself a farewell party for two hundred at Claridges. So that nobody could be wrongly dressed, Primmie borrowed a tiara and a ball gown, and I wore an open-necked shirt and my trousers, worsted gray.

All the guests had one thing in common: At some time in our lives they had been specially nice to us. It was a funny mixture: duchesses, policemen, actors, generals, privates, hospital nurses, taxi drivers and country squires.

I took a sadistic delight in standing at the door and personally winkling out the gate-crashers. "Please go away . . . you've never been nice to me in your life."

The evening cost a fortune but no matter; great days were ahead—we could save money later.

Next morning, I went to collect my sailing permit.

"Sorry, old man," said the official, "can't give you that till you show us your income tax clearance from the Inland Revenue."

Off I went to another dreary government office. Thick white teacups with "G. R." on them littered the untidy desks.

The man who interviewed me was a thin, self-important civil servant with a particularly active Adam's apple. He produced a file. "Now, let's see, you want to leave the old country, do you—emigrating, are you?"

"No. I'm coming back where I came from . . . to the United States. I have a contract to work there."

He turned the pages of a file. "Now let me see . . . in 1939 you left the United States to come back to this country. Why was that?"

"To join up . . . for the war."

"Yes, we all know that, we read the papers at the time, but nobody ASKED you to come, did they? It's not as if you were called up, is it? You paid your own way, didn't you?"

"Yes."

"Well, then, obviously you came here intending to reside again in Great Britain, so that makes you a resident of Great Britain for tax purposes and we are back taxing you on your world earnings from the time you left here in 1934."

The *Queen Mary* was sailing in two days' time and I had to have that sailing permit.

He was very generous. On condition that I did not come

back during that time, he allowed me to pay over the next three years, but it still cost me several thousand pounds which I didn't have for the privilege of spending six years in the British Army.

The *Queen Mary* carried fifteen thousand troops. We were packed like sardines. It didn't matter. We ate in shifts, slept in shifts and lay about in shifts. The teak rails of the upper decks bore the carved initials of countless thousands of GI's who had made the journey to Europe. How many, I wondered, were left behind forever?

On the night I landed in New York, my old employers at 21 gave a large cocktail party for me in the upstairs room of their establishment. At the end of it, I made a tour of my old haunts with John Huston.

I shopped for some badly needed clothes the next day and took a sleeper on the transcontinental train for California. I was feeling very tired and rather odd, so the trip would rest me up, I thought. David Selznick was on the train, and he brought me up to date on who was who now in Hollywood and what was going on. David was a friend who never minced words, however ominous.

"It's going to be tough for you," he said. "It's a whole new ball game now. A lot of new stars and new directors have come up while you've been away. You're lucky to have Goldwyn behind you."

At Chicago, a telegram was delivered from Eddie Goulding saying that he was giving me a welcome-home bachelor party of a hundred at Romanoff's on the night of my arrival. Another came from Goldwyn saying there was to be a big press luncheon the same day. I looked forward to it all, but I also dreaded it . . . I really was very tired and coughed a lot.

WELCOME HOME, DAVID!!

A big banner was strung across the main gate of the studio. Stage 8 had been transformed into a restaurant, and several hundred studio employees and members of the press listened to speeches of welcome by Goldwyn, Hedda Hopper, the head propman, Dave Chasen and others. The room was spinning, I was sweating, and I had a terrible headache. I wondered how I was going to get through it. I might have been Hollywood's first recruit, but I was being treated as if I had won the war single-handed.

After luncheon, "Willie" Bruce said, "I'm taking you home, putting you to bed, and getting you a doctor—you look awful."

"I can't let Goulding down," I said. "He's asked a hundred people tonight."

"Nonsense," said Willie, "if the doctor says you can go, all right—otherwise, bed."

The doctor took my temperature—it was 104—and told me I had bronchial pneumonia.

Goulding was marvelous when he was told. He came to see me and insisted on going through with the party without me. "I'll have a direct line to your room and an amplifier. You'll be able to hear what's going on and you can talk to old pals on the phone."

Among the hundred bachelors, Goulding rounded up most of my actor friends, including Clark Gable, Doug, Jr., Flynn, Gary Cooper and "Ty" Power. Also, I noticed from the book of photographs he sent me later of the proceedings, an impressive body of the Hollywood superbrass had also dusted off their dinner jackets, including Goldwyn, Selznick, Pandro Berman, Eddie Mannix, Billy Wilder, Howard Hawks, Mervyn Le Roy, Hal Wallis and even Harry Cohn.

There was a pipe band. My name was carved in a huge block of ice and the whole place was festooned with American and British flags. It was extremely generous of Goulding, highly flattering and completely unwarranted.

I convalesced in the desert at Palm Springs, and as soon as I was well enough, Goldwyn put me to work. He loaned me to Paramount to do a picture with, of all people, Loretta Young.

Primmie cabled that she hoped to get passage soon, and I went, frantically, house hunting.

The Fairbankses found it for me, right next door to theirs, exactly what she had always said she wanted—old and rambling with a big garden and a view of both the Santa Monica Mountains and the ocean. The basement had about three feet of water in it when the agent showed it, so I was able to buy it very cheaply. Vicki Baum, the author of *Grand Hotel,* had built it forty years before.

The day Goldwyn loaned me the money for the down
payment, I went off to celebrate with Doug and Mary
Lee. Halfway through our first glass of champagne, somebody rushed in and shouted, "The house next door is burn-
ing to the ground!"

We dashed out. I with my heart in my mouth. I was basely relieved to discover that it was the home of director
Sidney Lanfield on the other side of the Fairbankses' that
was going up in smoke.

The Pink House, as it was known for obvious reasons,
became of tremendous importance to me. It was the first
home I had ever owned, and with my adored family, I
longed to settle down at last. I seemed to have been running and running all my life.

I decided to give the place to Primmie as a surprise when
she arrived, then let her do it over, and with her wonderful
taste, decorate it in her own good time; in the meanwhile, I
rented a big Spanish-style monstrosity in Beverly Hills.

The picture at Paramount finished just in time for me to
fly East to meet my family. They had taken eighteen days
in terrible gales to cross the Atlantic in an old Liberty ship.
They finally docked in Portland, Maine.

Primmie looked radiant as she came running down the
gangplank. Little David was full of chat and questions. As
a typical war baby, when he noticed the skeleton of a house
being built, he said, "Look, Daddy, a bomb."

Jamie, now five months old, slept all the time in a carrying cot. The handle broke in New York and I dumped him
on his head in the middle of Penn Station, which may account for the fact that he became an extremely efficient
merchant banker.

Primmie fell in love with California on sight and was
over the moon when she saw the Pink House.

"The furniture will be perfect in it," she cried, her eyes
shining like a little girl's. "I am going to make it *so* beautiful
for you! You're going to be *so* proud!"

It was decided that she would do the house herself without telling me anything, and then, one day, when it was all
finished, she would let me carry her through the door.

She had brought Pinkie with her—a fresh-faced English
girl who had spent the war in an antiaircraft battery in
London. Pinkie adored the children and soon made the
Spanish dungeon shine like a new pin.

Goldwyn loaned me to Universal to make a historical film with Ginger Rogers. Ginger was to play Dolly Madison and I was to portray Aaron Burr—the two most unlikely bits of casting of the century. The script was gibberish, but I was far too happy and the prospect of, at long last, settling down with my family in my own home was too good to be ruined by renewed quarrels with Goldwyn and by suspensions which I could ill afford.

Larry Olivier had left behind a large black Packard when he had last been in California. I bought it by cable, left Pinkie in charge of the children, and with Clark Gable, Rex Harrison, Ida Lupino and Nigel Bruce, we set off in convoy for a week's golf at Pebble Beach. . . . They were golden days, and Primmie showed me a letter she wrote to Bill Rollo saying that she never imagined she could be so happy. We came back on a Sunday because I had to do wardrobe tests the next morning.

Ty Power and Annabella gave a small party for Primmie that evening. John McClain had just arrived from New York and all my closest friends were there. As I looked around at them and at Primmie's radiant face, I wondered how it was possible for one man to have so much.

Nearly everyone was working the next day, which meant being up by five or six o'clock, so we had an early barbecue around the pool. Ty cooked. Afterward, we went indoors and played some games. Someone suggested Sardines, an old children's game played in the dark. I was hiding under a bed upstairs when I heard Ty calling me. "Come down, quick, Primmie's had a fall!"

I rushed down.

In the dark she had opened a door thinking it was a coat closet. It was the door to the cellar, and she had fallen down a dozen steps. She was lying unconscious on the floor. We dabbed her head with water and she started moaning and moving a little.

Within twenty minutes the doctor arrived, and within another half hour she was tucked in bed in hospital.

"She's very concussed," the doctor told me after his examination, "but it's nothing to worry about. She'll have to stay absolutely quiet and in the dark for a few days. She'll be fine."

I went back to Ty's house and told everyone the good news. Then I went to the Spanish house and Pinkie helped me pack up a few things Primmie might need, a couple of nighties, a toothbrush, some perfume.

Back at the hospital, they repeated that she was fine, said there was no good I could do by staying and to go on home, and if I wanted to, to drop by before I went to work in the morning.

I was back about six the next day. They let me see her. She looked beautiful but very pale. Her eyes were still closed.

"She's had a good night," said the nurse.

All during the day I called from the studio. "Nothing to worry about. It's a bad concussion. All she needs is complete rest and quiet."

After work I went back to the hospital. They were most reassuring. I sat with her for a long time holding her hand. She was very still.

Suddenly, she opened her eyes, looked right at me, smiled a tiny smile, and gave my hand a little reassuring squeeze. It was the first time she had recognized me. The matron said, "Why don't you go on home and get some sleep yourself? There's nothing you can do. We'll call you at once, of course, if there is any change . . . go on home and don't worry."

Bob Coote was in the house, waiting for news, when I got back. I told him everything was going along well, that no one was worried, and we raided the icebox for a snack.

About eleven o'clock, the phone rang. It was the doctor. "I think you'd better come down," he said. "There are certain symptoms we don't like. I've alerted the best brain surgeon there is . . . we may have to operate."

Bob came with me. An hour later, they started the operation. Two hours passed before the doctors came down.

I knew.

I knew as soon as I saw them come out of the elevator.

I knew by the way they walked.

I knew by the way they stood murmuring together without looking at me as I waited across the hall.

She was only twenty-five.

14

Somehow the dreadful days dragged by—somehow into weeks and months.

Friends tried valiantly to cushion the despair and I was infinitely lucky to have them.

Ronnie and Benita Colman took me into their home, for I never again set foot in the Spanish monstrosity; then Douglas and Mary Lee Fairbanks gave me sanctuary. Joan Crawford took the children, with a stunned Pinkie, till they were settled on the Colmans' ranch at Montecito. Everyone tried to help, but there comes a time when friends must be allowed to get on with their own lives, so I went back to work at Universal, and occupying myself with such a disaster was some sort of relief from the alternative. Even so, after work I walked for hours alone on the darkened beach, hoping, perhaps, that a merciful tidal wave might sweep out of the Pacific. Then I went to bed to toss in torment till dawn when exhaustion took over. A couple of hours of deep sleep would be brutally ended by an alarm clock and smashing down once more came the awful realization that it had not been a dream.

Work on the Pink House continued. Not because I wanted to transform it into a shrine; it held no memories; we had never lived in it . . . so work went on. After a while, with the rest of the house still gutted, one room, the cook's, and the kitchen, were finished.

With a few belongings, I moved in among the cement and sawdust, coils of wire, unattached radiators and toilets, buckets of paint . . . utter desolation that seemed somehow symbolic.

The so-carefully-collected furniture and china arrived from England, but somewhere the container had been dropped and most of the contents were smashed beyond repair.

I had with me, for comfort, in the cook's room, a little case full of Primmie's most private things, childhood treasures, some photographs of our wedding and of the children's christenings, my letters written during the war and her tiny cache of inexpensive jewelry. While I was away at work one day, the case was stolen.

That night I nearly gave up.

The Pink House was finally finished, and upstairs a white carpet was laid.

That day, Rex and Lilli Palmer gave me a Boxer puppy to keep me company. Phantom, within an hour, had permanently changed the color of the carpet.

On Sundays, the house was full of people from morning till night. Every week Gable arrived accompanied by some gorgeous creature, while Lana Turner, Anita Colby, Rita Hayworth, Deborah Kerr, Ava Gardner, Ida Lupino and Patricia Medina set an unassailable standard of beauty and fun. Bob Laycock was stunned when he saw them. He came to California in his capacity of chief of British Combined Operations as guest of the American Pacific Fleet at San Diego and stayed with me for several days. It cheered me a lot to think that he took back to Bill and Kathleen Rollo good reports of their grandchildren.

Like the understanding Gable who had lately been through a similar family tragedy himself, John McClain was a staunch and thoughtful friend. One day he said, " 'Betty' Bacall is giving Bogart a surprise party tonight. It's time you got out of your house."

I didn't really want to go, but the alternative was still something I flinched from. Pinkie would relentlessly keep the children up till I came home from work so they could have a half hour's play with their father. It was torture for me and I dreaded seeing their gay, shining, trusting little faces.

After they had gone off to bed, it was worse: a lonely meal and then pacing about the house like a caged lion till bedtime. By now I was making an important picture for Goldwyn, playing the bishop in *The Bishop's Wife,* with Loretta Young as the wife and Cary Grant as the angel, so I was faced with getting up at six o'clock in the morning.

McClain, however, brushed aside all protests, and I found myself with forty others hidden in different parts of Bogart's house as a surprise for his birthday.

"Betty" Bacall was the perfect mate for Bogie: beautiful, gay, warm, talented and highly intelligent, she gave as good as she got in the strong personality department. Women and men love her with equal devotion.

Someone had been delegated by Betty to keep Bogie busy at the studio to give us all time to arrive and hide. When Bogie finally appeared, it was apparent how his busy time at the studio had been spent. He was loudly abusive and cries of "Who needs these bums!" and "Get the bastards outta here!" reverberated from the front door. For a few nervous minutes it was touch and go whether he would throw all forty of us out into the street, but Betty placated him or, rather, answered him loudly in the same vein and the party became a success after all.

Bogart was quite alarming to meet for the first time with his sardonic humor and his snarl that passed for a smile. It took a little while to realize that he had perfected an elaborate camouflage to cover up one of the kindest and most generous of hearts. Even so, he was no soft touch, and before you were allowed to peek beneath the surface and catch a glimpse of the real man, you had to prove yourself. Above all, you had to demonstrate conclusively to his satisfaction that you were no phony.

My test came soon. He asked me if I liked to sail.

"Done it all my life," I said blithely. "In fact I once represented my country in eight meters."

Bogie looked at me reflectively and sucked his teeth. "Okay, come aboard *Santana* Sunday."

Women were only infrequently made welcome aboard *Santana,* so Betty was not there when I boarded the sixty-five-foot ketch at Balboa.

Tough and often argumentative ashore, I expected Bogie to be a veritable Captain Bligh afloat. Far from it; he was easygoing, perfectly relaxed and highly efficient. I was lulled into a sense of false security and had no idea that this had been earmarked as the day of my entrance exam.

We were sailing along in a good stiff breeze, Bogie was at the helm, I was beside him, the solitary crew—a Dane he called Dum Bum—was forward keeping a sharp lookout because the stiff breeze was doing nothing to dispel a thick mist.

"Tuna boats ahead," yelled Dum Bum suddenly.

Sure enough, we were running fast toward a dozen big

drifters, each with its nets trailing out astern. It was a tricky situation that called for immediate action and because of the direction of the wind, there were only three solutions: one correct, the second risky, the third would have led to losing the mast.

Dum Bum was apprehensively looking at Bogie, and I was just thinking to myself that he was leaving things dangerously late when he let go of the wheel, gave me a wolfish grin, and said, "Take over, big shot. I'm going to the can."

He disappeared below.

Luckily, I knew what I was doing. I yelled a few orders which Dum Bum instantly obeyed, spun the wheel, and the danger was passed.

Christmas alone with the children was something I had dreaded. Although they never ceased asking others when their mother was coming back, some extraordinary radar system prevented them ever from mentioning her to me. I knew one day they would ask me the direct question, so until then I resolved not to broach the subject.

On Christmas Eve, with the lighted tree in the window behind me and a mountain of gaily wrapped presents from kind and even anxious friends beneath it, I was sitting on the patio steps swept suddenly by a wave of despair. A little arm went round my neck; they both stood there hand in hand.

"Are you very lonely?" asked the eldest, and when I just nodded, he said, "Mummy's never coming back, is she?"

"No, she's not," I said.

"Has she gone up to heaven?"

"Yes, that's right . . . she's gone to heaven."

The evening star was very bright over the distant ocean. He looked up. "I can see Mummy's eye," he said.

The Bishop's Wife turned out well. It, too, was chosen for the Royal Command Film in London, and Goldwyn kept me blessedly busy loaning me out all over town. I made pictures with Barbara Stanwyck and Jane Wyman. I played all sorts of roles, including a world-famous pianist. During my big concert scene an expert played the piano with his arms through my tailcoat while I rolled my eyes and looked soulful.

When a man is deeply unhappy, he brings out the very gentlest instincts in the very nicest women. They want to wrap him up, take him home, and look after him. They give all of themselves, but he, in turn, can give only in one direction, and inoculated by his unhappiness, he rides roughshod far and wide.

This happened to me in full measure, and I also believe at the same time, I went a little mad. I began to resent and avoid the married friends who had showered me with so much kindness and protection when I so badly needed it. Perhaps I was jealous of their happiness. Perhaps I was ashamed that they had seen me at my weakest and most vulnerable. This phase lasted several months, and bewildered and hurt, some wonderful people must have found my coldness most difficult to understand.

The Pink House in the spring was a dream place for the children. They took swimming lessons in the pool. Peach trees, avocados, pomegranates, cherries, oranges, limes, lemons and guavas were in full blossom. Phantom dashed about the lawn chasing hummingbirds, the bantams crowed, and the rabbits bred in great profusion. I planted a hundred rose bushes, and at last, I, too, began to feel roots going down and some happiness seeping back up again. The boys were settling down marvelously; and some pattern for the future seemed to be emerging. I was, therefore, appalled when Goldwyn called me in and told me he had loaned me to Alexander Korda to make *Bonnie Prince Charlie* in England. "You'll be away at least eight months," he said.

I begged him not to send me and pointed out that not only would it disrupt the children's lives, but also it would make new and hideous problems for me with the Inland Revenue.

He was adamant, so I refused to go. Immediately, I was put on suspension.

Knowing that I was up to my ears in debt because of the Pink House, Goldwyn sat back and waited for me to crack. It didn't take long, and in the autumn, Pinkie and I packed up two resentful and mystified little boys and started the long trek back to England.

Korda, whose home was the penthouse in Claridge's, quite understandably was surprised when I spurned the accommodation he had reserved for me in that excellent hostelry. I kept a room there for myself and moved the family into a country hotel near Shepperton Studios.

Bonnie Prince Charlie was one of those huge florid extravanganzas that reeked of disaster from the start. There was never a completed screenplay, and never at any time during the eight months we were shooting were the writers more than two days ahead of the actors.

We suffered three changes of directors with Korda, himself, for a time desperately taking over, and at one point, I cabled Goldwyn as follows:

> I HAVE NOW WORKED EVERY DAY FOR FIVE MONTHS ON THIS PICTURE AND NOBODY CAN TELL ME HOW THE STORY ENDS STOP ADVISE

He didn't. He didn't even bother to answer.

I loved Alex Korda, a brilliant, generous artist, but with this film he was wallowing around in his own self-created confusion. I felt sorry for him, but I felt much sorrier for myself as the Bonnie Prince who would assuredly bear the blame for the impending debacle and for Margaret Leighton and Jack Hawkins gallantly, against appalling odds, trying to infuse some semblance of reality into Flora MacDonald and Lord George Murray.

After nine frustrating months, the *Bonnie Prince* clanked toward its close. One more week, one more battle, one last mad charge and I would be rid of him. (Whenever we actors really started to breathe down the necks of the writers, Korda ordered another battle to delay us for a few more days.)

The director at this point was a robust, hearty and immensely nice ex-naval commander, Anthony Kimmins. No fool, he knew only too well that he was captain of a movie ship heading like an arrow for the rocks, but bravely he covered up and issued his orders to the several hundred extras as though he were Lord Louis Montbatten addressing the crew of a badly listing destroyer.

"Now, Bonnie Prince Charlie has just won a great victory! You brave Highlanders have captured the English colors! When he comes out of his tent over there, I want all you Highlanders to give him a big cheer! Let him know you all love him!"

The wild Highlanders, in scruffy red wigs and uncertain kilts, were almost entirely recruited from London's East End. As I came out of the tent for the first take, there was scattered cheering. Then, crystal clear in the morning air came a fruity Cockney voice. "Oi! David . . . we've got their fuckin' flag!!!"

The second happening on that most important day came during the charge itself. I was careering bravely along, skimming over the studio heather at the head of my Highlanders, pursuing the fleeing Redcoats, when suddenly, claymore in hand, I found myself flying through the air. I still believe Jack Hawkins tripped me. In any event, my sword sank deep into the leg of the Redcoat in front of me. It went in with an appalling "thonk" just behind the knee and pinned him to the ground.

"Cut!" yelled the director (an unnecessary observation). Several women, hairdressers and other camp followers screamed.

I pulled out the blade, trying not to throw up. The man got up and ran off with a pronounced limp. I chased after him.

"Are you all right? . . . I'm terribly sorry! . . . We'll get a doctor!"

"Wot's the matter, mate?" asked the man.

"Your leg," I blabbered, "my sword! . . . It went right in! We'll get a doctor!"

"Oh," he said "thought I felt something . . . not to worry though, David." He rolled up the bottom of his trousers. His name was Bob Head. He had lost the original leg at El Alamein.

Happenings go in threes. I was dismissed early that evening and hurried off to get changed so I could go and play with the children. Because of the hours we had been working, I hadn't seen them for days. The gateman stopped me. "Sorry, David. They just phoned up—they need you for one more shot."

Furious, I stalked back into makeup. Sullenly, I sat while the yellow wig was pinned on my resisting head, and once more, like a spoiled child whose picnic has been cancelled by bad weather, I glowered my way onto the set and snarled at the propman.

"Where the hell's my chair?"

"Over there, David. There's a lady in it."

"Then get her out of it!" I snapped.

"Take a look," whispered Hawkins in my ear. "Take a look."

The French have the right word—*coup de foudre*. I had never seen anything so beautiful in my life: tall, slim, auburn hair, uptilted nose, lovely mouth and the most enormous gray eyes I had ever seen. It really happened the way it does when written by the worst lady novelists . . . I goggled. I had difficulty swallowing and I had champagne in my knees.

Ten days later, we were married.

During the intervening time, there was quite a lot of activity. First of all, it turned out she was Swedish, which posed all sorts of strange problems with the marriage authorities. Also, she didn't speak English too well, which helped matters not at all when it came to explaining to them that she had landed in England en route from America to Sweden as the plane had been grounded because of sudden fog at London Airport and a friend on board had invited her to visit a film studio, et cetera, et cetera.

I had my problems too. I had to complete the *Bonnie Prince*, find gifts for all the crew, present Hjördis to Bill Rollo, who adored her on sight and was gay and happy for me through his own sadness; I also had to submit to a series of loathsome meetings with the Inland Revenue because I had returned without being away for three years.

"But I was sent, dammit, by the American company that employs me. . . . If I had refused, I would have broken my contract."

"Well, we should read the small print before signing these foreign things, shouldn't we?"

Also, I had to find a ring, track down Trubshawe, who was to be best man again, and make all the arrangements to return quickly to California, where Goldwyn was holding up the start of my next picture.

Small wonder that I had a minicollapse, and when the official at the Chelsea Registry office warned me pompously against the dangers of marrying a foreigner, I could barely croak at him to "shut up and get on with it." The number-one model of Sweden found herself married to a man with red eyes, a runny nose and a fever of 103°.

Audrey Pleydell-Bouverie gave us a wedding party in her little house strategically placed midway between the stables of Buckingham Palace and Watney's Brewery, and the next day we drove to Southampton to board the *Queen Elizabeth*.

Hjördis still swears that on the way there, I suddenly said, "Oh! I nearly forgot. There are a couple of little things I have to pick up." According to her, I disappeared inside a country hotel and emerged later with two small boys.

On the trip to California, we got to know each other a little better and the little boys adored her.

She loved the Pink House and rose magnificently to the hazard of being pitchforked into the middle of all my old friends. McClain, Coote and Mike Romanoff gave her a welcome party to make it easier, and her gaiety and beauty captivated everyone.

Life magazine had a spread of the ten most beautiful women in Hollywood, and Hjördis appeared on the cover. This generated a stampede of producers with offers of contracts, but, mercifully, she just laughed and said she was too busy getting to know her husband.

The Pink House came alive under her hand and became everything I had dreamed about as a home. At night the coyotes hunted in wierdly yelping packs in the canyon below; in the morning the deer grazed on the hills opposite; and the sunsets over the Pacific must have been ordered by the Chamber of Commerce.

Some highly decorative Scandinavian ladies now augmented the weekly gatherings: Viveca Lindfors and Signe Hasso were often present; also the latest Miss Sweden, Anita Ekberg, and the first naked female my sons ever saw was Greta Garbo swimming happily in our pool.

"Goldwynisms" had been so widely quoted—" . . . Include me out," "A verbal contract is not worth the paper it is written on," and of a fourteenth-century sundial, "What will they think of next?"—that for a while I was suspicious that Goldwyn might foster the legend by dreaming up new ones for himself, but I don't believe this was the case. I heard him let loose many of them, but I think his mind was so far ahead of what he was saying that he left it to his tongue to take care of thoughts he had left behind. In fact, he had a great dignity, but when thwarted, he tended to shout loudly.

After three months of my newfound happiness, the

pleasant routine was shattered. Goldwyn called me to his office and told me he had great news and that I was very lucky. "I've just loaned you to Alex Korda to make *The Elusive Pimpernel* in England. You'll be away six months."

Aghast, I told him that I didn't mind what he loaned me out for in Hollywood but that I had no intention of uprooting again so soon. Then the shouting began. He reminded me that he had picked me out of the gutter and given me my first break. . . . True.

I riposted by saying that with the enormous fees he was charging others for my services, I had already repaid him a thousand times over. . . . True.

Goldwyn pointed out that it would mean months of suspension if I refused. . . . True.

I said I looked forward to a good holiday anyway and I had plenty of money in the bank. . . . UNTRUE.

Goldwyn flicked a switch and said, "Find out how much money Niven has in the bank."

Within three minutes a disembodied voice came back, "One hundred and eleven dollars." . . . True, unfortunately.

Defeated, I prepared, once more, to make the necessary travel arrangements.

I lived in Hollywood for nearly twenty years without visiting a psychiatrist, but my behavior during the next few weeks was indicative of an unhinged mind and it was a pity I did not "get help."

I decided to make life unpleasant for Goldwyn which was tantamount to an eight-year-old with a peashooter assaulting Fort Knox. Everyone from Hjördis downward warned me. My agent was horrified and pointed out that in mogul-controlled Hollywood, one word from Goldwyn could sink me. I knew better, of course, and proceeded very methodically to wreck my own career.

At the last minute, I refused to fly to London to keep the starting date of Korda's picture and insisted, instead, on being sent by train to New York and by boat—eleven days to Liverpool. Hjördis remained loyal but mystified throughout the trip. Once in London, I cabled Goldwyn, reminding him that under the terms of my contract I had six weeks' holiday each year and unless I was given my holiday at once before *Pimpernel* started, the contract would be broken, as there would be no time left between the end of the picture and the end of the year.

TAKE SIX WEEKS HOLIDAY IMMEDIATELY GOLDWYN

came the answer.

THANKS VERY MUCH WILL TAKE HOLIDAY FROM TIME
YOU RETURN ME TO MY HOME IN CALIFORNIA   NIVEN

Poor, blameless Alex Korda, who wanted only to see his
picture started. found himself in the middle of this lunacy.
He offered me his yacht, *Elsewhere*, to go anywhere at his
expense, but my mental imbalance was such that I forced
Goldwyn to return me to the Pink House by boat and
train; then, the next day, I flew with Hjördis to Bermuda
for a delayed honeymoon.

Honeymoons are a great institution for getting to know
one's spouse, and the more I saw of Hjördis, the more
amazed I was at my good fortune. The luck, the unbelievable luck of one man to meet, fall head over heels in love,
marry within ten days, and be blissfully happy twice in a
lifetime.

I reveled in Hjördis' forthrightness, honesty and laughter, and the holiday sped by. Toward the end, a full-scale
hurricane hit the island—a nasty reminder of the impending storm with Goldwyn.

Six weeks to the day from the moment I had been
brought back to California, I reported to the studio for
work. Rather naturally, Goldwyn did not wish to see me
and I detected a certain coldness toward me all over the lot.
Behavior such as mine. spoiled-brat behavior of the worst
sort, was idiotic, conceited. indefensible and unforgivable:
the sort of thing that helped bring Hollywood to its knees.

Goldwyn, of course, had no further use for me and all
the direst predictions came true. When we came back from
England upon the completion of *The Elusive Pimpernel*, I
was immediately loaned out to play the heavy in a Shirley
Temple picture, a disastrous teen-age potboiler.

Big shots at other studios counseled me to break my contract with Goldwyn: "Just walk in there and tell him, the
hell with it! Tell him you want OUT . . . then come and
join us, we have a million properties for you!" I fell for
that—it was not my finest hour. I asked to see Goldwyn,
and as he sat expressionless behind his desk, I said, "Look,

Sam, we don't see eye to eye anymore. I have two years left of my contract. How about releasing me?"

He never took his eyes off me as he flicked his intercom lever. "Give Niven his release as from today . . . he's through."

15

Hjördis sounded doubtful when I told her the good news.

"Where will you work now?" she asked.

Where indeed? There is no question but that the blacklist existed in Hollywood at that time, but I have absolutely no proof that Goldwyn invoked its use in my case. On the other hand, the fact remains that the flattering studio big shots who had painted such glowing pictures of my future with them once I was free of Goldwyn were suddenly unobtainable. When I called their offices, the voices of their secretaries had changed subtly from fawning to evasive or even to faintly hostile.

Headlines put out by the Goldwyn Publicity Department were no great help:

> GOLDWYN DROPS NIVEN
> NIVEN FIRED
> BRITISH ACTOR NO LONGER GOLDWYN'S CUP OF TEA

Hjördis was nothing short of stoic because only too soon there was a shortage of cash. Nothing was coming in, everything was going out, and the reserves were melting like butter on a hot stove. Friends such as the Astaires and the Fairbankses tried to cheer me by reporting that at the latest Goldwyn dinner party, my photograph was still on the piano, but nobody suggested I should try a reconciliation.

Bogart, as usual, was down-to-earth. "Let's face it, kid. You've blown it! Keep going somehow, mortgage the house, sell the kids, dig a ditch, do anything but, for Christ's sake, never let them think they've got you running scared because somewhere in somebody's desk is a script that's right for you and when they dig it out, it's you they'll want and nobody else and everything'll be forgotten."

Bogie's life was either black or white—he had little patience with the grays—so he simply did not understand when I accepted the first offer that came along after months of near panic.

"You should've held out, kid. This is crap," he said when I showed him the script.

The film, *The Toast of New Orleans,* at M-G-M was a success thanks only to the fact that it launched Mario Lanza's golden voice and with the proceeds, Hjördis happily paid the bills one short step ahead of the sheriff. The next picture was even worse—an appalling travesty of a costume thriller. The result was so bad that the audience thought it was a comedy and as such it became faintly successful.

"Get outta town, kid," growled Bogart. "They gotta have time to forget that one."

I took his advice, rented out the Pink House for a year, took the whole family to England, and moved into a haunted manor house in Wiltshire on the edge of the Downs.

Hjördis somehow remained calm and outwardly unaffected by the rapid changes in our fortunes, but my new role as a country squire was hard for her to digest. I had a gun in the local syndicate dedicated to the slaughter of pheasants. I had a rod on the Kennet River for the purpose of killing trout, and I had a private pew in the village church (complete with hidden stove) for the good of my soul.

In the autumn, she came rushing to find me. "Hurry! Hurry! Hurry! The garden is full of dogs and men blowing trumpets!"

Philip Hardwicke and Philip Dunne as joint masters of the local foxhounds were merely following tradition. The opening meet was held each year at our manor house. Hjördis, in tight blue jeans and a white T-shirt with PALM SPRINGS RODEO written across her bosom, was a welcome if incongruous sight when I dispatched her outside with bottles of port and slices of fruitcake.

In England, we were able to catch up with Trubshawe, Coote, Noël Coward, and the Oliviers, who had moved into an Elizabethan abbey, near Thame. Arguments waxed and waned at Notley; causes were defended or attacked with vigor and professional reputations came under withering fire; but there were few tears and gales of laughter, particularly when, accompanied on the piano by a hysterical

Vivien, Larry would, dead seriously, sing *The Messiah*.

Friends were always championed to the death. One weekend, Larry, Vivien, Bobby Helpmann and Noël were trying to put Hollywood into its proper perspective for me.

"It's all very fine for you," I argued. "You are all theater people who occasionally make a movie . . . I have nothing *but* the movies."

If I had trodden on a wasp's nest, I couldn't have stirred up more action. Everyone started shouting at once, and when it died down, it was obvious that steps were about to be taken to get me started in the theater.

Within a week, John C. Wilson, the Broadway producer and longtime friend and associate of Noël's, offered me a play, *Nina*.

Gloria Swanson, who, the season before, in a spectacular comeback had been the toast of Broadway in *Twentieth Century*, had already been signed and the cast of three was to be rounded off by the excellent English character actor, Alan Webb.

"I'm terrified," I said to Noël. "I've only been on the stage once over ten years ago and I was fired for being gassed."

The Coward finger wagged immediately. "You will do it," he ordered. "You will do it well, and above all, you will do it sober."

The boys stayed on in the haunted manor with Evelyn Walne, their new governess, poised to join us if the play looked like running, and in October, Hjördis and I flew to the United States. First stop was to spend a weekend pheasant shooting with friends in New England.

I had by now seen Hjördis under a variety of conditions and had come to realize that one of the joys of being married to a "foreigner" is being constantly surprised; nothing is automatically predictable.

I was not thrown off balance, therefore, when she came down to breakfast on the first morning dressed not for the chase but for spending the day with an apple and a good book. "I am not coming to watch you shoot," she announced, "because I don't want to be shot."

The high-powered hunters and their wives tried to persuade her that it was perfectly safe, but she was adamant.

"I *know* I am going to be shot, so I stay home."

Finally, after much badinage about Scandinavian sixth

sense, trolls and spooks, she reluctantly consented to join us. "But I will be shot," she said sadly.

Less than an hour later, two guns turned to fire at a bird that was going back low and Hjördis fell to the ground, hit in the face, neck, chest and arm.

I rushed over, and as I cradled her, moaning, in my arms, a terrible thought went through my head: It's happened again.

Her beautiful face was a terribly swollen mask of blood; when she asked for a mirror, we pretended nobody had one. Within half an hour she was in the local hospital, where it was discovered that she had more than thirty pieces of lead in her, including one which to this day remains embedded in the bone of her eye socket.

She was given an anesthetic and they were preparing to remove the pellets when some strange force propelled me, uninvited, into the operating room.

"Stop, please!" I said to the astonished white-clad group. "I'm sorry, Before you cut her, I want another opinion."

I don't know what made me do it—some half-forgotten wartime whisper about shrapnel wounds perhaps—anyway, white-gauze masks were lowered and I was asked, icily, if I wanted to accept full responsibility. My host produced an ex-Navy surgeon friend who was paged at the local football game. He came and examined her and gave it as his opinion that if the swollen tissues were operated on at that time, she would be scarred for life.

"Many will work their way out," he said. "The ones in deep we can get later. She should be X-rayed frequently to see if any move, especially the one near the jugular."

Thank God for the U.S. Navy. Hjördis is, today, unmarked, but now when she hears those little Northern voices, I listen with great attention.

A battered Hjördis and I moved to the Blackstone Hotel, New York. In a tiny room next to us was lodged a doe-eyed waif, a young actress, also making her debut on Broadway that season—Audrey Hepburn. Together, we shook with fear as our opening nights drew inexorably nearer.

Nina was a translation from a big French success by André Roussin. It was directed by a comic Russian, Gregory Ratoff. In English, it was pretty bad.

Gloria looked marvelous and took great pains to remain

that way by eating the most loathsome concoctions of yogurt, yeast, wheat germ and molasses. She also had a fixation that every actor should have another string to his bow —some other profession capable of padding out the lean times.

"I have a clothing business myself," she said, "the Pilgrim Company. . . . All my clothes for this show will be made by Pilgrim."

We opened in Hartford, Connecticut, in front of a heavily partisan audience, most of whom had come up from New York to cheer us on, but among them was the usual sprinkling of carrion crows sniffing for the first scent of possible disaster and ready to fly back to Broadway, the bitchy bearers of grim tidings.

The show, at this point, went over quite well, and Otto Preminger, never a man to mince words, said he liked my efforts very much; but by the time we arrived in Boston a week later several scenes had been rewritten and the show was half as good. Two weeks and many rewrites after that, we opened in Philadelphia. The carrion crows had every reason to be delighted; there was no question: We were headed for big trouble.

Rex Harrison and Lilli Palmer answered my SOS and came down from New York to see the show and offer me some advice.

"Well, what do you suggest?" I asked over supper.

"Get out of it," said Rex.

When we arrived in New York, Hjördis tried her best to appear optimistic and Garson Kanin suggested questionable aid for first-night nerves.

"Go to the top of the Empire State Building. . . . Don't throw yourself off, just look down at all those millions of lights and remember that only one of them is the Royale Theater."

When the big night came, neither the producer nor the director made it to the theater and the last run-through was conducted by Biff Liff, the stage manager, who read out the final instructions with all the enthusiasm of an undertaker.

All the professional first-nighters and the dreaded critics were there. Also, Alfred Lunt and Lynn Fontanne, Tallulah Bankhead, and Rex and Lilli—gluttons for punishment.

The houselights dimmed and an expectant buzz faded into a pregnant silence. I stood quaking beside the stage manager, who made an abortive effort to bolster my sagging morale as he signaled for the curtain to rise. "Get out there, Dave. There's nothing you can do about it now—the horse has left the barn."

For a panic-stricken moment, I toyed with the idea of rushing madly out of the theater and throwing myself beneath the hooves of the mounted police, then I tottered onstage.

Webb and I played the first explanatory scene together, then the doorbell rang, signaling the entrance of Swanson. Webb, the husband, took refuge behind the curtain, and I, the lover, moved across stage to admit my mistress. I was ill prepared for what I saw.

She had, I thought, worn some rather odd garments in Hartford, Boston and Philadelphia, but now the Pilgrim Company had really excelled itself. Swanson stood there enveloped in a black-taffeta tent. She stepped forward and a gasp of horror mingled with the applause.

She smiled seductively at her lover, and I was supposed to smile back. I tried, but I was so nervous and my mouth so dry that my upper lip became stuck above my teeth and I stood there leering at her like a mad rabbit.

The Bedouin tent with Swanson's head sticking out of the top of it rustled across the stage and flung itself into my arms. Swanson is not tall. She is, to put it mildly, petite, so when I clasped her to me, the top of her head nestled just to the right of my breastbone.

Unfortunately, in my terror of the whole situation, I squeezed too hard in that initial clinch. There was a loud report. This was followed by a twanging noise, and about eight inches of white whalebone shot out of Swanson's chest and straight up my nose.

The audience was delighted—something new at last—they roared with laughter. Swanson half-turned to see what was happening, thereby stirring the whalebone around in my sinus. Tears of pain streamed down my face, but in my innocence of things theatrical, I thought maybe it didn't show; and with the whalebone crunching about among the scroll bones, and with my gopher teeth gleaming in the limelight, I carried bravely on with the scene.

The audience hooted, and the flop sweat broke out all over me like dew. Down in the area of my navel, Swanson hissed, "What the hell's going on?"

In the morning, Walter Kerr, the critic for the *Herald Tribune* wrote: "We understood from the program that Miss Swanson designed her own clothes . . . like the play, they fell apart in the first act."

Nina trailed along for three months, but by early spring we were all mercifully back in the Pink House. The movie business still wanted no part of me.

Hollywood is like a bird dog. When things are going badly, it tenses and sniffs at you. It scrapes away at the camouflage. It knows.

Hjördis told me not to worry because, she said, it made me put out an aroma of defeat. I must have been particularly smelly because she suggested a few days on a boat to take my mind off things. We chartered a small sloop and set off for Catalina Island with Garbo and a gentleman friend. An ex-Navy man completing the crew. Garbo was cook. Hjördis stewardess, and as befitted his background, the GF engineer and navigator. I was in charge of the sails.

For an hour he tinkered with the engine. I hovered nearby with useless advice while the Swedish members of the expedition drank schnapps and made crude Nordic jokes at our expense.

"I wonder," said Hjördis sweetly, "if you should give us a bearing because if we miss Catalina, the next stop is Japan."

Finally the engine sputtered into life, and as we chugged hesitantly west in the gathering darkness, the man pored over charts and poked about with calipers. Then he announced heavily, "Something's screwy here. According to my reckoning, we are eleven miles north of the Grand Canyon."

The seafaring Swedes showed no sign of panic. One of them—both claimed the honor—saw a pinprick of light far away to port. We changed course and hours later, with faltering engine, dropped anchor in a sandy cove.

Garbo during the weekend made up for some patchy and uninspired cooking by exuding sparkling fun and swimming, unself-consciously, every day Swedish style.

Television, in the early fifties, had begun to rear its ugly head. The major film studios, instead of grabbing it and making it their own, decided first to ignore it, then to fight it, and wound up, a few years later, being swallowed by it.

I picked up some sparse but badly needed dollars by doing guest shots on the Bob Hope and Jack Benny shows. Many people thought it was nothing short of suicide for a film star to fly in the face of the studio bosses and align himself with the enemy. I had no alternative. I was already dead. One well-known zany redhead did a show with me and over a very inexpensive supper at the Brown Derby confided that she was even more strapped for cash than I was. She turned out to be about as zany as General Motors: Within four years Lucille Ball had bought both the RKO studios.

In the spring, unable to raise another dollar in mortgage on the Pink House, I decided the sad moment had come: The Regency furniture had to go. I mailed carefully authenticated lists to Parke Bernet in New York and to the Shabbie Shoppe in Dallas, Texas, and enclosed a letter to each guaranteeing that their establishment was the only recipient of this golden opportunity. Their replies were sharp.

My own carelessness had saved me from losing my beloved collection. I had put the letters in the wrong envelopes.

In October I was offered a live TV show of *Petrified Forest* in New York. Hjördis and I worked it out, and after deducting air fares and three weeks' hotel expenses, we looked like clearing three hundred dollars, so we took off in a hurry.

It was a good show and 30,000,00 people saw it—a record at that time. Robert Sherwood sat in the control room watching us and professed himself delighted with our playing of his famous work.

Alex Segal directed it beautifully, and Lloyd Gough, Kim Hunter and Art Carney rounded out the cast; but by the end of it I was so exhausted by the tension that we decided to blow the three hundred dollars on a trip to Barbados whence Ronnie and Marietta Tree had bidden us come and visit them for two weeks.

The day after we returned to the Pink House, Otto Preminger called up and offered me the best part in his forthcoming picture, *The Moon Is Blue*. Something he had seen in my performance of *Nina* at Hartford had persuaded him that I was the actor he wanted. Hjördis and I were beside ourselves with excitement, but Otto had a great deal of opposition from United Artists, which was financing the picture.

"Niven is washed up!" they told him. "Get somebody else." but Otto is an immensely determined individual, and what Otto wants, he usually gets . . . he got me—bless him!

Many actors don't like working with Otto because he shouts even louder than Goldwyn and can be very sarcastic. I love it. Actors have a certain amount of donkey blood in them and need a carrot dangled in front of them from time to time. The directors I dread are the ones who say, "You've played this sort of thing before—do anything you want." . . . Otto dangles carrots.

A highly organized man, he made a German version of his picture simultaneously with the American one. The German cast arrived, the two companies rehearsed for a month, and the entire film was completed in two languages in eighteen days. It was also far ahead of its day in its attitude toward sex, was promptly banned by the Catholic Church in the United States, and the ensuing publicity helped enormously.

The Moon Is Blue became a very big success all over the world, and I, personally, was highly delighted to win the Golden Globe Award from the foreign press, The Best Comedy Performance of the Year.

William Holden and Maggie MacNamara played the lovers in the film. but before we started shooting, Otto asked me to play *The Moon Is Blue* for three months on the stage in San Francisco with Scott Brady and Diana Lynn.

While we were playing *The Moon Is Blue* in San Francisco, Charles Boyer was performing in an adjacent theater. The two of us were having supper together one night when Boyer told me that he and Dick Powell were thinking of forming a company to make films for television.

I was surprised, in view of the film studios' attitude toward the upstart television, that two such big names were prepared to risk so much; but I had little to lose myself, and the net result of that after-theater snack was the formation of Four-Star Television, Inc., which to date has made between two and three thousand films for home consumption.

The idea of *Four-Star Playhouse* was to have four well-known movie stars each appearing once a month in an anthology series.

We were unable to persuade a fourth star to join us in the venture, as most people were still too frightened of the studio bosses who uttered the direst threats against blacklegs; but during the first season, by doing guest shows, a few staunch friends helped us out: Ronald Colman, Joan Fontaine, Merle Oberon, Ida Lupino and others.

The three of us took nothing in salaries, and with the proceeds at the end of the first year, we bought the rights to the Somerset Maugham short stories and started a second series with Henry Fonda as host—he even had the guts to blow froth in the beer commercials. The third year, we purchased the Zane Grey stories and launched a third series, *Zane Grey Theater*. This in turn spawned *The Rifleman,* which spun off another new series, *Wanted Dead or Alive,* into which we put an instantly successful unknown, Steve McQueen.

So it went on, but it was not all smooth sailing by a long shot. Frequently, we overspent or underplanned; often sponsors were weeks behind with their payments. Once on a Friday, I pulled all my savings out of the Bank of America to meet the studio payroll, and the day before we were to start shooting a new series with Anita Ekberg as a female Tarzan, we received a very clear message from the right-hand man of Howard Hughes informing us that the luscious Miss Ekberg had left town indefinitely for an undisclosed destination and would not be available in the foreseeable future. We took the high-powered hint and hastily recast another beautiful body in the leopard skin.

Several of the owners of today's biggest names started their careers with us as actors or directors, and Jack Lemmon, Barbara Stanwyck, Steve McQueen, David Janssen, Chuck Connors, Robert Ryan, Robert Taylor, June Allyson, Gig Young, Ida Lupino, and many, many others made series for us. One year we were turning out fourteen different series at the same time—as big an output of film as any of the major studios had turned out in their heyday. We had become big business—nerve-racking big business.

My film career after *The Moon Is Blue* also climbed back onto a most satisfactory plateau of important pictures.

The boys were growing fast and had settled down well in California, although I always felt a tiny bit out of place with my polite hand-clapping Hollywood Cricket Club background when I found myself at Chavez Ravine, wedged between two cap-wearing, gum-chewing, mitt-thumping, raspberry-blowing little Dodger fans.

The days were full of promise and the friends were near-by with whom I could savor them.

Fred Astaire is a pixie, timid, always warmhearted, a sentimentalist with a Lefty Flynn-type penchant for schoolboy jokes. He is also a racehorse *aficionado* who owned a winner of the Hollywood Gold Cup.

Early one Sunday he called me. "I've done a terrible thing. I don't know what possessed me, but at four o'clock this morning, I got out of bed and drove all over Beverly Hills, painting the city mailboxes with my racing colors."

Freud might have had an explanation for Fred's behav-ior—well-to-do ladies often abduct sausages from super-markets—so when one day a voice on my telephone said, "Good morning. I am the Bishop of Los Angeles." I replied knowingly, "And I am the Mother Superior. How's your cock?"

A quick intake of breath followed by a longish pause alerted me to the fact that it was not Fred. When the bish-op had recovered from the unaccustomed greeting, he told me what was on his mind.

"We have a convention of several thousand Anglican clergy coming to Los Angeles from all over the world. We are holding a service in the Hollywood Bowl and we would be very happy if you would read the Second Lesson."

He explained that it was several weeks away, and when I inquired why he had selected me, he told me that as the Archbishop of York was coming from England, it had been decided to invite what he kindly described as a prominent British resident of Los Angeles.

The day approached, and what had for some time seemed no more than a minor chore now assumed the pro-portions of a major hazard. I had meetings with the bishop and inquired about my wardrobe for the occasion: dark suit.

We discussed the script: Galatians 4.

I did not understand it . . . "What is *un*circumcision?"

He explained patiently and told me with a smile not to worry about who was to read the First Lesson. "You won't have to follow Bob Hope . . . I will be reading that myself."

On the night before my appearance at the giant Hollywood Bowl, I was so nervous I was unable to sleep. In the morning, I had a high fever and had completely lost my voice.

Hjördis telephoned the bishop and explained while I listened on an extension . . . I could tell from the disappointment in his voice that he was having a hard time being a believer, so I went down there anyway to let him hear me croak, I think. He said gently, "You could try it. They will understand that you have something wrong with your voice and they will be terribly bored if I read them both lessons."

When the moment came, with my knees clanking together like castanets, I walked out onto the desertlike stage while the thousands of clerics rustled themselves into a seated comfort. A massed choir of hundreds stood in tiers behind me as I turned to face the vastness of the Bowl.

Somebody up there loved me that day. I opened my mouth to whisper the announcement of the lesson and out of my hitherto totally constricted throat came the deepest and most resonant sounds I had ever heard.

On the Fourth of July in the United States American friends point out, with unholy glee, that the crack of each firework is symbolic of the breaking of a Redcoat's neck. Bogart was always at his most sardonic on this occasion, but once, in celebration, he broke all his rules and invited women aboard *Santana*.

Betty, calling her husband Captain Queeg after the half-mad sadist he had portrayed in *The Caine Mutiny*, came along to keep Hjördis company. We dropped anchor in Cherry Cove and Frank Sinatra moored alongside us in a chartered motor cruiser with several beautiful girls and a small piano. After dinner, with Jimmy Van Heusen accompanying him, Sinatra began to sing. He sang all night.

There were many yachts in Cherry Cove that weekend, and by two in the morning, under a full moon, *Santana* was surrounded by an audience sitting in dozens of dinghies and rubber tenders of every shape and size.

Frank sang as only he can, with his monumental talent and exquisite phrasing undimmed by a bottle of Jack Daniels on top of the piano.

He sang till the dew came down heavily and the boys in the listening fleet fetched blankets for their girls' shoulders. He sang till the moon and the stars paled in the predawn sky. Only then did he stop and only then did the awed and grateful audience paddle silently home.

Noël Coward was about to appear in Las Vegas. He was sitting in a deep sofa at Bogie's one evening, discussing the problems of his show. Bogie and I were facing him in two easy chairs. Suddenly, we realized that little Stevie, the five-year-old Bogart son and heir, was stalking Noël from behind, his target, obviously the top of Noël's head. In his hands he bore a large brass tray. The impending assault was so horrible that Bogie and I just sat there unable to move like two dogs watching a snake.

Little Stevie raised the tray high and brought it down with a crash on Noël's unprotected cranium. His head almost disappeared into his shirt.

Noël never looked around. His voice never changed nor did the rhythm of his speech alter. "Bogart, dear," he said, "do you know what I am going to give darling little Stephen for Christmas? A chocolate covered hand grenade."

The famous "Sinatra Rat Pack" should now be put in perspective. All sorts of people were for years stuck with this label—Dean Martin, Sammy Davis, Jr., Shirley MacLaine, Peter Lawford, Tony Curtis and Janet Leigh, to name a few. They were guiltless.

During Noël's appearance at the Desert Inn, Sinatra invited a few friends to go with him to Las Vegas for the opening. When anything is organized by Sinatra, the arrangements are made with legendary efficiency and generosity. We boarded a bus outside Bogie's front door. Caviar and champagne sustained us during the drive downtown to the Union Station, and there, with a cry from our leader of "Yellow armbands, follow me," we trooped aboard a private coach on the train for the overnight trip to Las Vegas. The group consisted of Betty and Bogie, Mike and Gloria Romanoff, Ernie Kovacs and his wife, "Swifty" Lazar, Sid Luft and Judy Garland, Angie Dickinson, Hjördis and myself.

Sinatra provided individual apartments for everyone at the Sands Hotel and a large communal suite with hot and cold running food and drink twenty four hours a day; a big bag of silver dollars was presented to each girl in the party to gamble with.

We saw Noël's triumphant first night, and on subsequent

evenings we visited all the other shows in Las Vegas. We gambled endlessly, only occasionally poking our noses outside to sniff the desert air and gauge the time of the day. After three days, Judy Garland slipped me something that she promised would keep me going. It was the size of a horse pill, and inside were dozens of little multicolored "energy" nuggets timed to go off at intervals of forty minutes.

After four days and nights of concentrated self-indulgence, the only one of the party who seemed physically untouched was Sinatra himself. The rest were wrecks, and it was then that Betty Bacall, surveying the bedraggled survivors, pronounced the fatal words: "You look like a goddamned rat pack!"

A week after we returned to Los Angeles and forced ourselves back into some semblance of good health, the Rat Pack gave a testimonial dinner to Sinatra in the private room, upstairs, at Ramanoff's. A surprise package, tied with pink ribbon and flown down by Jack Entratter, the entrepreneur of the Sands Hotel, awaited everyone of us. Inside each was a white rat. Several escaped during the unpacking and hot-footed it into the restaurant, sowing instant alarm among the chic clientele and eagle-eyed columnists below stairs—thus heralding the end of the short, happy life of Sinatra's Rat Pack.

So much has been written about Sinatra, of his talent, his generosity, his ruthlessness, his kindness, his gregariousness, his loneliness and his rumored links with the Mob that I can contribute nothing except to say that he is one of the few people in the world I would instinctively think of if I needed help of any sort. I thought of him once when I was in a very bad spot; help was provided instantly and in full measure without a question being asked. It was not, incidentally, money.

On New Year's Eve of 1956, Anne and Charlie Lederer stretched a striped awning across their back garden, boarded over their swimming pool, and gave a very beautiful party for a couple of especially glamorous visitors, the Shah and the Empress of Iran. *"Le Tout* Hollywood" turned out in force.

Hjördis and I were dancing, and beside us, Betty Bacall, a particularly active and dedicated exponent of modern dancing, was gyrating, bumping and grinding around the guest of honor—a comparatively subdued performer.

In an effort to reestablish some sort of contact with his partner, the incumbent of the Peacock Throne said, "You are a wonderful dancer, Miss Bacall . . . you must have been born to dance."

Betty tossed back her mane of tawny hair, gave one more convulsive heave, and answered loudly in her husky-sexy voice, "You bet your ass, Shah."

Betty Bacall was the perfect wife and companion for Bogie. I don't know how long she knew he was seriously ill, but she was courageous and dedicated through the whole heartbreaking period. I had heard his nightly coughing bouts on my last trips with him in *Santana,* but he said it was just his smoking, nothing more. Then he began to lose weight, but he never had been much interested in food.

Suddenly, there was an emergency seven-hour operation and the slow slide began.

"If I put on weight, I've got it licked," he told me.

Hjördis and I went away to Rome for three months while I made *The Little Hut* with Ava Gardner and Stewart Granger, and afterward we spent a short time together in Sweden. From there, I brought back the radical plans and specifications of a new yacht that I thought might interest Bogie and took them to his house. I was shocked at the change.

We spent a day aboard *Santana,* but it remained tied up alongside her dock. She never put to sea again with Bogie.

He no longer referred to his illness, and with Betty in permanent attendance, preserving somehow, God knows how, her marvelous gaiety and fun, he slowly wasted away. When he became too weak to make the trip downstairs for his ritual evening drink with his friends—now invited only one at a time and carefully selected by Betty—they converted the little service elevator, took out the shelves, and sharp at six o'clock Bogie would have his terribly emaciated frame carefully dressed and be lowered below, sitting in his wheelchair.

One of us would always be waiting—Huston, Sinatra, Harry Kurnitz, Nunally Johnson, Joe Hyams, "Swifty" Lazar, a few others, and on special occasions, Dum Bum.

At four o'clock one morning, Betty called us and said very quietly, "My darling husband is gone."

16

One Sunday afternoon, the phone rang in the Pink House. "This is Mike Todd. I'm over at Joe Schenck's. I wanna see you. Get your ass over here."

I was halfway through a polite excuse before I realized that he had long since hung up. I had never met Todd, but I had heard a hundred stories about the legendary master showman, gambler, promoter or con man—everyone saw him from a different angle.

We had a houseful of friends that afternoon, and the consensus of opinion was that, whatever else, Todd was always interesting and I should indeed get my ass over to Joe Schenck's.

When I arrived, Todd was by the pool. Of medium height and perfect proportions, he was tanned dark mahogany. He wore the briefest of swimming slips. On his head was a white ten-gallon hat, in his mouth was a cigar of grotesque proportions.

He had no time for preliminaries. "Ever heard of Jules Verne?"

"Yes, of course."

"Ever read *Around the World in Eighty Days?*"

"I was weaned on it."

"I've never made a picture before, but I'm gonna make this one. . . . How'd you like to play Phileas Fogg?"

My heart bounded. "I'd do it for nothing."

Todd tossed aside his hat and cigar.

"You gotta deal," he said and disappeared beneath the surface of the pool.

From that moment till the time, six months later, when the picture was finished, I lived in an atmosphere of pure fantasy. Nobody knows where Todd raised the necessary $7,000,000, and he certainly didn't raise it all at once because several times production ground to a halt while strange, swarthy gentlemen arrived from Chicago for urgent consultations. For weeks on end we went unpaid. Todd induced S. J. Perleman to write the screenplay and employed John Farrow to direct it.

The Mexican bullfighter-comedian Cantinflas arrived to play my valet, Passepartout, and Shirley MacLaine was signed to play Princess Aouda.

"But who the hell do we get to play Mr. Fix, the detective?" said Todd, chomping on the inevitable cigar.

"How about Robert Newton?" I suggested.

Todd was enchanted with the idea and immediately put in a call.

"But I warn you, Mike," I said, feeling every kind of heel, "Bobbie is a great friend of mine, but he does drink a lot these days and you must protect yourself. Lots of people are scared to employ him—he disappears."

"I want to see Newton," said Todd firmly, "and when he comes in, I want you here in the office."

"For Christ's sake, don't tell him I said anything," I begged. "He'll never forgive me."

A little later, Bobbie Newton shuffled in. I hadn't seen him for some weeks, and it was obvious that he had been on a bender of heroic proportions.

Todd went into his routine. "Ever heard of Jules Verne?"

"Ah, dear fellow," said Newton, "what a scribe!"

"Eighty Days Around the World?"

"A glorious piece, old cock."

"How'd you like to play Mr. Fix?"

"A splendid role," said Bobbie, rolling his eyes. "Do I understand you are offering it to me, dear boy?"

"I might," said Todd, and I felt like the slimiest worm when he continued, "but your pal, Niven, here says you're a lush."

"Aah!" said Newton. "My pal, Nivèn, is a master of the understatement."

He was immediately hired and gave his word of honor to Todd that he would go on the wagon for the duration of the picture. He stuck manfully to his promise.

On location at Durango, Colorado, Bobbie and I went off every evening after shooting to catch big, fighting rainbow trout in the mountain lakes. One cold autumn sunset, with streaks of blue woodsmoke clinging to the surface of

the water and the last rays falling on the glorious colors of
the aspens and beeches, Bobbie confessed to me that his
promise to Todd had not really been all that difficult to
give because that very morning his doctor had warned him
that one more session with the *bottle* would almost certainly be fatal. Two weeks after we finished the picture, Todd
called some of us back for an added scene on a ship. Bobbie
Newton was required for only one day, but when he arrived for work, a roaring delivery of "Once more unto the
breach . . ." announced alarming news. "Oh, Bobbie," I
said, "what have you done to yourself?"

He put his arm around my neck and tears rolled down
his swollen cheeks.

"Don't chide me, dear fellow, please don't chide me," he
said.

Within a very few days, the doctor's warnings to that
warmhearted, talented and wonderful soul proved tragical-
ly correct.

If Todd had difficulty in raising money for his epic, he
seemed to have none persuading the biggest names in show
business to play small cameos for fun. We started shooting
in Spain with Louis Miguel Dominguin playing himself in
the bullring, and there, after a falling out, Todd replaced
the director John Farrow by the young Englishman Michael Anderson.

In London, more cameo parts were played by Noël
Coward, John Gielgud, Trevor Howard, Robert Morley,
John Mills, Beatrice Lillie, Hermione Gingold, Hermione
Baddeley and Glynis Johns, and back finally in California
for the major portion of the work, I became inoculated
against surprise when I found myself playing scenes almost
daily with different distinguished visitors—among them
Ronald Colman, Charles Boyer, Marlene Dietrich, Frank
Sinatra, George Raft, Red Skelton, Victor McLaglen, Andy
Devine, Joe E. Brown, Cedric Hardwicke and Buster Kea-
ton.

Somehow Todd also found time to collect someone especially for himself, and radiant with happiness, Elizabeth
Taylor became a permanent fixture.

Nothing fazed Todd. . . . When a flock of several
hundred sheep stopped our car on the way to location in
Colorado, he bought the flock.

"Great idea!" he said. "We put the sheep in front of the train to hold it up."

The sheep had been on their way to market, so now feel had to be provided at great expense to keep them alive till their big moment.

When it came, far from stopping the train, they scattered before it like chaff.

"Sell the goddamned sheep," ordered Todd, "we need a herd of buffalo." He found them too, in Oklahoma, and the scene was reshot with several hundred gigantic beasts stampeding in every direction.

In Paris, when the police moved in to stop us from shooting, Todd promptly paid two taxi drivers to stage a head-on collision in the Rue de Rivoli, and during the ensuing diversion, he completed his shot.

Todd needed all the luck at his disposal when he took over the Place Vendôme and ordered cars towed away in the early morning which might interfere with his day's shooting.

One of the offending vehicles turned out to be the property of a cabinet minister who was spending the night away from home. Todd nearly wound up in jail.

In London, he stole a shot of a company of Guardsmen marching out of Wellington Barracks and separating on either side of his camera by the simple device of camouflaging the machine on a vegetable barrow and pushing it directly in front of the oncoming soldiers at the last second—that, not surprisingly, proved to be our final day's shooting in the streets of London.

At Balboa, Todd converted an ancient sailing yacht into a paddle steamer of the period by building on deck a large superstructure which housed the ponderous engine of a San Francisco cable car to turn the paddle wheels. Not only was the yacht now dangerously top-heavy, but, as we chugged out of the harbor, full laden with actors, crew, lights and cameras, it was made clear to us that a nasty passage was ahead. I pointed to the storm warnings being raised by the Coast Guard at the end of the breakwater.

"I can't see a goddamned thing," said Todd. "I'm Nelson."

In the end, the boat proved too dangerous to turn around

in the heavy seas and we had to go all the way to Catalina before we dared try it.

With gorgeous Elizabeth by his side, Todd remained undefeated to the end, even when the sheriff of Los Angeles locked up the finished footage of his picture, thereby immobilizing his only asset within the state of California till various local creditors had been mollified.

Todd was allowed to assemble and score the film during the daytime under the watchful eye of a sheriff's deputy, but at night, back it went into the vault.

Somehow, Todd staved off the enemy, and, at last, the picture was ready for presentation. The sheriff was persuaded to allow the film to travel to New York for its big gala opening at the Rivoli Theater.

"You gotta get your ass back East," Todd told me. "You gotta be there at the payout window."

Todd sent air tickets and installed us in the most expensive apartment in the St. Regis Hotel. There was a present for Hjördis when we arrived and the rooms were full of flowers; champagne and caviar were waiting for us.

The opening was a Todd bonanza; mounted police held back the screaming crowds as the audience of a thousand famous people in evening dress filed into the theater. Every member of the audience received a beautifully bound and illustrated program, embossed in gold on the cover with the name of each recipient. After the showing, Todd gave a champagne supper for fifteen hundred at the Hotel Astor.

Where did he get the money for all this? The answer, according to Bennett Cerf of Random House, who produced the program, was that he didn't. The morning after the opening, his check made out to the publishers bounced.

No matter, Gambler Todd had got right to the wire with his last penny, and when the audience had finished cheering and the ecstatic reviews were being read, there he was, standing happily at the payout window.

The picture won the Academy Award as the Best Picture of the Year and became one of the biggest money spinners of all time.

Todd married Elizabeth and gave her a diamond the size of a skating rink. He bought himself a twin-engined plane.

Hjördis and I, with peculiar logic, decided that with a lot of good pictures now being offered to me, it was the ideal moment to go away from Hollywood for a few months, so we flew off around the world.

Shirley MacLaine came with us to Tokyo, and with her husband, Steve Parker, as guide, we saw the best of Japan. The four of us went on to Hong Kong.

Shirley is a great traveler and a spectacular companion. She is also a lady of formidable crusading opinions and her antiestablishment observations reverberated around the Crown colony.

When she and Steve flew back to Japan, Hjördis and I continued on to Thailand, India and Turkey. In Greece we decided to splurge, so we chartered a small yacht and the boys flew out to spend their holidays with us in the Islands of the Aegian and Ionian seas. Hjördis caused a stir in every land we visited not only because of her spectacular beauty but because her idea of traveling light was to order a local costume in each country in turn. Somehow, her purchases always seemed to be delivered on the day of our departure: consequently, she contrived to be a country behind in her clothing. Her cheongsan from Hong Kong was, however, a huge success in Bangkok, and her sari from Jaipur nearly caused a riot at a football match in Istanbul.

Back once more in the Pink House via Sweden and England, I made *My Man Godfrey* at Universal before we decided to visit the scene of the Rat Pack inauguration.

The operator at the Sands Hotel located me at a blackjack table and told me Mike Todd was calling me from New York.

"Get your ass over to Palm Springs," he said, "Liz and I are flying out tomorrow, Come and spend the weekend."

I explained that although Las Vegas is separated from Palm Springs by only a hundred miles as the crow flies, the bird would have to cross a hundred miles of mountains and desert to make the trip.

"Hold the phone," said Todd. After a while, he was back on the line. "Okay, I'm sending the plane out there to pick you up—we'll come on out on a commercial. See you tomorrow night for dinner." He hung up.

The following day, Todd's twin-engined, twin-piloted pride and joy arrived from New York, picked us up, and half an hour later, we were in Todd's Palm Springs pad.

Elizabeth Taylor has always fascinated me. I met her

first when she was fifteen and got to know her well during her marriage to the gentle, self-effacing Michael Wilding. Her incredible beauty, her talent and her violet eyes have been the subject of endless paeons of praise; less well known are her courage, her down-to-earthiness, and her staunch defense of friends. That she is completely unspoiled and natural is a miracle when one remembers that with all the attendant sycophantic adulation, she has survived being a major world movie star since she made *National Velvet* at the age of ten.

She was gay and relaxed during the weekend but made no secret of her annoyance that she would have to stay behind and work in Hollywood when Todd flew back to New York in a few days' time to attend some testimonial dinner.

On the Sunday evening, we all returned to Los Angeles in Todd's plane. Hjördis and I needed little persuading when Todd suggested that we pick up our car and drive back to Palm Springs to relax in his beautiful house till the following weekend when he would be back again.

On the day we reinstalled ourselves in his desert home, Todd called us and said how he wished he could be with us and how little he relished the idea of going back to New York.

"Get out of the dinner," I said. "Come on down."

He said he couldn't, as he had promised to attend. With typical thoughtfulness, he called again just before he took off to make sure we had everything and repeated once more how much he wished he didn't have to go.

Four hours later, his plane crashed in New Mexico.

The word "playwright" is spelled that way for a very good reason. Shipwrights build ships, wheelwrights fashion wheels, and playwrights construct plays. If they construct them badly, they quickly fly apart at the seams.

Terence Rattigan is an actor's playwright. To perform the characters he has invented is a joy because they are so well drawn and the plays that present them are so well constructed that so long as you can remember your lines and don't bump into the furniture, you can't go wrong. *Separate Tables* is one of Rattigan's best plays and the Major is one of his best-written characters, so I was, naturally, overjoyed when I was offered the part in the film version. Burt Lancaster, Deborah Kerr, Rita Hayworth, Wendy Hiller,

Gladys Cooper, Cathleen Nesbitt, Rod Taylor and myself rehearsed for two weeks under the expert eye of Delbert Mann—one of the best of the new brew of young directors who had been making names for themselves in live television in New York. It was a dream company to work with.

When the shooting was completed, Hjördis, who had just suffered through yet another miscarriage, was particularly delighted when we took off for a long-planned two-week holiday with Noël Coward at his home near Port Maria in Jamaica. On the first evening over rum drinks, having just heard sad news from England, I said to Noël. "It's terrible. I've arrived at the age when all my friends are dying."

"Personally," said Coward, "I'm delighted if mine last through luncheon. . . ." "Incidentally," he added, "you don't look too good yourself."

I wasn't, it is true, feeling very well—feverish—and Hjördis had just discovered some spots on my back—they itched. By the next morning more spots had appeared on my face and chest and my fever had soared.

"I'm terribly sorry, Noël," I said, "but there seems to be a faint possibility that I may be coming down with chicken pox."

Noël eyed my flushed face with mounting distaste, then spoke very slowly and distinctly. "I want to make one thing crystal clear: You cannot come down with it here."

The next day when Hjördis counted my proliferating spots and reported to Noël that on my face and chest alone she had found more than two thousand, Noël sighed resignedly. "It's high time I wrote another play," he said, "and painted some more of my excellent pictures, so we will now pull up the draw bridge, fly the Yellow Jack . . . and the hell with it."

He then fetched a bottle. "The village postmistress," he said, "swears that pure rum will stop the itching and bring down the fever."

While Hjördis watched apprehensively, he anointed my spots and gave me a hefty tot to drink for good measure. The result of this piece of folklore was instant delirium and two attempts, bravely frustrated by Hjördis, to climb out of the window into the sea.

By the time, weeks later, that I was well enough to travel, Noel had indeed painted many excellent pictures. He had also written a very successful play, *Nude with Violin*.

His real resilience, however, is demonstrated by the fact that he invited us to stay with him again.

Children's diseases are not to be recommended to adults. It was weeks before I could go back to work. When I did, I started *Ask Any Girl* with Shirley MacLaine.

On the set one day, Shirley was called to take a phone call from New York; she let out one of her traffic-stopping shrieks. "Hey, David! Come here quick!" she yelled. "You've just won the New York Critics' Award for *Separate Tables*."

It was a tremendous surprise. I didn't even know I was a candidate. There were, I believe, fifteen voters, and apparently after three ballots, I had just scraped home over Spencer Tracy in *The Old Man and the Sea*. Bosley Crowther, the influential voice of *The New York Times*, had voted against me which, of course, he had every right to do, but finding himself in the minority, he behaved like a spoiled brat and devoted his Sunday article to saying what a disgrace it was that I had won.

Shirley got me all excited. "If you win the New York Critics, you are almost bound to be nominated for the Academy Award! Hey! You may get the Oscar!!"

I tried to be cool and accepted congratulations all over town as unsmugly as I could, but the weeks before the announcement of the five nominees for Best Performance by an Actor were endless. When it finally came over the radio, I was on my way home from work and my receiver was on the blink. The attendant at the gas station gave me the good news when I stopped to fill up. When I arrived at the Pink House, Hjördis had the champagne out. The phone never stopped ringing. Basically, the awards system is a good one. For the nomination, five in each category, one's peers vote. The actors nominate the actors, the directors nominate the directors, the writers the writers, the cameramen the cameramen, and so on. Then the whole lot, all three thousand members of the Academy, vote for the winners.

The other nominees in my category were Spencer Tracy, Paul Newman, Sidney Poitier and Tony Curtis.

I had ten weeks to wait before the final result, and I started out by telling myself that at best, I was a four-to-one shot. I also felt a bit of a fake because playing the role of the Major had, thanks to the way it was written and directed and the formidable help I had received from that high-powered cast, been far easier than I could have imagined.

As the ten weeks dragged by, the pressure built up. The winner of the Academy Award is supposed to add $1,000,000 to the potential of the picture he is in. His next film, too, is supposed to benefit largely. The advertising campaigns start in earnest one month before voting day. Film companies and some individuals spend thousands of dollars pushing their wares; everyone is speculating.

"Tracy will win because everyone loves him. . . . Newman will win because he is always so good—and it's time he did. . . . Poitier will win because he's black and Hollywood is color conscious. . . . Curtis will win because he's Jewish. . . . You can't win because you're British and they gave it to Alec Guinness last year," etc., etc. It was all very nerve-racking, but as the day came nearer, I found that I wanted that Oscar desperately.

My estimate of my chances was not very high at the best of times, but it dropped to zero on the very day that the three thousand voters received their ballot sheets. There in the Hollywood *Reporter*, the local bible which would be read by all of them, was a reprint of a story by the eminent film critic and columnist of the Washington *Daily News*, Jim O'Neill. It stated that a well-known Hollywood producer had told the columnist that the one person he would never vote for would be me, because I had copied Eric Portman's stage performance entirely, had seen the play forty times, and had haunted Portman's dressing room till I had to be thrown out of the theater bodily.

I was sunk. I cabled O'Neill in Washington and pointed out that not only was I not clever enough or stupid enough to copy anybody's performance, but it so happened that I had seen the play precisely once, four years before in London.

O'Neill checked with Portman, who kindly corroborated this and wished me luck, and he then, very graciously, apologized to me in print for "irresponsible reporting." He quoted Portman's cable and for good measure told me, over the phone, the name of the Hollywood producer, "as the very least I can do."

It was far too late to hope to put the record straight, the votes would already have been cast, and I had really given up any hope. However, I called the "well-known producer" and thanked him for his help.

After a lot of spluttering, he said, "Jesus! I'm trapped. I did it but I heard it from So-and-So. So-and-So told me it had come from 'thingumabob.' " and so it went on.

Out of curiosity, I tracked it back through eight people and there I found who had originated the story; a publicist in the publicity department of a rival studio, whose job it was to further his man's chances, had decided that the best way was to chop down the opposition.

When there is $1,000.00 at stake, Hollywood has never believed in kid gloves. The actor, of course, had no idea it had happened; he would never in a million years have condoned it.

The night before the Awards, someone gave a large party for Ingrid Bergman, who, after years away from Hollywood and a romance on Stromboli which had shocked or titillated the world, had reappeared to make one of the presentations. Everyone at the party seemed to have voted for me; they didn't say so in so many words; they were content to signal the fact across the room by making a cross in the air and pointing to their own chests and winking knowingly.

I was greatly encouraged until I caught the eye of Rosalind Russell, a nominee for Best Actress, for whom I had not voted . . . I found myself winking and pointing and drawing crosses in the empty air.

The night of the Awards finally was upon us. I was slightly anesthetized because for the hour-long show, Bob Hope, Jack Lemmon and I had been pressed into service as the three masters of ceremonies, and this preoccupied me with a great deal of hard work. At Grauman's Chinese Theater on Hollywood Boulevard, the scene was set.

The traditional searchlights weaved back and forth across the purple night sky and the bleachers were jammed with thousands of excited fans as the bearers of well-known faces arrived and popping flashbulbs blinded their well-known eyes.

I had to be there early. Before I left home, our Celtic and Nordic blood sent us dashing superstitiously about the house gathering up good-luck charms. Distributed about my person were several rabbits' feet, a silver pig that one of my sons had given to me, some heavy Swedish coins, a Hebrew inscription on beaten bronze which I hoped might have captured the Jewish vote, a Buddha with a tiny diamond in his navel which Hjördis had found in Thailand, and my other son's first fallen tooth.

Hjördis looked spectacular and, munching tranquilizers like popcorn, arrived later with Suzanne and Peter Ustinov.

My chores as a master of ceremonies over, I found my seat with them and sat knotted with indigestion as the show dragged on. I watched wretchedly as the happy recipients of Oscars made their carefully prepared acceptance speeches (more superstition had stopped me from preparing even one line—just in case.). Ranged around the walls of the packed auditorium were five television cameras, each focused on a nominee and each ready to capture and flash to millions of viewers all over the world looks of expectancy, disappointment, joy, studied indifference or tears.

Irene Dunne was finally introduced, and I carefully composed my generous-hearted-loser face, for she it was who would open the big white envelope, sealed in guaranteed secrecy by Price Waterhouse and Company and containing the name of the winner of The Best Performance by an Actor.

She opened the envelope and, after an interminable pause, read out my name. There was a roar. I didn't wait to diagnose whether it was a roar of approval or rage. I kissed Hjördis, leaped to my feet, and with tailcoat flapping, I cantered down the aisle. I thought, "I've got to get there quick before she changes her mind."

Such was my haste to get on that stage that I tripped up the steps and sprawled headlong. Another roar rent the air. Irene helped me up, gave me the Oscar, kissed me on the cheek, and left me alone with the microphone. I thought the least I could do was to explain my precipitous entrance, so I said, "The reason I just fell down was. . . . " I had intended to continue, "because I was so loaded with good-luck charms that I was top-heavy. . . ." Unfortunately, I made an idiot pause after the word "loaded" and a third roar raised the roof. I knew that I could never top that, so I said no more on the subject, thereby establishing myself as the first self-confessed drunk to win the Academy Award.

So many ingredients go into one individual winning an Oscar—the material, the direction, the other actors, the photography, the editing, even the music—that in reality it's a team effort, but whatever the background and however sentimental the vote, it's a lovely feeling to accept first prize.

Cables and messages and scripts poured in from all over the world. . . . King for a Day? Certainly! After that, it's back to the old drawing board.

The message I cherished the most was an invitation to go to see Samuel Goldwyn at his home. He opened the door himself and put his arm around my shoulders. It had been eight long years since we had parted company.

"I don't give a goddamn about your award," he said. "I've seen the picture and I want you to know I'm proud of you."

In the drawing room, Frances caught me looking, surreptitiously, at the piano; there in its silver frame stood my photograph in uniform sent from England during the war.

"Sam never took it down." She smiled.

Live television, during its reign, proved one thing: that many actors are masochists. Without exception, the most ghastly torture ever invented for people in my profession, it incorporated all the worst features of films, radio and the legitimate theater.

Before an unseen audience of millions, overdressed and underrehearsed actors struggled with badly written scripts in front of cameras which collided with sickening regularity and scenery that wobbled and often collapsed while the whole mess was directed by egomaniac directors drunk with power in front of consoles studded with switches and buttons.

The actor's nightmare was ever present: the dread of forgetting the lines without any possible hope of being prompted back onto the track. My partner, Dick Powell, was the genius who overcame this on one occasion. When forgetfulness set in, he continued mouthing silently and all over the country hundreds of thousands of viewers frantically twiddled their dials and phoned their repairman.

Fortunately, film and tape gradually eliminated the live monster, leaving it to cope most efficiently with news, talk shows, and sports, but while it was in its final throes, masochist me could not resist one more exposure to its well-known dangers, so off I flew to New York.

It was an important show, but the material was the usual

gibberish. I was a spy or a doctor or a Congressman, I forget which—it would not have made the slightest difference. The strange thing was, I didn't really need the money that badly. It was an irresistible urge to be frightened, like skiing, but this time I was determined to be calm. After all, I was the star of the show and the major part of the burden was mine. My idea of being calm was this: I left my hat, coat and briefcase (my spy, doctor or Congressman equipment) in my little dressing room just off the sound stage and with only five minutes to air time, I wandered nonchalantly about in shirt sleeves.

An hysterical assistant rushed up. "David! . . . For Christ's sake! . . ."

"Calm yourself, please," I said, trying not to throw up, "we have five, lovely, long cool minutes before we have to act this very bad play in front of several millions of people but, in the meanwhile, let us all relax. . . ."

"David! For Chriss—"

"Please," I said, "don't raise your voice. All I need is two minutes during which I will go to my room, put on my coat and hat and pick up my briefcase."

"David!" the assistant pleaded. "*Please*, you've just got two minutes!"

"Okay," I said, "no sweat," and followed by a forest of admiring eyes and with the slow measured tread of a London bobby, I stalked to my little dressing room.

I had locked myself out.

Immediately, I was transformed into a shrieking, babbling banshee. "HELP! HELP!"

A quivering announcer started to extol the sponsor's wares against a background accompaniment of studio firemen hacking down my door, and eventually, I made my entrance with my hat on back to front, my coat wrongly buttoned and covered in wood chips. I wouldn't remember a word.

Orson Welles once said to me, "We have now acted in theaters, on radio, in films and on live television. They *can't* think of anything else, can they?"

Oh, God! I hope not.

I stayed on in New York to make a film.

In this journal, I have, by now, firmly established myself as a name-dropper so I can, with equanimity, record that apart from reestablishing contact with McClain, the New York Giants and many other old friends, the only occurrence of note during the time I was filming in New York was my good fortune in getting to know Senator J.F.K. of Massashusetts and his beautiful wife, Jackie.

One night with a small party, we visited El Morocco and were seated, at J.F.K.'s request, in the Champagne Room at the back. I was dancing with Jackie in the main room and remarked on the fact that her husband had remained out of sight all evening.

"Why's that? Doesn't he like to dance?"

"He wants to be President," she replied.

The picture finished, I returned to the Pink House just in time for the boys' summer holidays. I had many offers. Four Star was mushrooming, the mortgage was paid off and the Oscar was gleaming on the mantelshelf. I should have known from experience that I was headed for trouble.

The astute reader will have noticed fewer references to Hjördis in the pages covering the last few months. Unfortunately and almost imperceptibly, that had become the pattern of our lives at that time.

I had fallen into the well-known trap of becoming so wrapped up in my career, myself and, lately, my success, that I had been taking the most important thing in my life for granted.

Hjördis told me that she was leaving me.

17

With complete honesty, Hjördis explained that she had to find out if she was still an individual, a human being in her own right, or just the trappings of someone else. It was very painful. Once Hjördis makes up her mind, that's it! She rented a small house nearby and moved into it to live alone and find out if she still "existed." The boys were nonplussed and refused to believe it had happened. Irreverently, they named her new residence The Summer Pink House and visited it daily on their bicycles.

Hollywood is an impossible place to work out family problems. There several hundred resident correspondents peer through their microscopes at an ever-changing handful of goldfish who are news. Rumors flew; so we put out the traditional nauseating statement about "a trial separation" and voiced our pious hope that "friends would understand while we attempted to reconcile our differences."

Looking sadly at an empty chair was no way of spending the summer holidays, so I took the boys to Honolulu to try our luck on the surfboards. Forty-eight hours later, the Los Angeles papers were full of pictures of my being helped from the sea with blood streaming down my face——the result of a head-on collision with a rock.

Urgent inquiries from Hjördis—a good sign.

After six weeks, I returned to the Pink House and diplomatic relations were reopened between the two establishments, mostly in the form of SOS messages relayed by the boys.

"The boiler's burst. She wants to know what to do."

"Somebody's stolen the mowing machine and the landlord is suing her. Who does she call?"

I went to work at M-G-M with Doris Day making *Please Don't Eat the Daisies,* and three months to the day from the start of our trial separation, I took my lunch box at midday and paid my first visit to the Summer Pink House. Hjördis was sunbathing in the garden when I walked in demanding beer to wash down my sandwiches. By the time I went back to the studio the war was blessedly over.

It was a horrible experiment, but by anyone as completely honest as Hjördis, it could never have been undertaken except as a last resort. Most importantly, it worked and a whole new lease of life was given to our happiness entirely thanks to her having had the courage of her convictions.

As soon as I was through with the picture, we took off on a second honeymoon.

We had been invited to Brazil as guests of the government. I was to be presented with the key to the city of Rio de Janeiro by President Juscelino Kubitschek. We went via New York, and while Hjördis busied herself finding clothes for the visit, I misguidedly enrolled myself at the Arthur Murray School of Dancing for a crash course in the tango.

For hours, closeted in a tiny cubicle, I nestled between the bosoms of a large, dark lady and swooped and dipped like a madman. If anybody was still dancing the tango in Brazil, they certainly were not doing so during our visit. I never had a chance to display my virtuosity.

North American hospitality is justly famous; the South American variety is exuberantly overpowering. It was a fascinating experience. Very few Hollywood faces had, thus far, been seen in that land of ardent moviegoers and we were feted, cheered and mobbed wherever we went.

When the president, at the palace, presented me with a colossal key, Hjördis said as a joke, "What about me? Can't I have a little one too?"

With great gallantry, he ordered a small golden replica to be made specially for her and delivered the same afternoon.

A fascinating man with a most attractive family, his pride and joy was the controversial city of Brasília, which was then only half built. On the spur of the moment he said, "We go up there together tomorrow."

We flew up in the presidential plane accompanied by his wife, daughters and the architect of Brasília, Oscar Neymeyer, who sat white-faced and miserable throughout the trip—he is, frankly, terrified of flying.

When we arrived in Brasília the president put us in his helicopter and pointed delightedly as we flew between the half-built skyscrapers of his new capital, landing finally on the lawn of the only finished structure in the city, his own Palace of the Dawn, there to spend the weekend. "Tomorrow," he said, "you and I will officially declare the lake to be filled with water."

In a dinghy with an outboard motor, dodging in and out of the half-submerged tree trunks, we made the grand opening tour of the huge half-filled man-made waterway.

After another week of being royally entertained in Sao Paulo, we spent a few days by ourselves in Bahia.

Soon after we got back to the Pink House, my birthday loomed up, and Hjördis said, "Let's go down to some little place on the beach and have lunch together."

It was a Sunday and the weather was glorious, and dreading the bumper-to-bumper traffic, I advanced every excuse, but she was adamant. So I took my place resignedly behind the wheel and we headed out toward Malibu.

She pointed excitedly. "Let's go in there . . . it looks sweet."

The Frigate Bird was a well-known whorehouse with a very unsavory reputation. I explained this to Hjördis.

"Oh, *please,*" she said, "I've never been in one before. Please, do take me in there . . . and look . . . it says DINING ROOM!"

Still chastened by our short separation, I gave myself a good mark for being attentive to my wife, although luncheon in a brothel seemed a strange way to demonstrate it, and turned into the driveway.

As we entered, a parrot in a cage gave a wolf whistle and a sleazy madame greeted me with, "Look who's here! Well, hullo there, Dave! . . . Long time no see!" A libelous and erroneous statement as it happened, but I pretended not to hear and pressed grimly on toward the dining room. There I froze. In the gloom, I saw the well-known back of a close friend. His arm was around a blond girl's waist . . . Laurence Olivier.

"Quick!" I hissed to Hjördis. "We've got to get out of here." Then as my eyes became accustomed to the semi-darkness, I spotted another even more easily recognizable form . . . Peter Ustinov was pinning a dark girl to the wall. My head spun. My friends had gone mad; what a lunatic risk to take! I grabbed Hjördis by the arm and dragged her down the passage; the parrot whistled again, a peal of well-known laughter followed us—Patricia Medina!

Only then did I catch on. My surprise birthday party in surprise surroundings was a complete success.

In the spring of 1960, we had an overpowering urge to move. This urge became more and more pronounced, and we knew with certainty that this was not something being signaled to our brains by our pathologically itchy feet. We knew that we wanted to make a big and permanent change. When I told my agent and my business manager that we were thinking of moving back to Europe to live, they were dumbfounded and lost no time pointing out that my career had never been in better shape and asked what sort of pictures I thought I'd make over there.

"You'll be sitting on top of some goddamned mountain," they said, "praying for the phone to ring."

They talked ominously about the boys' schooling, hinted darkly about my obligations to Four Star. . . . They told me quite frankly that they reckoned I had gone mad, but the more they reasoned with me and the more valid their arguments sounded, the more certain I became that we would be going.

Hollywood had completely changed. The old camaraderie of pioneers in a one-generation business still controlled by the people who created it was gone. The mystique had evaporated. Wrong it may have been, but when Joan Crawford, Norma Shearer and Marlene Dietrich had graciously consented to give interviews to the press, it was on the strict understanding that the copy would be submitted and could be altered to their taste before it was published. They created and perpetuated their images and they became immortal.

Now the inevitable reaction had set in, and upon us was the era of the vicious, apparently lawsuit-proof columnist of *Confidential* magazine and the telephoto lens. The pipe dream was gone—the lovely joke was over. The asphalt jungle of highways was proliferating everywhere through the once lovely California countryside, the famous sunshine was dimmed by automobiles and industry, and the scent of fear was attacking the smog-filled lungs of the professional film makers, already resigned to the fact that their audience was brainwashed by television. It was time to go, but even so and with our European roots tugging at us, it was a tough decision to make. Although we had lately received a nasty shock from the tax authorities who had taken all our savings to pay off a hefty reassessment of taxes from four years before, we still needed a clear sign that we should actually start making our reservations.

The message was delivered nearby in tragic and brutal fashion . . .

On a bright Sunday during the Easter holiday, David and Jamie were on the patio helping me with the barbecue; Hjördis was indoors baking the potatoes. The garden was vivid with blossom and the yellow orioles had come back to nest once more. Around us the hills were misty and the blue jacaranda trees were in full bloom. In the distance Mount Baldy on one side reared its snow-topped head above the industrial haze of the Los Angeles basin; in the opposite direction, Catalina and the Santa Barbara Islands floated in ghostly isolation far out on the Pacific.

I don't think we even heard it; if we did, we would have dismissed it as the backfire of an automobile. It was a revolver shot. Four youths, junkies, had come up from downtown in a taxi. After paying the fare, they had cased our street for suitable victims and had settled on a neighbor's house a few yards away.

They rang the bell. The son of the house, a boy about the same age as mine, opened the door. They shot him.

While he was dying in agony on the threshold, they held up the distraught parents, took their available cash, and then, inexplicably, allowed them to call a doctor.

They all were arrested within half an hour and, receiving the sentences reserved for juveniles, have, presumably, long since been once more let loose on society.

Los Angeles is a violent city, so I don't mean that we stampeded in panic as a result of this single tragedy, but it certainly tipped the scales because we had lately decided to adopt and we wanted to bring up a new family somewhere in peace and quiet.

Finding a good home for the Pink House was our primary consideration. Many unknowns wanted it badly, but we sold it much less advantageously to an old friend who loved it and who has lived there happily with his family ever since.

I resigned from the board of Four Star, put the Regency furniture in storage, and when the boys went back to boarding school, we flew off to find a new home and a new life in Europe.

First stop, Klosters in Switzerland to catch the tail end of the skiing and to ask the advice of Deborah Kerr and her husband, Peter Viertel.

They were adamant that we should follow their example and make Switzerland our base, so when my agent finally trapped me after days of frantic search, offering me several months in Greece and England making *The Guns of Navarone,* I left for the island of Rhodes and Hjördis stayed behind combing the Alps for a suitable chalet.

She was brilliant and within a few weeks found exactly what we wanted, a comfortable cuckoo clock in a quiet farming village fifteen minutes from the ski resort of Gstaad.

The Guns of Navarone was a long and physically very arduous picture culminating with five weeks in England in November simulating a storm at sea by working nine freezing hours a day in a huge tank full of filthy water.

After nine months, Gregory Peck and I were left alone with two weeks of exhausting night work still to do, shooting from dusk to dawn, filming the actual finale of the picture—the blowing up of the guns. As my character had been built up as "a genius with explosives . . . the only man who can do it," it will readily be appreciated that without my presence during those crucial last two weeks, the colossal $7,000,000 epic could never be finished. With only three days to go, I picked up a fearsome infection via a split lip and at two o'clock one morning was carted away with what in the grim times before antibiotics was known as general septicemia. I lay dangerously ill for days while the experts from Guys Hospital struggled to identify, isolate and eliminate the bug that had struck me down.

The picture ground to a halt amidst general consternation. The big brass of the company arrived posthaste from America. They called a meeting with Carl Foreman, the producer, Lee Thompson, the director, the head of the finance department, representatives of the banks and insurance companies and various assistants.

One of those present reported the scene to me later.

Foreman read out the latest ominous bulletin from the doctors; murmurs of sympathy and alarm arose on all sides. After a suitable pause, the biggest brass spoke. "We gotta problem here, fellers . . . so David is very, very sick . . . That's tough on him . . . and we all love him . . . but wadda *we* do if the son of a bitch dies?"

"The son of a bitch," pumped full of drugs, went back to work against the doctor's orders far sooner than was prudent, completed the crucial three days' work, and suffered a relapse that lasted seven weeks.

The big brass never even sent me a grape.

While I was recuperating in the chalet, Hjördis busied herself looking for the baby girl we had both set our hearts on. One day the miracle happened. A little round bundle, a few weeks old, was delivered into her arms. It promptly went purple with rage and tried to scream the house down, but one look at the Madonna-like serenity of Hjördis' face was all I needed. We were entering a period of pure joy.

Two years later, another little creature appeared, and while Hjördis remained calmly confident, relentless competition for the affection of these two diminutive blond bombshells set in between myself and my two sons. It continues, unabated, to this day; no holds barred.

After a while in Europe, the twin calls of sun and sea increased in volume. Hjördis, once again, was brilliant, and this time, after combing the whole northern Mediterranean basin till she knew every rock by name, she found an old monstrosity perched in an olive grove on a little promontory of its own on Cap-Ferrat.

Any actor who voluntarily supports two residences should have a psychiatrist permanently installed in both of them.

However, the Regency furniture was sent for, and the house was officially declared open by the more-beautiful-than-ever Grace from next door in Monaco who sat on a packing case with her enchanting husband and ate sardines by candlelight.

During the next few years, we returned a few times to Hollywood, including once to make a picture about two crooks with Marlon Brando and once to shoot the pilot of Four Star's most ambitious television series, *The Rogues*. The eye must really have been in on the day when producer Collier Young and I did the casting because we chose as my leading lady a complete unknown, Sally Kellerman.

Brando, contrary to what I had heard, was easy, sympathetic and generous to work with and a great help on a tricky political occasion.

Hjördis and I had received a message from the White House. Jackie was giving a very small surprise party for the President.

The producer of the picture, a staunch Republican, saw no particular reason to arrange the schedule to get me off a few hours early on Friday evening. Brando, a super Democrat, viewed it quite differently and the matter was quickly arranged. We flew to Washington; on arrival, we were smuggled by Fifi Fell into a small hotel, where we changed, and then boarded the Presidential yacht at a heavily guarded dock.

Apart from Fifi, ourselves and a Senator from Florida, it was entirely a family affair: the R.F.K.'s, the Shrivers, the Smiths and so forth. Jackie had provided a small orchestra. When it struck up "Happy Birthday to You" as the President boarded for what he thought was a quiet dinner alone with his wife, his face, luckily, lit up with pleasure.

We cruised up and down the river, followed by a Secret Service launch . . . a gay, happy family evening. We gave presents and in the early hours of the morning played some fairly strenuous Kennedy games.

During one of these physical encounters, the entire left leg of Senator E.K.'s trousers was ripped off at the crotch. At 4 A.M. we came alongside for landing, and it was evident that several marines, Secret Service men and others were standing there to receive us.

"Please take my pants," I said, "it'll cause no stir if an actor comes ashore half-dressed, but it might look odd if you do."

"The hell with it." Teddy Kennedy laughed. "It happened, didn't it?" and with white underpants on the port side flashing bravely, he stepped jauntily ashore.

The next day, J.F.K. was in his office at eight sharp before attending a Decoration Day Service with his small son. At eleven, we had a rendezvous in his Oval Office.

"See how it feels," he said, smiling, and I sat for a moment at the Presidential desk.

With Jackie and the two children, we were whisked away in the Presidential helicopter to spend the rest of the weekend swimming, walking and skeet shooting at Camp David.

On the way up there, with a Secret Service helicopter in attendance, I noticed, at the President's elbow, a brightly colored telephone. He saw me staring at it and started to laugh.

"Is that *the* one?" I asked. He nodded.

"Is that the one you pick up if you want to blow up the world?"

"That's it," he said, then he looked down at the glorious, green countryside passing below us, glanced at the attendant chopper flying beside us, and laughed again.

"You know," he said, "a guy could get to like this!"

Countless volumes have been written about this extraordinary human being and the earthshaking moments he lived through and often controlled. I shall never forget him for his simplicity, his humor, his kindness, his interest in other people and, above all, his love of life.

The end of the journal is now in sight, so I will attempt to reward the reader's patience and loyalty by bringing it swiftly to a close without making it sound like my obituary.

Since the war, Trubshawe had tried his hand at many things, including becoming a publican. He had been the landlord of several hostelries, including a small inn, The Lamb, at Hode in Sussex. The honest burghers of Brighton, taking their Sunday drives over the Downs, were astonished to see a newly erected billboard that stated simply:

TRUBSHAWE HAS A LITTLE LAMB
—12 MILES.

Now he has given up that line of business and become an actor—a very good one too. He swiftly made a name for himself in television and one of his earliest screen appearances was in *The Guns of Navarone*—a lovely bonus for me.

Bill Rollo died. He died exactly as he would have planned it, except that he had every intention of living forever. He worked hard all his life and put all he could afford into his delightful small farm in Rutland. Fox hunting was his joy and his extravagance. Long since remarried, he spent all the time he could spare with Dinie at Barleythorpe. At the age of seventy, mounted on his favorite hunt-

er, on a glorious autumn morning, with the scent breast
high and the Quorn hounds in full cry, he put his horse at a
big thorn fence. It fell. Bill's neck was broken.

I was filming in Spain, Hjördis was visiting her family in
Sweden; David was at the University of Florence; and
Jamie at school in Switzerland. We converged on London
and the next day drove north for the funeral.

In London, it had been a happy family reunion, but as
the miles sped by and Barleythorpe came nearer, the terrible sadness of the real reason for our coming together
swept over us. We all had adored him. He had been inde-
structible. The little village church was packed with his old
hunting and shooting friends sitting silently and stoically in
their grief. In the family pew, the Niven contingent wept
unashamedly. After the service, we walked miserably out
into the pale sunshine. The Duke of Beaufort, a close
friend of Bill's, approached.

"I take it you will be spending the night with Dinie?"

"I can't, I'm afraid, I said, "I have to go back to Spain—
I'm shooting in the morning."

"Ah," he said, "they've got a lot of birds down there this
year, I hear."

I didn't try to explain.

The boys completed their education in Switzerland,
France, England and Italy. Jamie returned to the United
States and after leaving Harvard married a very special girl
from Philadelphia. He now works in New York, David in
London.

Lately, Betty Bacall arrived to spend some time at Cap-
Ferrat with us. She brought with her the score of *Applause*
and for ten days sat at the end of our promontory, belting
out her numbers. The fishermen deserted the rocks below,
the sea gulls departed and certain species of fish are no
longer to be found in our waters, but when she opened on
Broadway, she scored the greatest triumph that has come
to any actress in the last ten years.

Well, that about rounds it off. . . .

What else is there? Oh, yes . . . the movies! I almost forgot about them. Well, in the ten years since I left Hollywood, my itchy feet have spurred me, usually accompanied
by Hjördis and the girls to make films in Greece, Spain,
England, France, Israel, Ireland, United States, Monaco,

Switzerland, Austria, Mexico, Italy and Lebanon—and more than one film in many of these countries.

During that time I have been directed by the highly intelligent such as John Huston, John Frankenheimer, J. Lee Thompson and Peter Ustinov and by the professionals, the heavy-handed, the hysterical and the half-wits. I have also worked with drunkards and those who prefered pot, speed or horse.

As a result of these travels and all the exposures, nothing really fatal happened, but there was one extremely painful near miss.

We were shooting *The Pink Panther* in the Italian Alps. The following day I was required to do something very simple on skis, and the producer, not knowing that I would rather ski than eat, told me to take the afternoon off and practice with a ski teacher. So anxious was I to profit from his rash instruction before he realized I might break a leg, that I bustled off up the mountain in my thin movie ski outfit, half-wittedly ignoring the fact that on the top it was 35° below zero . . . so cold in fact that no one else was skiing.

Halfway down and traveling fast behind the instructor, I suddenly got a feeling of absolutely nothing in precisely the spot where I should have been warmest . . . something had gone badly wrong amidships. A neon sign flashed on in my brain FROSTBITE, and cupping my hands over the danger area, I inadvertently put myself into the racing position and streaked past the astonished instructor. At the bottom three morose and mauve-colored guides were warming themselves over a fire of fir branches.

"*Catso gelato!*" I yelled in my shaky Italian. "Put it in the snow," they shouted, plucking feverishly at my zipper. "Put yours in the snow," I gibbered. "Mine's cold enough."

My instructor arrived. "Alcohol!" he commanded. "We must put it in alcohol!"

We clambered into his ancient car, and I was driven through the main street of Cortina d'Ampezzo, one of the choicest resorts in the Alps, lying in the back with four horny-handed mountaineers, trying to keep the circulation going in my stricken friend.

In the bar of the Hotel de la Poste, smartly dressed clients finishing a late lunch gaped in amazement as we clumped into the bar and yelled at the barman to fill a balloon brandy glass to the brim with whiskey, *"Prohtissi-mo!"*

In the lavatory, while the Italians formed a solicitous clucking semicircle, I faced the agony of the thaw and prised out of my ski pants a pale-blue acorn. Into the whiskey it went, and the pain was excruciating. This moment was chosen by a smart Milanese nobleman whom I happened to know to enter with a view of relieving himself. He took in the tableau at a glance.

"David," he asked in a horrified voice, "what *are* you doing?"

"I'm pissing in a brandy glass," I muttered between clenched teeth. "I always do."

Apart from that, nothing much happened in my wanderings.

I have been knifed (by mistake) in a Spanish production and nearly shot dead by a bedouin in Israel when the World War II rifle he was handling still had one up the spout. The bullet passed between our heads as I was talking to Duncan MacRae.

I have been knocked senseless by falling scenery in an English studio and overturned in a canoe into the loathsomely infested waters of a Mexican jungle . . . all in all, about par for the course.

The results, too, have been average. Some pictures the critics loved and the audience hated; some despised by the experts were greatly appreciated by the paying customers. One effort became one of the great money-makers of all times; another broke the record at the Radio City Music Hall; and a third was so bad that it never got shown anywhere—even on the airlines.

The whole movie industry, at the moment of writing, is in disarray; some say it will never recover.

When it was booming, nothing was put into research. With people, today, cavorting about on the moon, it is incredible to think that films are still made and distributed in much the same way as they were in the days of D. W. Griffith, Chaplin and Buster Keaton. If the film companies had been making motorcars or false teeth, they would have been bankrupt forty years ago. When the businessmen took over from the old-time moviemakers and started chasing trends, disaster followed as the night the day and now there is little money left with which to make new pictures.

Fingers of blame have been freely pointed in every direction, including at the people who pulled in the customers.

Sitting in their yacht in Monte Carlo harbor, I was discussing the situation with the Burtons. "What about the people who got a million dollars a picture?"

Elizabeth's reply was as down-to-earth as usual. "If someone was stupid enough to offer me a million dollars to make a picture, I was certainly not dumb enough to turn it down."

The movie business has often before proved its resilience and it will do so once more. In these days of supercommunications, it makes no sense to think that the greatest form of mass entertainment ever invented will just fade away.

Actors have a problem: Often we don't know how to get "off."

"How do I finish this story?" I asked a writer friend.

"Quite simple," he replied, "just bring it up to date, then stop writing."

After he had departed, I was left in my London hotel staring at a blank sheet of paper digesting his brilliance and wondering how to avoid being sentimental while at the same time underlining my wonder at the ease with which two baby girls had altered my priorities and changed the whole process and meaning of my life when the phone rang.

"Uncle David!" said a sweet voice. "This is your goddaughter!"

Noël Coward has twenty-seven godchildren—five more than I (eighteen of mine are girls). Noël would never have floundered as I did; his record for patience and helpfulness is legendary . . . example: "Uncle Noël! Look at those two little doggies! What *are* they doing?"

"The little doggie in front," said godfather Noël, "has just gone blind, and his friend is pushing him all the way to St. Dunstans."

"I have a friend with me," said my unidentified goddaughter. "He's dying to meet you. . . . Can we come up?"

When she walked in and embraced me, I remembered her. Eighteen years old, long blond hair, Indian headband, willowy wasp-waist figure, suede jacket, fringed skirt, green eyes and a gorgeous smile.

Her companion was considerably less prepossessing.

"This is Big Top," said my goddaughter offhandedly, as she indicated a morose, bearded creature lurking behind her. He sported an Afro hairdo, a grave error for a red-headed Caucasian. He, too, was festooned with love beads and his heliotrope bell-bottoms were kept up by a broad leather belt, the buckle of which was fashioned in the shape of a penis. Dirty, horned toenails jabbed out belligerently from between the thongs of his questionable sandals.

"You wanna blow some grass, man?" he demanded, his flat north country voice winning easily over a phony American accent. He ignited a joint and passed it to my goddaughter.

"You dig today's pictures?" he asked me. "How come you only work for those creepy has-beens, man? I've got something that'll really blow your mind, very groovy."

"What's it about, Big Top?" I asked, groaning inwardly.

"Just be cool," he said. "Be cool. . . . If you wanna be in something really far out, really specific, something really against your bag . . . I have this story about this old guy, rich and weirdo: His daughter has freaked out, see, and shacked up with a spade who drops acid, who's a big wheel in some corny new African state. . . ." He droned out the rest of the well-known rubbish, then delivered a long lecture.

It was cats like me, it seemed, who had ruined the movie business with our bad taste and lack of imagination. The only way we could atone for our sins was by coming up with some heavy bread for his production company.

He finally withdrew, leaving my room smelling like a haystack. I opened the windows.

"Isn't he awful?" My goddaughter giggled. "I won't do that to you again . . . I got trapped." She looked at me speculatively and took a long draught of champagne. "Want to take me to a party? It's just around the corner."

In the lobby many heads turned in her direction as she clung to my arm.

The party was located in a studio above an antique shop. A glassy-eyed transvestite admitted us and pointed limply into the gloom of a sickly sweet haze . . . "There's wine over there."

The place was illuminated by carriage lamps; on the walls were garish posters, large colored numbers, and blown-up photographs of Che and Mao. Through an open bedroom door to the right, I could see two young Lesbians making slow, unhurried love. Our host offered us some pills from a Georgian snuffbox.

"We have it all, man," he said, ". . . California sunshine even."

Out of the gloom a tall girl rose, kissed me on the lips, said "Peace," and sat down again.

Around the walls, on cushions, couples sat and smoked and stared at nothing in particular. From a record player, a female voice—Joan Baez, I think—was singing a sad ballad about children.

Nothing much happened for an hour, then a 16-mm film was thrown on a portable screen. It was about homosexuality in Algerian prisons. The warders played prominent parts and the close-ups were quite repulsive. As the film unfolded, my blond green-eyed goddaughter became aware of my increasing restlessness.

"This isn't your scene, is it?" She giggled. "Do you want to split?"

She was giggling a lot by now, and in the reflected light of the screen, I saw that her eyes were brightly out of focus.

Gratefully, I grabbed the offer, and ducking under the beam from the projector, I went quickly down the stairs. In the street, like a man who has just run a four-minute mile in thick mud, I leaned against the railings, gulping down great drafts of clean, windy spring evening.

After a while, I looked up at the scudding clouds above, and suddenly and unexpectedly, up there above the chimney pots, I beheld an old childhood friend, sailing calmly and confidently through a clear patch of sky:

who knows if the moon's
a balloon, coming out of a keen city
in the sky—filled with pretty people?
(and if you and I should

get into it, if they
should take me and take you into their balloon
why then
we'd go up higher with all the pretty people

than houses and steeples and clouds:
go sailing
away and away sailing into a keen
city which nobody's ever visited, where
always
it's
Spring) and everyone's

in love and flowers pick themselves.

INDEX